SHARON NAYLOR

HOW TO PLAN AN
ELEGANT
WEDDING
IN 6 MONTHS OR LESS

Achieving Your Dream Wedding
When Time Is of the Essence

PRIMA HOME
An Imprint of Prima Publishing
3000 Lava Ridge Court ♦ Roseville, California 95661
(800) 632-8676 ♦ www.primalifestyles.com

Library of Congress Cataloging-in-Publication Data
Naylor, Sharon.
   How to plan an elegant wedding in 6 months or less : achieving your dream
      wedding when time is of the essence / Sharon Naylor
   p.   cm.
   Includes index.
   ISBN 0-7615-2824-5
   1. Weddings—Planning.   I. Title.
HQ745.N389   2000
395.2'2—dc21   00-048303

00 01 02 03 DD 10 9 8 7 6 5 4 3 2 1
Printed in the United States of America

HOW TO ORDER
Single copies may be ordered from Prima Publishing, 3000 Lava Ridge Court, Roseville, CA 95661; telephone (800) 632-8676 ext. 4444. Quantity discounts are also available. On your letterhead, include information concerning the intended use of the books and the number of books you wish to purchase.

Visit us online at www.primalifestyles.com

CONTENTS

To Rose, Anna, Helen, Millie, Minnie, Connie, and Annie:
The Butterfly Club.
With eternal love and gratitude

ACKNOWLEDGMENTS

IT WOULD TAKE ME more than six months to thank all the people who, in some way, contributed to the makings of this book and the makings of the author. I must begin by thanking my wonderful editors at Prima, Denise Sternad and Michelle McCormack, as well as my agent and longtime friend, Elizabeth Frost Knappman.

Immense gratitude goes to my father, Andrew Blahitka, an unsung hero and role model for all the success I have attained. Money isn't everything, he taught me, family is. Remember that when you're making out your wedding budget and when the seating chart has to be arranged.

Mom, thank you for your listening ear and for being my personal thesaurus.

Steve and Leanne, thank you for your support, for always calling to see how my book signings went, and for creating my Web site. Steve, you are the future of film, and I have no doubt that you will find yourself at a podium someday.

Karen and Greg, my love and thanks go out to you.

Madison and Kevin, thank you for your tired smiles, your ready hugs and kisses, the joy and wonder in your eyes, and the sound of your laughter. You will never know how important you are to me and how much I adore you.

To the most loyal and loving friends in the world—Jill, Jen, Pam, and Susan—thank you for a long history of trust and laughter. To have one true friend is the greatest of blessings. I have four, and am grateful every day.

I would also like to thank the many newly married couples and wedding professionals who gave their time and input to this project.

And, most importantly, I would like to thank Kathryn DeGuire and Lee Suckno for keeping me in it.

INTRODUCTION

"Y OU'RE PLANNING A wedding in less than *six months? Are you crazy?"*

You're going to hear that a thousand times—if you haven't already—so let me ease your mind. No, you don't have to be crazy to plan a wedding in less than a year. In fact, you just might be smarter for it. No matter what nightmare stories you've heard about brides who tried to pull together an elegant wedding in less time than it takes to grow out a bad haircut, you actually are in a far better position than brides who give themselves a year (or two) to plan their weddings.

Think about it. The average bride who chooses a date far in advance does all of the major planning and booking in the first month or two, and then she has the rest of the year to sweat out her decisions, waffle on them, change them, argue with her mother and mother-in-law about them, and make each little detail such a big deal that she's a frazzled wreck by the time the wedding comes around. She may even just want to get the whole ordeal over with, so tired is she of even hearing the word "wedding."

You, on the other hand, have a great advantage. Because your time is limited, you don't have the luxury of waffling and changing your mind a million times. You know what you want, you get in, you make your plans, you get out, and on to the next task. Your wedding is therefore more efficient and enjoyable, focused on the fact that you're getting married, not on whether or not the ice sculpture will be swans, cupids, hearts, or a likeness of the two of you. While brides with plenty of planning time go practically insane with all those idle hours, you smartly avoid the conditions that make for bridal horror stories.

This, of course, is not to say that your wedding planning experience is going to be (pardon the pun) a cakewalk. Planning a wedding in less than six months is going to take some extra time and effort, especially in our current age of rushing around and having more responsibilities in our lives. You wouldn't be able to do it without a good guidebook and the benefit of inside advice from wedding professionals and real-life brides who planned beautiful weddings in six, three, and even one month.

Yes, it will be a lot of work. You will need to be smart about your steps and decisions. You are, after all, entering the world of the wedding industry, where everything is pretty much planned according to a set schedule—that is, a year in advance. You will find that the best catering halls have been booked for two years. You will find that some gowns have to be ordered nine months in advance. You will find that some florists, bakers, and limo companies will just be too busy on your wedding day. I can hear you sighing from here. *Why bother then?* My answer, from years of experience as a wedding author and syndicated wedding writer, is that it can be done. It just takes a little extra legwork, a whole lot of patience, flexibility, creativity, diplomacy, a good support and help network, and the ability to work the wedding industry from a knowledgeable standpoint. With this book, you are armed and ready, and will be able to plan the wedding of your dreams in less than six months . . . and will probably have more fun and more positive memories than brides who lose a year or two of their lives to the planning process.

Less time = More Money?

THERE is one drawback, however. Planning a wedding in less than six months will most likely mean that you will have to spend a bit more money for it. After all, the most fair-priced of the high-quality wedding professionals and sites have already been booked. The wedding industry is a word-of-mouth one. All brides who happen upon a gem of a photographer whose work is good and whose prices are affordable refer him to all their friends and family. The gems that exist within the industry get booked up quickly, leaving the fool's-gold selections to the rest of the brides. So, since you're getting into the game virtually halfway through, your choices will be something like these:

- ◆ The outrageously overpriced, five-star professional who just did Mariah Carey's last party.

- ◆ The professional with the attractive ad in the Yellow Pages with a history of bad service and small-claims suits against him from earlier disgruntled brides and grooms.

- ◆ The just-starting-out professional right out of Johnson and Wales with no client base or advertising, but amazing possibilities.

- The mediocre professional who will raise her prices because she knows you're desperate.

- The absolute professional with a rare opening right when you want it.

Sounds frightening, I know, but that's the nature of the industry. There are sharks out there, and they usually bite the brides and grooms who feel they *have* to book somebody, anybody, and don't take the time to do the necessary research. You may not have a lot of time to plan, but you don't have the time *not* to do your homework. That would cost you money and happiness. Obviously, in this situation, you want the best quality and dependability you can get for your money. You know enough not to go for the too-good-to-be-true option that costs next to nothing and delivers even less. You'll instead hunt for the gem that wasn't already taken by the scavengers who came before you. And it is possible to find that true professional, though you may well have to spend a little more for what you want. Fortunately, this book takes that into account and offers plenty of ideas on how to save money, to get the best for less, to stretch your wedding budget, and to get some things for free.

You'll Need a Little Help

THE best action that you could take for your own well-being, especially at the start of your wedding planning time, is to ask for and accept help from others. Most brides I've spoken with said the six-month time frame was no problem, because they delegated smaller tasks to their mothers (who were dying to help out anyway!), their bridesmaids, their fiancé's mom (for brownie points!), and even the groom. If you're smart about handing out little to-dos, the work gets done quickly, and the list gets checked off smoothly.

There are some rules, however, for depending on others to help you plan your wedding. Too many brides have gone about this the wrong way, winding up with poorly done tasks, forgotten requests, and ruined relationships over the correct design of the wedding programs. For the best start to your delegating process, follow these guidelines, remembering to use the "Task Delegation List" in the back of this book to keep you organized.

- *Ask whether the person has time to help you out.* If you know your sister is in the middle of studying for the bar exam, don't burden her with the task of hunting all over town for salmon-colored ribbon.

- *Delegate the little things.* Ask someone to help by calling places for brochures, booking appointments for fittings, and so on. Do not assign someone something that will matter very much to you.

- *Put the request in writing, such as in a letter or e-mail.* Sometimes people forget conversations, and you don't want to have to argue about verbal agreements being legal and binding.

- *Be understanding of others' limitations.* Always say, "If you can't do this, just let me know by next week."

- *Give them a deadline.* Tell them the calls have to be made by Friday. If you don't set a deadline, people can put the task off and forget about it.

- *Tell them to get back to you with the results of their task.* It's always a good idea to make sure people have your e-mail, since that's an easy way for them to just drop you a quick line.

Speaking of helping out, gone are the days when the groom would just show up in his tux, smiling, on the day of the wedding. Now grooms are getting involved in the planning of the wedding from decision one onward. Your fiancé may or may not care about the wedding plans—he does, after all, just want to be married to you—so approach him with your invitation to voice his opinions. He may be happy about being freed from the macho, male mentality that "guys don't do weddings," and he'll just take it as his part in planning a really big celebration. Everyone wins. He gets to feel included, his choices are a part of the day, and you have one more person to help with the long list of things to get done. Most brides report that their grooms were more than happy to do tasks such as these:

- Design the wedding program (or invitations, in some cases) on the computer
- Keep track of RSVPs (a big job!)
- Make maps for inclusion in the invitations
- Help plan the catering menu
- Go for cake and catering tastings
- Choose the wines and liquors for the reception

- Do the initial honeymoon researching
- Buy cigars for the reception
- Design the wedding ring (for example, Oksana Yurchuk wears an exquisite ring that her husband, Dorian, designed and created)

You Make It Sound So Easy!

OH, no—it's not going to be easy. Planning a wedding very rarely is, no matter how much prep time you have. In your situation, planning a wedding in less than six months, you'll have to work very hard to get what would be half a year's worth of work done in the first month. Most major decisions and purchases will have to be done in the first month to get you on track to the rest of the planning process. From ordering a gown to booking a ceremony and reception site, to booking your honeymoon, to finding a photographer—all will have to be arranged in the first month for best results. While some of the finest caterers do pull off beautiful weddings in a week, they could put their children through college on what they'll charge for that feat. So be smart, get the bulk of the major tasks completed as soon as possible, then enjoy the rest of the planning process—with an air of celebration, not stress.

Can't a Wedding Consultant Do It for Me?

IF you're one of those brides with a grueling job, small children to take care of, or you live far away from the place where the wedding will be held, getting a wedding consultant can be a great idea. Again, things have changed in the wedding industry over the years, and you won't see the frantic little hyper-planner like Martin Short's character in the remake of *Father of the Bride*. Now, wedding consultants offer several types of packages to help you plan your wedding. You can book them to plan everything in your wedding from start to finish (if you don't mind handing the reins to someone else and watching their interpretation of your vision take place). Or your consultant may simply provide you with brochures and videos from their recommended wedding vendors, or just show up on the wedding day to orchestrate the events. The choice is yours.

Fees for wedding planners vary almost as much as do the services they provide. Some planners do not charge a fee, but instead take a cut of the fees you pay to the vendors you hire through them. Others charge a flat fee for their help, still others a certain amount per wedding guest (including children!), and then there are those who charge you anywhere from 10 to 20 percent of the total cost of the wedding. Time is money, and you're paying the planner for his or her time and expertise. If your wedding is scheduled less than six months from now, this could be a good option for you. On the other hand, many brides who have gone this route later regretted leaving themselves out of the joy of planning for the sake of time and convenience. So consider carefully: If your schedule and responsibilities leave you no other choice, or if you love the idea of having a professional do some (not all!) of the work, then consider hiring a professional wedding planner based on the following criteria:

- *He or she must belong to a professional organization such as the Association of Bridal Consultants.* That organization has strict rules about education in the field, experience, ratings, and positive reviews, and membership in ABC is a gold star for your selection. Avoid any planner who is not a member of such an organization.

- *Get referrals.* Ask recently married friends, or friends of friends, who they used, and whether they would recommend that person.

- Choose a planner who is willing to sit down for a free first consultation.

- Be sure you have good rapport with this person. He or she will be a very important part of the most important day of your life, and you must get along in a friendly manner. Avoid a planner who seems rushed, talks down to you, or is not patient with your questions.

- Choose a planner whose workspace is professional and who shows what he or she is capable of doing for you.

- Ask to look at pictures and samples from actual events this person has worked on.

- Ask how many weddings he or she will be planning for your

time frame. If it seems like a lot, move on to the next planner. You don't want a harried planner mixing your order up with another bride's.

- ◆ Ask if the planner has done weddings with this short an amount of lead time. If this person has never done a rush job before, it might be overwhelming.

- ◆ If you're planning an outdoor wedding, or a wedding on a beach, ask if he or she has ever done that kind of wedding before. As you'll read later, untraditional weddings have detailed criteria lists and present a list of challenges that any good planner can handle with expertise.

- ◆ Arrange a check-in schedule with your planner. Let your planner know you'll be calling once or twice a week to check on progress. See how he or she takes this. Some planners are artists and do not want to be bothered, and others are happy to discuss the plans with you, get your input, and work together.

- ◆ Always get a written list of their fees, including what extras go beyond the standard rate.

- ◆ Create a solid contract with the planner, and feel free to add in any changes that you don't see in the contract, such as special arrangements that you make

The benefit of having a wedding coordinator is that someone else does the busywork. To truly create the wedding of your dreams, the coordinator has to know exactly what you want and exactly how you want it. So you must be clear about your vision. Bring in pictures from magazines. Describe your dreams. Ask for ideas if you have few. And learn from other brides who regret handing over a blank check and giving a planner total creative freedom. Be involved with the plans.

But There's No Time to Have Fun!

NONSENSE! This is the planning of your wedding! Don't fall into the trap that many brides do of taking everything too seriously, turning a simple decision into a power struggle, stressing, crying, moaning to the groom, and basically acting as if the planning of your wedding is a series of root canals. Many brides who have planned in less than six months actually report that they enjoyed their planning process far more than did their friends who took a year. Problems were laughed at, decisions were a snap, and—best of all—the people around them believed they were under so much pressure (even though they weren't) that they respected their space and were quite agreeable at all times. The "sense of urgency" actually helped the bride and groom avoid a true sense of urgency!

So remember at every step of the way that each task is part of a greater whole, that the wedding will come together, that hard work put in now will pay off, that money isn't everything, and that the whole idea behind what you're doing is getting to the "I Do!" part faster, so that you and your groom can begin your wonderful life together.

RELAX!

During your planning of the wedding—from your first minute through the rush and hurry of booking available vendors, making all the little decisions, and finally walking down the aisle at the ceremony site—you'll be facing the ups and downs of stress. Your family may pressure you to invite certain people, include certain customs, hold the wedding at a garish hall you hate. Your bridesmaids may turn moody and jealous, delaying and fighting every step of the way. Your flower order may get canceled. Your gown may come in two sizes too small, and you'll have to make hundreds of phone calls.

So you don't lose your mind, or give it all up and run away to Bali; instead, practice these healthy stress-busters to keep yourself in check. These tips go for the groom as well.

+ *Get plenty of sleep.* The brain does not work well on fewer hours of shut-eye than it needs. Make sure you're getting your rest.

+ *Get plenty of exercise.* Just because you have appointments lined up doesn't mean you should give up your running routine. Exercise produces the body's feel-good hormones, and you'll want to be in good shape for your wedding.

+ *Try yoga or meditation.* I know, your brain may be racing with the details and fears of planning a wedding, but you may be able to slow down a little bit. You can find tapes and videos in the library if you don't want to commit to a class right now.

- *Eat well.* Choose nutritious foods that make you feel good. Stay away from sugar and caffeine, which are unhealthful and make you jittery.

- *Avoid mood enhancers, such as alcohol, drugs, cigarettes, even chocolate donuts.* Starting or increasing a bad habit now can put strain on your well-being and even become a problem in your marriage.

- *Take bubble baths.* Make it a ritual to set aside undisturbed time to soak your cares away.

- *Get a massage.* Either have your partner knead your sore neck muscles, or get a licensed pro to give you the full treatment with eucalyptus oil, Native American music, candles, and soothing instructions.

- *Take a mini-vacation.* When things get tense, go away, just the two of you, to a hotel for the weekend and pretend you're just dating again.

- *Make wedding talk off-limits at certain times.* Give yourself a break from the subject, so that your whole life does not revolve around the details and hassles of the reception.

- *Laugh!* Be sure you include lots of enjoyable activities in your week, and that you and your fiancé are still having fun together. Watch funny movies, television shows, go to comedy clubs, crack each other up. Laughter keeps you relaxed, and will melt away the frustrations of the more ridiculous aspects of the planning process.

- *Try aromatherapy.* A sniff of lavender will make your shoulders come down from up around your ears.

- *Keep it all in perspective.* It's just a wedding, not the end of the world. It's a time-limited planning event, one that will become what you make of it. Enjoy the process, and limit your stress by being flexible when you have to be, firm when necessary, and diplomatic when to the situation demands it. Respect your own choices, and set your boundaries from the beginning so others know they can't walk all over you.

TIMELINE

Your Very Own Timetable

USE this as you go along to remind you of unfinished business, and to keep you on track throughout your engagement.

SIX MONTHS BEFORE THE WEDDING . . .

- ✓ Announce your engagement.
- ✓ Attend engagement parties.
- ✓ Discuss as a couple what your shared wishes are for the wedding of your dreams.
- ✓ Begin looking through magazines and books for wedding-day ideas.
- ✓ Choose the wedding date (and backup dates for booking purposes).
- ✓ Inform your family and friends of the wedding date.
- ✓ Assess your wedding budget.
- ✓ Decide who will pay for what.
- ✓ Decide what part of your budget will get the most money (for example: gown, reception, or flowers).
- ✓ Decide on a level of formality.
- ✓ Make up your guest list.
- ✓ Select and book your ceremony location.
- _____ Select and book your ceremony officiant.
- ✓ Find out about your ceremony site's regulations.
- ✓ Select and book your reception site.
- ✓ Choose the members of your bridal party and inform each of his or her role.
- veil ✓ Choose and order your wedding gown and veil.
- _____ Choose and book your bridesmaids' gowns.
- _____ Hire a wedding coordinator (if you so choose).
- ✓ Choose a florist and meet with the floral consultant.
- ✓ Choose and book a caterer.
- _____ Choose and book a cake baker.
- ✓ Choose and book a photographer.
- _____ Choose and book a videographer.
- ✓ Choose and book your reception entertainment, DJ, or band.
- _____ Choose and book a limousine or classic car company.
- _____ Choose and book a rental company (if you so choose).
- ✓ Start looking at invitation samples, and select your desired design.

_____ Place engagement photo and announcement in local newspapers.

✓ _____ Notify your boss about your upcoming wedding and arrange for time off for the wedding week or weeks.

FIVE MONTHS BEFORE THE WEDDING . . .

✓ _____ Find out your local marriage license requirements.

_____ Choose and book your honeymoon.

✓ _____ Order your invitations.

✓ _____ Order wedding rings.

_____ Have wedding rings engraved (if you so choose).

_____ Reserve all rental equipment (tents, chairs, tables, linens, and so on).

✓ _____ Choose and reserve a block of rooms for your guests at a nearby hotel.

✓ _____ Book your honeymoon suite for the wedding night.

_____ Order pre-printed napkins, matchbooks, and so on.

_____ Create maps to ceremony and reception locations for enclosure in the invitations.

FOUR MONTHS BEFORE THE WEDDING . . .

_____ Choose and rent men's wedding wardrobe.

_____ Begin gown fittings.

_____ Choose shoes and accessories for wedding day.

_____ Help bride's and groom's parents choose their wedding day attire.

_____ Choose children's wedding day attire.

_____ Consult with wedding coordinator for a "halfway there" update.

✓ _____ Consult with caterer or banquet hall manager for a "halfway there" update.

THREE MONTHS BEFORE THE WEDDING . . .

_____ Write your vows.

✓ _____ Register for gifts.

_____ Begin bridesmaids' fittings.

_____ Choose ceremony readings and music.

_____ Submit song "wish list" to DJ or band you've hired.

_____ Submit picture "wish list" to photographer.

_____ Arrange for a babysitter to watch guests' kids on the wedding day (have several babysitters if you expect a lot of children).

TWO MONTHS BEFORE THE WEDDING . . .

_____ Address invitations to guests.

_____ Mail invitations to guests.

_____ Order or make wedding programs.

_____ Order wedding favors.

_____ Choose and purchase your "going away" outfit and honeymoon clothes.

_____ Meet with ceremony musician about song list.

_____ Have attendants' shoes dyed in one dye lot.

_____ Formally ask friends to participate in wedding, such as give readings, attend the guest book, transport wedding gifts from reception to home, and so on.

_____ Send for all name-change documents, such as passport, credit cards, driver's license, and others.

ONE MONTH BEFORE THE WEDDING . . .

_____ Get marriage license.

_____ Get necessary blood tests, medical exams. (Note: Check your state's requirements to be sure you give yourselves enough time!)

_____ Plan the rehearsal.

_____ Plan the rehearsal dinner.

_____ Invite bridal party and involved guests to the rehearsal and rehearsal dinner.

_____ Confirm honeymoon plans.

_____ Get all incoming guests' arrival times at airports and train stations.

_____ Arrange for transportation of guests to their hotel.

_____ Make beauty appointment for wedding day.

_____ Do fitting for gown.

_____ Attend showers.

_____ Write thank-you notes for shower gifts (by hand, no shortcuts!).

_____ Make up seating chart for reception.

_____ Pick up honeymoon travel tickets and information books.

_____ Make up welcome gift baskets for guests.

_____ Arrange for wedding-day transportation for the bridal party if they will not be in limos.

_____ Make wedding favors (if you so wish).

_____ Purchase unity candle.

_____ Purchase garters (get two—one for keeping, one for tossing).

_____ Purchase toasting flutes.

_____ Purchase cake knife.

_____ Purchase guest book.

_____ Purchase post-wedding toss-its (birdseed, flower petals, bubbles, bells, or other) and decorate small containers, if you so choose.

_____ Purchase throwaway wedding cameras.

_____ Visit hair salon for "tryouts" of hairstyles for wedding day.

ONE WEEK BEFORE THE WEDDING . . .

_____ Confirm all wedding plans with all wedding vendors, by asking each to tell you what date, time, and place he or she has on record.

_____ Caterer (give final headcount now!)
_____ Florist
_____ Cake baker
_____ Photographer
_____ Videographer
_____ Ceremony musicians
_____ Reception entertainers
_____ Officiant
_____ Ceremony site manager
_____ Reception site manager
_____ Wedding coordinator
_____ Limousine company
_____ Rental company agent
_____ Pay final deposits for all services.
_____ Place tips and fees in marked envelopes for such participants as the officiant, ceremony musicians, coordinator, valets, and so on).
_____ Drop off guest welcome baskets at hotel.
_____ Pick up wedding gown.
_____ Pack for honeymoon.
_____ Break in your wedding day shoes.
_____ Remind groom to get new shoes for the wedding day.
_____ Arrange for house- and pet-sitters.
_____ Get travelers' checks (if you so choose).
_____ Plan wedding day brunch, and inform bridal party about it.
_____ Purchase bridal party's and parents' gifts.
_____ Wrap bridal party's and parents' gifts.
_____ Bride and groom buy gifts for each other.
_____ Write out guests' place cards and table numbers.
_____ Get ahead on wedding thank-yous by sending notes out to those who have sent gifts.
_____ Submit address change notification to the post office (if you will be moving after the honeymoon).
_____ Attend bachelorette party (be sure to tell bridesmaids and friends that this week would be good for you, as you do not want to be out the night before your wedding).

THE DAY BEFORE THE WEDDING . . .
_____ Make sure everything you need is packed.
_____ Lay out all wedding day wardrobe and accessories.
_____ Very important: Discuss with all residents in your home the shower-time schedule for the next day!
_____ Assemble emergency bag with extra stockings, lipstick, pressed powder, emory boards, and so on.
_____ Arrange to have any emergency items such as aspirin or insulin in the emergency bag.

Manicure/pedicure

_____ Put a cell phone in the emergency bag.
_____ Gas up the cars.
_____ Go to the beauty salon to get waxed.
_____ Place last call to caterer or coordinator to answer last-minute questions.
_____ Attend rehearsal.
_____ Attend rehearsal dinner.
_____ Get a good night's sleep!

ON THE WEDDING DAY . . .
_____ Attend bridal brunch.
_____ Have hair and nails done at beauty salon, and have a massage there as well.
_____ Have photos taken at home.
_____ Make sure someone responsible has arranged for your suitcases to go to your hotel room or in the car that will be taking you to the airport.
_____ Make sure someone has the wedding rings.
_____ Make sure someone has the car keys.
_____ Relax and know that everything will be fine!

WHAT KIND OF WEDDING DO YOU WANT?

CREATING YOUR DREAM VISION

At the very start of your planning process, you'll of course need to figure out exactly what kind of wedding you want. Do you want a grand, elaborate, traditional wedding with a horse-drawn carriage, doves, ice sculptures, and a harpist playing throughout the cocktail hour? Do you want an intimate wedding at home? Do you want to get married barefoot on a tropical beach? Your initial vision has to be defined, as this is the cornerstone of all of your plans. If you want a traditional wedding, for instance, certain prescribed steps must be taken, certain decisions made. If you'll be married at home, you'll have an entirely different list. Plus, your decision will determine the formality level and, ultimately, the budget of your wedding.

You might be confused right now, thinking that since your time is limited, so are your options. Nonsense! You can have whatever kind of wedding you want—whatever your dream is—and you don't have to limit yourself to what's easy and quick. You would be cheating yourself by settling for less—which, by the way, is the number one complaint of brides who planned their weddings in less than six months without the information you have at your disposal right now. You may not be able to pull off the most elaborate of affairs (this is reality, you know), but there is no reason your wedding cannot be of the same quality—or better—as that of any other bride's.

Even if you *think* you want your wedding in your backyard, please read the descriptions of the wedding types from which you can choose. You'll get a true picture of what it takes to plan that particular type of event. Some of the hidden costs and headaches may surprise you; at the very least, you'll become even more clear about what your original style idea entails.

While a wedding can take any shape or form, the following major "categories" will be explained in depth:

+ The Traditional Wedding
+ The Outdoor Wedding
+ The At-Home Wedding
+ The Destination Wedding

At this point, many brides ask, "Which one is easiest to plan?" Again, your decision should not be based on "easy." No one choice is inherently easier than another. An at-home wedding can be just as involved as a destination wedding. A formal outdoor wedding can require even more planning than a traditional wedding—and often does. So take each choice as an equal, and judge based on the merits of the individual style. Each choice can be a simpler affair within that category, or can be grandiose, depending on what you want and what your budget allows. So don't even ask the "Which one is easier?" question. This section will help you focus on what kind of wedding you want. And, yes, we will discuss the details of each wedding type in chapter 4: Choosing the Locations

The Traditional Wedding

THE traditional wedding—a ceremony in a church or synagogue, followed by a reception in a banquet hall or other site—is the most common and most well-known. The planning of this type of wedding is pretty much standard: You make arrangements with the officiant and the reception hall manager, make your choices, hand over a dozen checks, and show up for the big day.

This kind of wedding is described in every bridal magazine and wedding book out there; it's the one you see on the *In Style* wedding special on television, and the type that every one of your guests has attended many times. It's standard, traditional, prescribed by etiquette, and probably the kind of wedding you've fantasized about since you were a little girl.

The Outdoor Wedding

THIS kind of wedding is increasingly popular, as people fall in love with the romantic images from well-produced insurance commercials and pictures of Cindy Crawford's wedding on the beach. While a garden or beach wedding may seem easier to plan, it actually brings up a host of questions that the traditional wedding does not usually present. What if it rains? What are the backup plans? Very often, planning an outdoor wedding can require twice the legwork, as you'll have to plan the outdoor event and also arrange what everyone will do if the weather does not cooperate.

Many brides report that while their outdoor wedding was lovely and magical, they endured an extra dose of pre-wedding nerves as they watched for every rain cloud and checked the Weather Channel for five-day forecasts that changed dramatically every day.

Aside from the weather question, outdoor weddings seem to mean more to the couples who choose them. They are surrounded by the beauty of nature, flower gardens, the roar of the nearby surf. Their guests appreciate a wedding that is unlike the usual. Their pictures are not staged poses on the steps of a chapel or at the altar. Outdoor weddings bring plenty of natural light to a wedding, and may very well fit your vision.

The At-Home Wedding

YES, your backyard is easier to book on short notice, and the at-home wedding can be a wonderfully intimate, meaningful affair. After all, you may have grown up in that house. You may have descended the staircase you now navigate in your wedding gown as a little girl playing "bride" with a pillowcase pinned to your head. An at-home wedding fills the family abode with priceless memories and a level of joy that seems to stay in it long after the wedding is over.

While the at-home wedding is another wonderful choice, it too presents its own collection of issues that need to be addressed. Is there enough room for all of your intended guests, or will you have to pare down your guest list? What about parking? What about power? Is the oven big enough for the caterer's trays? Who is going to clean up? You're unlikely to face these questions with the other styles of weddings, but they simply represent a different list that requires an equal amount of effort.

> ## Wedding Day Reflections
>
> We're pretty informal people ourselves, so we decided to have an informal wedding. My parents weren't happy—they wanted the whole big splash wedding—but at the end of the day, as we looked around and saw all of our guests happy at their little candlelit tables, and we were completely relaxed, we knew we had made the right decision in planning a wedding that matched our style, instead of what anyone else wanted us to do.
>
> —Danielle and Jeremy

The Destination Wedding

THE destination wedding comes in two forms: the elaborate wedding you plan for a location far from your home, such as in your old hometown where your parents live, or a trip to a vacation spot such as Hawaii, Las Vegas, or the Caribbean. Cruises fit into this category as well.

The destination wedding, depending on what you want, can be a huge effort if you're making all the traditional-type plans from a distance; or it can be as simple as one phone call to a wedding coordinator at a well-known resort spot. Several brides say that they were perfectly happy with their plan of attack: They called the wedding planner at a Las Vegas resort, took less than an hour to explain what they wanted, and a week later they were married in Vegas. It all depends upon your vision.

What serves you well at this point is that the destination wedding is becoming extremely popular. More established and high-quality resorts are catering to this upsurge in interest; therefore, service and choices are better, and many establishments even have packages for entire families. This can be a wonderful idea if you and/or your fiancé have children of your own, as these resorts have programs to keep children occupied during the rest of your visit, as you honeymoon together.

One major drawback is that planning from a distance can be difficult. You may not have the level of involvement you want, your choices are not as wide-open as they would be closer to your home location, arranging travel may be a hassle for you and for your guests, and some destinations have strict rules about residency, legalities, licenses, and other details. As in all weddings, you'll have to choose wisely during your planning process and consider the grander picture of what the final result will be.

> ### *Wedding Day Reflections*
>
>
>
> W*e thought we were making it easier by planning an informal wedding. We planned an outdoor picnic. It was decorated beautifully, and the ceremony was lovely, but afterward, I looked around and it was like any other barbecue day. In trying to make it simpler, we really ripped ourselves off.*
>
> —Tara and Dan

Smaller Is Not Necessarily Better

WHEN deciding what kind of wedding you want, you'll also have to decide how big your wedding will be. Because the size of the guest list often determines the location, budget, and other details, you'll have to decide right up front whether yours will be a smaller, intimate wedding of 30 to 50, or if you'll invite everyone from your clients to your college roommates to your manicurist.

Here again, many brides confuse themselves, assuming smaller is better. It may be—if an intimate wedding is what you're after—but a smaller wedding can be just as involved as a larger one. You can face as many details, plans, and decisions while putting together a wedding for 50 as you will for a wedding of 250. The answer, then, is to make your decisions on the issue of involvement rather than solely on the issue of size.

A smaller wedding, if you so choose, is going to be more intimate. Many brides who have little time for planning do select this option, saying that smaller weddings take less time. There are fewer invitations to address, fewer favors to wrap, fewer trips to the airport to pick up incoming relatives. They report that a smaller, more intimate wedding was a better choice, not only for so-called ease of planning, but because they were more relaxed at their own weddings. The guests were not crowded into a room. There was plenty of space on the dance floor. They did not spend all night hopping from table to table, chatting with a few hundred guests, most of whom neither bride nor groom knew all that well.

In terms of saved time, a smaller wedding does provide a slight edge.

Brides who planned a larger wedding in a short amount of time report that the biggest headache was finding a reception site big enough to suit their needs at this late date. It took a while longer, but they did find a location. Also, finding lodging for visiting friends and relatives with only a few month's notice was more

Say the Word

Speak with your fiancé about what he wants as well. His input is important, too, and more and more grooms are getting involved with the planning of their weddings. He may not have been dreaming about the big day since he was seven, but he undoubtedly has some feelings about whether or not he can help you pull off a lavish wedding in just a few months. Your fiancé probably understands by now that the short planning time will be stressful, and you should explain that you'll need his help and support. You'll have enough stress on your mind. Making your life partner your partner in planning your wedding is a smart move.

difficult, and some brides say they had to put some relatives in one hotel and others in another hotel farther away. (The distanced guests were miffed, apparently because they saw themselves as not important enough to stay at the hotel where the reception was taking place! Such problems!)

So, contrary to popular opinion, it is possible to plan a large wedding in less than six months. It will just take more effort. You may feel strongly about having the big picture wedding, or you may agree with the many brides who feel that a smaller, intimate affair will not only be less time-consuming to plan, but will also be more enjoyable.

The Guest List

IF at this point you've decided to have a smaller wedding, now you'll face one of the most difficult tasks of the wedding: creating your guest list. Obviously, you must figure out the exact size of the wedding in order to make all the other decisions. Determining the size of your wedding is the foundation of your planning.

TINA AND RICH'S STORY

Tina has an enormous family. Her fiancé, Rich, also has an enormous family. When they tallied their prospective guest list, they came up with 350 people. After all, they couldn't leave anyone out! So they started their planning process by facing this monumental headache: Where would they fit so many people? An at-home wedding was out. All of the biggest banquet halls had been booked a year ago. None of the beautiful estate homes in the area would allow more than 150 guests.

In her frantic state, Tina considered avoiding the whole thing by eloping with Rich, but she knew she would spend the rest of her life disappointed that she didn't get the dream wedding she'd always wanted.

I spoke to Tina about her options. She didn't want to hold the wedding at a later date when the banquet hall would be available. I don't blame her. We talked about outdoor weddings, perhaps at the beach or at a park, and together we came up with the idea of having her wedding at an arboretum. The nearby site was available, room for guests was unlimited, they had indoor banquet rooms suitable for rain-outs, and she would save thousands on her florist bill by depending upon the natural décor of the site. She never would have considered this option if it weren't for the size of her guest list, so what began as a problem actually led to a wonderful solution.

Stress Relief

Warning! Most brides report that the guest list is where they got the most outside pressure from family members. You wouldn't be the first bride to hear, "But you have to invite them—you were invited to their wedding in 1981!" The bottom line is that this is your wedding. Even if your parents are paying for it, which may or may not be the case, you'll have to explain that since this short planning time presents special circumstances, you must limit the number you invite to the wedding. Stand firm, and don't be bullied. This job is difficult enough without outside pressure.

Most brides report that they plan their guest list in tiers, as in "ranking" guests in order of importance. In your own life, for example, you have people to whom you're close, who you wouldn't dream of leaving out of your wedding. Then, you have a scattering of peripheral people who you "should" invite, then your parents' lists, and all the other people you've ever met in your life.

Using this common tiered method, spend some time now making up your guest list. Use your address book to make sure you don't leave anyone out, and when you are through with your list, then approach your parents and future in-laws with your request to submit their lists. Explain in polite, diplomatic terms that space is limited and that you have only invited x-number of people. Give them a firm limit, explain about the tier system you're using to prioritize your list, ask

The Tiers of Guest List Construction

Instructions: Use this tier list to classify your guest list, and draw a line where the limit ends. For instance, most brides draw the line after first cousins (making exceptions for individuals from the "lower tiers" with whom they are especially close). Left-out family members will understand that you had to "draw the line" somewhere.

Both sets of parents (or multiple sets of parents if divorce and remarriage
    is involved)

Siblings and dates

Grandparents

Aunts and uncles

First cousins and dates (if cousins are over eighteen—and yes, we know kids
    "date" at age twelve these days, but they don't get to bring their boyfriend-
    of-the-week!)

Great aunts and great-uncles

Best friends and dates

High school and college friends and dates

Bosses and coworkers

Favorite neighbors

Family friends

Children of guests

Others

them to adhere to the same rules for fairness, and give them a short deadline for delivery of the list.

Once you get both sets of parents' lists and cross off duplicates, make your selections, and accept their extra choices, you'll have your working head count. This is the number you'll need to know for the selection of your ceremony and reception sites, your catering order, your floral order, lodging, transportation, and most of the other decisions. So this working number is a big factor. If you're truly limited in site choices, your number may have to become smaller. At that point, you'll cut out a tier or two.

Buying Time

In the interest of time (your most precious commodity right now!), don't worry about getting everyone's addresses and phone numbers—just the names are enough at this point.

Choosing a Level of Formality

THE more formal an event you have planned, the more rigid the rules of etiquette. For instance, a black-tie wedding will require your male guests to rent tuxedoes and your female guests to wear long gowns. For an ultraformal wedding such as this, you'll pull out all the stops, offering champagne and caviar to your guests, and hiring an orchestra to play

---

Brides' Insider Secrets About Semiformal Weddings

You can wear a gown you bought off the rack or a simpler dress (No nine-month ordering times!)

Caterers are more likely to supply you with the selections of your choice

They're far less expensive than formal weddings

They're not the usual wedding everyone has been to—with the same food, the same music, the same everything

Everyone is more relaxed and has a better time

It's more about the marriage than about the party

at your reception. Since it's unlikely you'll have the time—or the inclination—to plan a wedding of such magnitude in a short amount of time (although it can be done), we'll look at the more common levels of formality from which you're more likely to choose. Remember, too, that the level of formality also depends upon the time of day and the type of wedding you want. Again, it's mix and match. You can have a semiformal or informal home wedding, or a semiformal or informal outdoor wedding. It's up to you.

Your gown should match the level of formality, so if you want to wear a big, puffy ball gown, you're in for a formal wedding. If your wedding will be informal, then your gown should be more of a dress style. All the factors should fit together.

At this time, you must also choose the level of formality of your wedding so you can make the next decisions. If you've decided on an informal wedding, you won't be looking at any grand ballrooms. Your search list will instead include gardens or your own home. You know your likes and dislikes, and you know what you'd like to have at your own wedding. Most brides with fewer than six months to plan opt for the semiformal wedding.

> ### *Say the Word*
>
>
>
> *Every bride has to deal with the occasional rude guest who requests to bring a date, or to allow a preteen to bring a "friend" so the child will be more comfortable. Some guests want to bring their children because they don't ever leave them with babysitters. This is a tough one for most brides, and most report that they hated themselves afterwards for giving in. Do not make that mistake! Simply explain that space is limited, and offer the example that you couldn't invite some of your own friends because there is no space available.*

The Legalities

You know you'll have to get a license no matter what type of wedding you plan, but did you know that the style of wedding you choose may also involve some tricky legalities? For any short-time wedding, you'll have to do the important thing first: Make it legal. Check right away with your town hall for your state's requirements for marriage licenses, blood work, physicals, and necessary documents. There are as many sets of rules as there are states, so you have to make sure you find out exactly what you'll need and when. Getting a license may have to be done within a certain time period before the wedding, for instance, as will the blood work. You may need to get copies of your birth certificates, divorce papers, death certificates, or even valid photo IDs. Depending upon your age, you may need to get parental consent. The rules vary widely, so you'll need to be highly organized and efficient in order to get these necessary tasks done.

> ## Stress Relief
>
>
>
> Do not *depend on the Internet for marriage license information. Rules change every day, so be sure to call someone at your town hall, ask about marriage licenses, get the details, and write everything down. For further protection in case of argument or mixup, write down the name of the person you spoke with and the date and time you spoke with them. In some cases, your ability to explain a snafu may help the clerk complete your paperwork more efficiently.*

DESTINATION WEDDING LEGALITIES

No other wedding is more involved with regard to legalities than the destination wedding. Depending on the site you choose, you may have to do some extra work to get all the documents you'll need. You may need to gather—*and have notarized*—the following:

+ Birth certificate

+ Passport

+ Voting registration

+ Photo IDs

+ Social security cards

+ Divorce certificate (from previous marriage)

+ Annulment papers (from previous marriage)

+ Death certificate (if previous spouse is deceased)

Even more complicated is the fact that some destinations will require you to bring along a witness who has known you for a certain amount of time. That person or persons must have some of the above documentation as well, as will any children or other guests you bring along. Do not find yourself in the position that some less-informed brides have been, where they were standing on a cliffside in Fiji, ready to be married, and the local officiant would not perform the ceremony without proof of divorce. And finding a fax machine in remote areas of Fiji can be difficult.

Another element of the legalities is the need for blood work and inoculations. Some destinations will require you to get shots for any number of conditions. At the very least,

?

How much time will it take to get all the information we'll need for our marriage license?

Start *working on this right away! Some locations take weeks to get back to you with information requests, and some take months to file your applications!*

you will most likely have to get blood work done. Avoid getting caught in a common trap by finding out ahead of time whether that location accepts blood work from your home state or only from their domain. You may have to get the blood work done at your destination, which could mean arriving a week or so ahead of time. Speaking of arrival time, some locations require that you be in the locale for a certain amount of time, racking up a "residency" for a certain number of days. The rules are tricky, and different from location to location, but you can easily find out the rules by making a call or two to that destination's board of tourism or consulate. As in all your wedding planning, have your questions ready, get confirmation in writing even if you have to ask them to mail you their information packets, get the name of the person to whom you spoke, and confirm everything shortly before the wedding. Be organized. Have the dates of the medical and legal appointments in your calendar, and don't let these details slip by.

PERMITS

Another legality that you may face, especially when planning at-home, outdoor, beach, or specialty site weddings is permit requirements. Check with the town hall of the place where you're holding your wedding and inquire about any permits that will be necessary. Some beach areas require permits for use of the beach, for outdoor cooking, liquor consumption, and more. The list of possible permits includes:

- Parking
- Outdoor cooking
- Liquor consumption
- Bringing in extra electricity
- Construction of tents
- Use of fireworks
- Public gathering

Again, get all information on the necessary permits in writing. Ask at the town hall, at the police department, even the fire department. Never go by what a clerk "thinks." Many brides have had their receptions ruined by receiving incorrect or outdated information from a clerk who was too lazy to look up the new town regulations. Recognize that the town hall may not get this kind of request every day, and be kind and diplomatic when asking them to do a little research for you.

Stress Relief

One of the most important things you need to ask about is the noise violation rule. Some locations have "curfews" for noise, such as 9:00 P.M. or 10:00 P.M If you're planning your party to go on into the night, you certainly do not want the police showing up either to tell everyone to be quiet and shut down the band, or to hand you a "disturbing the peace" summons.

WHAT KIND OF WEDDING DO YOU WANT? 🐾 15

RELIGIOUS REQUIREMENTS

If you will be having a religious ceremony—as opposed to having a justice of the peace or the captain of a ship perform the rites—you will undoubtedly face a list of religious requirements before the priest, pastor, or rabbi can perform the ceremony. Many religious institutions require an application, an interview, and proof of divorce or annulment before they will "accept" you for services. One frightening aspect of this, as reported by some brides, is that they have actually been turned down by some churches! Some officiants say no if neither the bride nor the groom is a recognized member of the church, or if they are church members but don't attend enough! Some clerics turn down couples they do not feel should be getting married. One bride said that a priest felt she and her fiancé had not known each other long enough, so he would not perform the service!

The solution to this is to begin your search for a ceremony site and officiant right away. Make the necessary appointments, have the necessary meetings, and book your date as soon as possible.

If you are lucky enough to get the officiant you want, you may be required to attend some pre-wedding classes or counseling. The Catholic church has Pre-Cana classes, which is a series of courses any marrying couple must take to discuss their values, child-rearing ideas, and other major marriage topics. Discuss this requirement with your officiant, especially if you or your fiancé live far away or have an involved work-travel schedule. Some churches will not perform your wedding ceremony until you complete their courses, and some will allow you to take courses at your location.

?

My fiancé and I are planning to be married on a yacht. I've heard that captains of ships are certified to perform weddings, but how can you tell whether they're legitimate?

If you will be married on a boat, find out the captain's credentials, whether or not he or she has ever done this before, and what the paperwork requirements are. Then check with your state's board of marriages about the legalities in your area.

So now that you know the major factors involved in each style of wedding, you probably know what kind of wedding you'd like to plan. You know your wedding size, formality, whether it will be traditional or outdoor, and what legal issues you have to pursue. You know what you'd like. Now, the big question is: How much money can you put into it?

2

THE MONEY ISSUE

CORRESPONDING LIMITED TIME AND BUDGET

ALMOST ALL BRIDES are limited in their wedding plan choices by their budget constraints. Unfortunately, brides planning a wedding in less than a year are at a greater disadvantage in the budget department, as products and services are likely to cost more at this late planning time. After all, the best-valued, moderately priced wedding professionals were booked a year ago. What's left in the selection pool are the higher-priced pros and places that will charge a rush fee as they sense your desperation and need for quick booking. You will not have much time to comparison-shop—an essential in the world of wedding-budgeting—and you will not have the time to order less-expensive items that take a while to come through. No, this is not an ideal financial situation. But while the relatively brief planning time will mean extra expenses in some categories, you can find ways to make the most of your budget and get more wedding for your money.

How's Your Cash Supply?

ONCE the basics—size and formality—are decided, the key factor in the rest of the wedding decisions will be how much money is available.

How much will you need to create the wedding of your dreams? What can you get for what you have?

The average wedding today costs $20,000, according to the American Society of Bridal Consultants. Remember, that's average nationally. Figured into this amount is the total spent on the lavish Upper East Side weddings you read about in the society pages. Remember, too, that there are gorgeous $50,000 weddings and gorgeous $5,000 weddings. You should not hobble yourself by comparing your wedding to any other, you shouldn't start off your married life deeply in debt because you spent way too much on the event, and you should not cheat yourself by planning an itsy-bitsy wedding for next to nothing just because you feel you have no choice. None of these options are acceptable. What you must do is figure out how much money you can afford to spend, and then find a way to make your vision happen with that amount.

> ## Penny-Wise
>
> ——— $ ———
>
> *When considering your wedding budget, do not be lured by credit card companies that promise special wedding loans. On some wedding sites, well-known credit card companies are offering special lines of new credit for brides-to-be, and that's just one more way to get yourself deep into debt.*

Follow the two steps described below to assess just how much you can spend:

STEP 1: DETERMINE YOUR CONTRIBUTION AS A COUPLE   Look at what you and your fiancé have to spend on the wedding. If you're planning a wedding that will take place in less than six months, you may not have had a lot of time to save extra money for this occasion. So, you may be somewhat more limited than brides who've saved for two years. Be realistic about the amount of money you can devote to this wedding. Remember to respect your college loans, car loans, insurance premiums, and other expenses. You don't want to cause more problems by draining your bank accounts for a five-tiered instead of a three-tiered cake.

STEP 2: DETERMINE PARENTAL CONTRIBUTIONS

Find out whether or not your parents will be helping out with the expenses. Not all brides get their parents to foot the bill these days, although it is still fairly common for brides to get the free ride. In some cases, grandparents, godparents, and surrogate parents do contribute heavily to the wedding expenses. Do not assume this, however, as you never know your loved ones' financial positions or their true willingness to follow through on their good-natured offers at the engagement stage. Plan to sit down with your family to discuss what they will be willing to contribute to the fund. Arm yourself with this list of traditional rules for who pays for what, and assure your family that this list is negotiable. If the groom's family wants to pay for the cake, that's fine.

> ### Penny-Wise
>
> ——— $ ———
>
> While it is smart to make all your wedding purchases with a credit card—for safety's and potential refunds' sake—do not go nuts and max out all of your cards. After you pay the interest, you may find you've spent twice as much (if not more) than your wedding actually cost. Only charge what you can afford to pay off quickly.

Before you assign budgeting responsibilities, first look at the budget according to your own priorities. On what do you want the most money spent? The reception menu? Your dress? Flowers? Some brides imagine a wedding awash in a sea of pink roses, and they'll allocate a large portion of their budget to the florist. Some want the Vera Wang gown, and all other expenses get chopped way down. It's time for you to think about the wedding you envision, to choose where you want the most money to go—what you want to feature—and *then* you can complete your budget.

JESSICA'S STORY

After all the weddings she had been to, Jessica knew what she wanted and what she did not want. She wanted flowers. Tons of flowers. Exotic flowers. She wanted a bouquet that would make the world stop and look. She wanted centerpieces that would make her reception look like a royal event.

Facing a limited budget, and a realistic view of what flowers actually cost, she knew that she would have to do some tweaking of her budget to get the one thing she wanted most for her big day. So, being careful not to cut too deeply into other areas, she trimmed a little here and a little there. She hired the videographer for only one hour of the reception, choosing to schedule the cake-cutting earlier in the evening so the videographer could leave without missing anything important. She went to her second choice for favors, booked a party bus for her bridal party instead of four limos, and chose less expensive invitations.

After a while, as her success mounted, Jessica found ways to manage her budget without too much compromising. And she did create a floral vision that wowed her guests and fulfilled her wishes and dreams.

Here is a list of the major wedding expenses. In the right-hand column, place them in order of importance to you:

PRIORITIZING YOUR EXPENSES

Expense	Order of Importance
Engagement announcement	
Engagement party	
Ceremony site	
Reception site	
Wedding gown	
Bride's accessories and shoes	
Groom's clothing	
Wedding coordinator	
Invitations	
Programs	
Caterer's menu	

Expense	Order of Importance
Liquor	
Cake	
Flowers	
Reception entertainment	
Photography	
Videography	
Limousines or classic cars	
Favors	
Gifts	
Honeymoon	

Many brides report that sitting down with parents to decide what they'll pay for was difficult. Egos were often bruised, decisions taken out of the hands of the bride and groom, and the two families established a resentful relationship—especially when one family had significantly more money than the other. Only brides and grooms who pay for the entire wedding avoid this conflict. Here are some ways to help you start off on the right foot with a diplomatic meeting:

1. *Schedule a joint planning session.* Plan to sit down as a couple with both sets of parents, with the express intent to discuss the wedding budget. Your parents should not be ambushed, and a proper amount of time should be given to this task.
2. *Choose a relaxed, neutral atmosphere.* Many brides and grooms like to hold this meeting at a quiet restaurant, where Dad is less likely to make a scene about what things cost. In his own home, he may feel entitled to run the show.

Do Your Homework

It is a good idea to do a little bit of research before you begin the aforementioned task, as you want to start off with some idea of the average item or service costs. Be realistic about your budget from the outset, so you can plan your wedding with a minimum of financial hassle.

3. *Begin on a positive note.* Start off by proposing a toast, expressing gratitude that both sets of parents are agreeing to participate in the planning. (Some brides throw in the fact that they are happy to avoid the familial nightmares that brides with less loving parents have to endure. That ought to do it!)

4. *Be the leader.* Don't just put the paper on the table and say, "You choose." It helps if you already have ideas concerning whom you want to pay for what.

5. *Show them the traditional list discussed on the next page.* That way, they know what is traditionally their domain, and it gives them an out if they can't spend more. Some parents are relieved to see that they are not responsible for the more expensive aspects of the wedding, and a written list excuses them from the obligation. Of course they want to help as much as possible, but when it comes to money, it may be a touchy issue for them. Handled well, the presentation of a list of what's expected can be a relief to them.

6. *Avoid alcohol, or drink in moderation.* Do not get drunk—any of you! This is not a time for people to make decisions they won't remember later.

7. *Be prepared to deal with stress.* If the discussion gets tense, take a break and have some salad or bread. Say you'll get back to it after the appetizers. Change the subject to something non-wedding.

Stress Relief

Just watch out—many brides report that allowing certain family members to foot a bill usually means that family member wants free reign over the decisions. You may get something like "I'm paying for the cake, so you will have the cake topper I've chosen." A better idea is just to budget an amount, get the check from the parents, and order the cake yourself. And don't be a pest if the actual amount turns out to be $20 over what they gave you; just go ahead and pay the difference.

Who Pays for What? The Traditional List

Remember, this is the traditional list that's been around for years. Today's brides and grooms and their families are far more flexible, not bound by these rules, so you're free to allow the monetary participants some freedom in what they'd like to pick up.

BRIDE'S FAMILY

- Wedding announcements
- Engagement party
- Bridal consultant
- Invitations
- Wedding gown and veil
- Bride's accessories and shoes
- Reception site
- Catering
- Flowers
- Photographer
- Videographer
- Reception entertainment
- Limousines
- Tips

GROOM'S FAMILY

- Officiant
- Marriage license
- Bride's bouquet
- Boutonnieres
- Rehearsal dinner
- Honeymoon

8. *Be sure to pick up the tab for this dinner.* It's the least you can do if your parents are about to pay for a big wedding.

9. *Confirm the decisions made.* After dinner, print up what everyone agreed to and send them each a copy. Keep one for yourself as well.

Note: If one family has far less money than the other, do not have this meeting. When Daddy Warbucks puts his initials next to everything on the list, the less wealthy parents will feel terrible. Simply ask the less loaded but equally loving set of parents about the items they will handle, if any.

The Top Ten Mistakes Brides Make Regarding Money

1. Asking unreliable friends to take on a wedding day task, only to have it botched
2. Planning to cater the wedding themselves
3. Ordering a gown with delivery scheduled too close to the wedding date (A delayed delivery could mean you're out a dress!)
4. Taking the first available vendor rather than researching the options (That's the best way to get scammed!)
5. Not getting referrals from friends
6. Waiting too long to book sites or services
7. Not reading contracts carefully
8. Making decisions in haste or out of frustration
9. Planning too elaborate a wedding for the amount of preparation time
10. Being unorganized—for example, forgetting whether or not deposits were placed, paying twice, or losing contracts (Your life can get hectic during these few months of planning, so have a good organizing system and stay on top of it!)

WEDDING BUDGET

Item/Service	Who's Paying	Budgeted Amount	Amount Actually Spent
Engagement announcement			
Engagement party			
Ceremony site			
Ceremony décor			
Officiant's fee			
Reception site			
Rentals for reception site			
Wedding gown			
Wedding gown fittings			
Bride's accessories and shoes			
Bride's manicure, pedicure, and hairstyling			
Groom's clothing			
Groom's accessories and shoes			
Wedding coordinator			
Invitations			
Postage			
Programs			
Thank-you notes			
Caterer's total bill, including food, service, cleanup, and so on			
Liquor			
Cake			
Flowers			
Reception décor			
Reception entertainment			

(continues on next page)

WEDDING BUDGET, CONTINUED

Item/Service	Who's Paying	Budgeted Amount	Amount Actually Spent
Photography			
Videography			
Wedding cameras			
Limousines or classic cars			
Other guest transportation			
Favors			
Gifts			
Honeymoon			
Tips			

We've already mentioned that a wedding planned in less than six months is apt to be more expensive, and have touched on why. Throughout the book, as you read about each planning category in detail, you will learn several ways to save money on your wedding plans. These budgeting tips are from my book *1,001 Ways to Save Money and Still Have a Dazzling Wedding,* as well as from the many brides and grooms I have interviewed for this book. In addition, in the Resource section in the back of the book, you will find lists of Web sites and toll-free numbers to use to find your own savings.

3

CHOOSING THE DATE

ARE SOME DAYS BETTER THAN OTHERS?

SELECTING THE DAY of your wedding can be a little tricky. Even brides who have left themselves a year or so to plan their weddings may find it difficult to select a wedding date on which both their ceremony and reception sites are open. At this late time, you may find very few sites available for the day or days you want, and that the availability of ceremony and reception sites do not match up. This can be very frustrating, and juggling dates and times to make something fit may take quite a bit of effort.

Brides who have gone before you (some planning their weddings in as little as a month) suggest that you make life easier by scheduling the ceremony and reception site in the same place. Many beautiful reception halls can be arranged with an altar and chairs set up in one area and the reception in another. A garden wedding is perfect for this setup, as are home and beach settings. In general, if your hunt for sites turns up mismatching days of availability, you would be best advised to select one available site that you can use for both your ceremony and reception.

What Month?

THE most popular months for weddings are June, August, and September. Sites book up a year in advance for these months, so you will be traveling a hard road if you want to get married during those peak times. Availability is low as a rule, and prices are high. You would be much better off having your wedding in the off-season, such as February, April, March, or November.

What Day?

CERTAIN days of the year should be avoided, for obvious reasons. Some days are so popular due to holiday status and vacation time that they are booked years in advance. Such days include:

- New Year's Eve
- Valentine's Day
- Columbus Day weekend
- 4th of July weekend
- Memorial Day weekend
- Labor Day weekend

Other days are off-limits for common sense reasons:

- Tax time
- Friday the 13th
- A negative family anniversary, such as the anniversary of a death or a failed marriage
- Inclement weather seasons, such as your region's tornado time or usual string of days 100 degrees or more

♦ Religious holidays that have meal restrictions (One bride who scheduled her wedding during Lent realized that her religious guests did not eat meat on that day. They had to order vegetarian pizzas!)

Of course, Saturday weddings are still the most popular, but you'll find the Friday night wedding gaining ground. Even brides who have tons of time to plan are setting Friday night wedding dates, knowing this option is less expensive and enables them to leave for their honeymoon on a Saturday without taking the red-eye. Friday night weddings are becoming popular, and you may be able to find a wonderful location open on that day.

CARRIE AND BEN'S STORY

With just a few months of planning time, Carrie wasn't surprised that none of her site choices were available for the weekends she wanted. After a dozen or so calls to banquet halls, estates, and even VFW halls, she realized her mistake. She was asking only about Saturdays

Once she switched to asking about a Friday night wedding, her options opened up substantially.

The Friday night wedding is becoming more common, but hasn't yet taken over the popular Saturday all-day event. Right now the budding opportunity in the wedding industry means that Friday night may be your saving day.

Another option is the Sunday wedding. Churches and synagogues are usually open for 2:00 P.M. to 3:00 P.M. ceremonies—so that you miss the regular church crowd—and the timing gives you the perfect excuse to have an earlier (and less expensive) brunch, lunch, or cocktail party reception. After all, you are taking your guests' travel plans into consideration, and many brides report that this option is a wonderful one if all family and friends have spent the entire weekend together as an extended celebration of the upcoming wedding.

A new change we're seeing in the wedding industry is the smaller, more intimate wedding planned for a Thursday night. This is, of course, perfect for the bride and groom who are hosting a small celebration of ten to twenty guests, and whose friends and family are all located close by. Very often, these special dinners are held in the finest of restaurants, with only the couple's closest loved ones, the finest of foods and wines, and slow dancing at the Steinway grand piano—an unforgettable experience.

> ## ?
> ### Can we really have a non-dinner wedding?
>
> Yes! Many brides are turning to the option of lovely brunches or teas that are every bit as beautiful as the usual traditional reception. One of the loveliest weddings I've attended was a tea party in the garden of a historical estate. Displaying elements of class, distinction, and elegance, it transported guests to an uppercrust ambling, rather than to the usual disco-ball, hyped-up reception where they do the Macarena and the Chicken Dance.

What Time?

THE availability of your selected sites may determine the time of your ceremony and/or reception, or it may be up to you to choose. Many brides and grooms choose a reception that begins immediately after the service (and most guests report that they appreciate that choice more than having to kill three hours at a lounge near the reception site!) or they schedule a little time between the events to relax and take pictures. It's up to you, and up to the availability of your reception location.

Again, just as style and formality fit together and prescribe certain rules for your wedding, and just as budget determines what you can include, the time of day you select is a very important factor in completing the picture of the wedding you'll have. When you tell your guests what time the reception will be, you're also telling them how to dress and what they can expect to eat. An 11:00 A.M. reception will mean either a brunch or a luncheon, 2:00 P.M. will mean either a luncheon or a cocktail party, 5:00 P.M. means a cocktail party and dinner, 8:00 P.M. means a formal dinner, and 9:00 P.M. means a champagne and cake gathering. These are the standard rules, and you would be best served by following them. You don't want your guests complaining that they are starving after the finger sandwiches and crumpets have been devoured. Be sure, too, that your time matches your formality and style.

Some Things to Think About . . .

IF you are planning an outdoor or destination wedding, you will have to pay careful attention to the conditions attached to the date you pick. While the traditional wedding is usually indoors and exempt from the laws of nature, your wedding may present some issues with regard to season.

FOR OUTDOOR WEDDINGS

- What will the weather be? Cooler in the evening? Rainy? Muddy even if you miss the rain? Humid?

- Will it be mosquito season? Or will guests be encountering bees?

- If at the beach, is it early in the season, when the winds pick up and the sands are blowing?

- Is it high tourist season, when the city is jammed with visitors and your beach wedding will be cheered and jeered by teenagers cruising around in open-topped Jeeps?

FOR DESTINATION WEDDINGS

- Is it high tourist season, when nothing is available and everything is twice as expensive?

- Is it low tourist season, when nothing is open?

- Is it hurricane season?

- What are the social situations? Is there a coup brewing? Some destinations have been flagged recently for being dangerous to tourists. One honeymooning couple ventured off the fenced-in grounds and was robbed by locals.

- Is it the time of a religious holiday in that destination? If so, some local customs may preclude some of the wedding activities.

- Is it too late to book a honeymoon package?

?

We have a great location with a lovely view overlooking the ocean. What's the best time of day to make use of it?

W*hen choosing a time for your wedding, you may want to plan according to your most romantic image—at sunset, for example. Whether you're at the beach as the sun is setting over the oceanic horizon or over the tops of faraway mountains, sunset is a lovely time to tie the knot. Check the Resources for a Web site where you can check the precise sunset location anywhere in the world at any time of the year.*

The Most Important Factor . . .

SINCE you are planning the wedding at a relatively late date, you must consider all the loved ones you want at the wedding. This will mean not only giving them as much notice as possible—within the first week you are sure of the date—but considering what might preclude them from being able to attend. Many late-planning brides report that the biggest letdown of their weddings was the fact that some people just couldn't get vacation time, or couldn't attend because of their children's commitments. Ask yourself these questions when considering your guests' availability:

- What are everyones' work schedules? Can they get a few days off? Will they be traveling on business at that time?

- Is anyone studying for a big exam, such as for the bar or medical licensing?

- What about the kids' school schedules? Will they be off on vacation? (Many brides plan their wedding for the downtime of April/Easter vacation for kids.)

- Do they already have vacations planned for that time?

- Will any relatives or friends be extremely pregnant or likely to have a newborn near that date?

- Do any of the guests have medical conditions or scheduled tests or surgeries for that time?

- Are any other weddings or special events in the family planned at that time?

- Is that a brutal travel weekend? Will your guests be apt to be stuck in crowded airports or in traffic on the interstate for hours trying to get to you?

Expect that some people will not be able to come. That happens to all brides, no matter when the wedding is scheduled.

You can't please everyone, so you should do your best to plan a wedding date that works for you and for as many people as possible.

Say the Word

If you are planning a destination wedding, inform the guests you will be inviting of the location and booking details at least twelve weeks in advance, if you can. The standard advance notice for weddings is six to eight weeks, but if you're asking people to travel or change their own plans, you ought to give them more notice than that.

How Many Dates Do We Need?

SINCE you will be scrambling to set up sites according to your wish-list days, try to have five from which to choose. That sounds like a lot, but you'll have more to work with if you select and prioritize possible dates. You will make one fit as you search for locations available to you and as you consider your guests' commitments.

If you follow the advice of some recent brides, you will inform your wedding vendors that you are trying to piece together a ceremony and reception on the same date, and that you are trying to match availabilities. A good vendor will understand and try to

Say the Word

Both you and your fiancé should tell your bosses now about your wedding date and honeymoon time-off needs. Make sure you have enough vacation days available, and if you do not, then negotiate to earn some extra time off. Make the notification right away—especially if your situation is similar to that of the bride who got a new boss two weeks before her wedding! The new boss may have no way of knowing what your previous arrangements were.

accommodate your needs, allowing you to place 24-hour reservations on a date until you can get confirmation from the other locations. Just learning which days are open at a site is not good enough. You should block the time for yourself, while respecting the vendor's need to keep his days open for other brides should you select another site. Simply ask for this service, and follow through with a solid booking and erasure of the other dates when the second half of your plan is revealed. Remember, go no more than 24 hours without calling the vendors to confirm your reservations. They are doing you a huge favor to hold a date, and you should not take advantage of their efforts.

4

CHOOSING THE LOCATION

FINDING A PERFECT—AND AVAILABLE— WEDDING SPOT

IF YOUR FIRST choice of ceremony or reception sites does not work out, such as every church and splashy reception hall for miles around has been booked for a year, do not lose heart. This actually presents you with the opportunity to choose from a list of alternative sites, which will make for a wedding that is unique, beautiful, and fun for your guests. Again, choosing an alternative site often means that you will hold your ceremony and reception at the same place, which many brides report was a wonderful solution that cut down on travel needs (no need to get everyone from the ceremony to the reception hall!) and even money (only have to pay one site rental fee instead of two!).

Many brides—not just short-time planners—are choosing to go the alternative site route. Perhaps because they are not exactly church-going people, or because they want their ceremony to reflect their own personalities. For instance, a couple who met on the beach at Wildwood Crest, New Jersey, four years earlier during summer vacation with their families chose to hold their wedding ceremony on the beach site where they first met. It was a meaningful location and a wonderful decision for them.

Here, then, is a list of possible alternative wedding sites. Check these ideas carefully and consider whether any seem suitable to your wishes:

- *Beaches.* Many brides are holding their weddings on beaches with the roaring surf in the background, the sun setting over the horizon, and the relaxed atmosphere of an outdoor celebration. Beach weddings often work well with receptions held on beautifully decorated decks or terraces of beachside restaurants.

- *Gazebos.* With strings of lights and greenery adorning each rail and the roof in the center of town or at a park, gazebos are popular for smaller, more informal events.

- *Parks.* Some parks have lovely lakes great for picture taking! Swans and ducks swim by in their natural habitats; lush, green lawns invite barefoot walking; and at the right time of year, the colors of the trees provide a nice backdrop for a natural, outdoor wedding.

- *Historic Homes, Estates, or Mansions.* A wedding in a historic mansion lends an air of elegance as your guests mingle by the ornate fireplaces, admire the priceless artwork, and descend brocaded staircases. Estates may also have perfectly manicured gardens suitable for cocktail hours, and they may provide a guest capacity greater than you'll find in a more sought-after reception hall. Just check with your town's historical society for a list of nearby historical homes and estates that offer public use, and then research your options well.

- *Museums.* Museum weddings are becoming popular, as the surrounding paintings, sculptures, and architecture of the building itself provide an amazing backdrop and some interesting focal points for your event. (You'll be the masterpiece in this very classy setting!)

- *Arboretum or Botanical Gardens.* At each of these locations, breathtaking flowers and décor are already in place, saving you money. Some botanical gardens offer a variety of settings, from sunflower-strewn courtyards to butterfly gardens to rainforest atmospheres. Plus, many offer private, thematic rooms to adhere to the style of your wedding. At the Botanical Garden in New York, for example, several private rooms are available for smaller or larger groups, and you may choose access to any number of garden areas.

♦ *Country Clubs.* Even if you're not a member of the elite golfing team, you may find a country club is the ideal place for your reception. Many clubs offer exquisitely appointed event rooms with large picture windows overlooking the course, lake, hills, or landscaped gardens.

♦ *University Clubhouses.* If you're an alumnus, check to see whether you can get that great sunroom in the clubhouse or the president's mansion gardens.

♦ *Scenic Overviews.* Many towns and cities provide tourism lists of beautiful scenic overviews. Some may be distant visages of the cityscape at night, the ocean, or mountainsides that create amazing silhouettes with each hour of the setting sun. Check with your local tourism board for a list of public-access spots or permit requirements.

♦ *Seaside Resorts.* A highly recommended seaside resort, or even a charming oceanside bed-and-breakfast may provide just the atmosphere you're looking for.

♦ *Panoramic View Sites.* Top floors of buildings often have an incredible panoramic view of the city, such as Windows on the World in New York City. Check your area for the best elevated views, and provide your guests with an uplifting experience.

♦ *Lakeside Restaurants.* Some have great decks and grounds where you can enjoy the view of the sun setting over the lake, sailboats gliding past, and ducks and swans swimming by.

♦ *Exclusive Social Clubs.* Some may open their doors to nonmembers at the right price.

◆ *Elks Halls.* Gone are the musty old Elks halls of our grandfathers' era—the ones that smelled of cheap beer and cigars, with an ancient pinball machine and dartboard tucked in the corner. Newer Elks halls are like upscale lounges, as is the one in North Arlington, New Jersey, where the upper floor is a well-designed party room complete with a glass wall overlooking a seascape and marina. Don't discount options based on name recognition; first see what they have to offer.

◆ *Historical Landmarks.* Some brides love starting their own history as a couple in a place that has its own history. For instance, one bride reports that the circa-1900 mansion she chose for her wedding had a long and winding history of an old-money family, a great love story, and even mention of a haunting or two. For those who aren't afraid of friendly ghosts, this option may be for you. Other historical landmarks may be old music halls with a list of golden-age celebrity clientele.

◆ *Jazz Clubs.* Just rent the entire club for the night, so you're not sharing the space with a crowd. Your guests will love the cozy atmosphere; the plush couches; the piano bar; and the relaxing, soulful music.

◆ *Penthouse Suites.* Smaller weddings of twenty or so can be held in an extravagant penthouse or president's suite at a major four- or five-star hotel, such as the Hilton, the Four Seasons, the Plaza, or your town's "best" location. Many of these suites feature designer-style gathering rooms, several adjoining rooms, and a wonderful view of the city or town. It's the perfect place for an upscale gathering of ten to thirty of your closest guests.

◆ *Boats.* Holding a wedding on a yacht is becoming one of the fastest-growing options out there. Brides and grooms love the idea of setting sail to start their new life together, enjoying beautiful views of the cityscape as the sun sets.

♦ *Cruise Ships.* The cruise wedding options out there are limitless, as the wedding and boating industries have joined forces to create all-encompassing wedding packages with four-star chefs and great entertainment, lovely décor, and professional service that at times cannot be matched on land. For example, if you're in the New York area, you might choose the Bateaux New York cruise, an elegant boat that holds 300 people, offers an unobstructed view of the city from within the boat through its windows and glass ceilings, and charges $200 per guest for a five-hour cruise (see the Resources for contact information).

If you are interested in booking a cruise wedding, you will be best served by following this advice offered by brides who have researched boats for their locations:

♦ *Be sure there's adequate shelter from bad weather.* Since you never know what the weather will hold, make sure the boat has indoor covered space as well as an open deck. One bride who booked a schooner was mortified when the rains came down and all her guests crammed into the bathrooms, the smoky galley, and the musty under-deck crew's quarters to get out of the rain.

♦ *Make an appointment to tour the boat.* Do this when it's docked and not being used. Do not simply book a boat you were on five years ago, as you have no way of knowing whether the crew has kept up the boat. One bride tearfully shared her story of having wonderful memories of family cruises aboard a boat that had shiny brass rails, beautiful white sails, scrubbed mahogany decks and doors. On the day of her wedding, however, as she and her guests walked down the pier to the boat, she saw that it had been "let go." The dingy and torn sails were not even put up for the event, the ladder steps were broken and hanging from delicate hinges, the mahogany deck was faded and worn, and the deluxe meal that once featured lobster tails and bacon-wrapped scallops was little more than a barbecue with champagne served in cracked plastic cups. So be sure to tour the boat, checking in particular for:

1. Basic cleanliness
2. Full, clean sails (ask the captain to raise them for you!)
3. Sanded and polished decks
4. Clean windows
5. A good entrance bridge (Some brides were shocked to see that their guests would have to walk a two-foot-wide board without handrails to get on the boat. Even worse, when the tide was lower at the end of the evening, the guests would have to negotiate that narrow board up a steep incline!) Always make sure the boat offers a secure bridge with handrails.
6. A working restroom that's up to current standards

♦ *Be sure there is enough seating for guests.* A good schooner or yacht will provide plenty of bench space along the railing and masthead with cushioned seating so your guests can sit down and eat their meals. You don't want your guests to stand all night, especially when the boat encounters wakes from other passing vessels.

♦ *Be sure that your handicapped guests can gain access to the boat.* If you have a relative who is in a wheelchair, inform the captain and ask if the boat is wheelchair accessible. If your guest occupies a larger-than-standard wheelchair, or a personal transportation device other than a wheelchair, be sure to find out the full width measurements and weight of the machine so the captain can adequately inform you of accessibility. You do not want a loved guest stuck on land while you sail off into the sunset.

♦ *Find out what entertainment is offered on board.* If you're booking a riverboat, you might want to close the gambling option, or your guests may spend all night at the roulette table, gambling away your wedding gift. Many brides choose, in this instance, to offer gambling for a short amount of time, and then they close the tables.

♦ *Be sure to rent a boat with a crew!* Many brides forget that they'll need someone to drive the boat, serve the food, and so on; they sign a contract for the boat rental, unaware that rental of the crew is extra. Always get a package in which the crew comes with the boat.

♦ *Be sure the boat provides safety measures.* Life vests or other flotation devices are essential, as is a fire extinguisher.

♦ *Be sure the boat is reliable.* Ask for evidence of engine maintenance and the vessel's seaworthiness.

♦ *Be sure the boat and captain are licensed and the ship is Board-of-Health inspected.* You don't want any little four-legged, hairy creatures coming along for the ride.

♦ *Minimize potential for seasickness.* Bring Dramamine for your guests who don't have sea legs. Since motion-sickness medications do not work for everyone, and since there may be a fair amount of alcohol consumption on board, discuss with the captain your need for the ship to remain in calm waters such as a bay or calm river. This is not the time to set out for the open sea.

KARA'S STORY

Kara knew she wanted her wedding on a yacht. She lives near the Baltimore Inner Harbor, and spent many lazy summer days lying out on the green, where she had watched radiant wedding parties boarding an amazing enclosed yacht decorated with roses. Tuxedoed crew helped the guests aboard, handing them crystal glasses filled with champagne as they stepped onto the shiny wood deck. Kara would dreamily watch the wedding guests assemble, the bride make her entrance, and the ship sail off into the sunset. "Someday," she vowed back then, "I'll be married on that boat."

The moment her fiancé placed that two-karat ring on her finger, she called the yacht company and spent weeks trying to find an available day for her event on that boat. Once the date had been agreed upon, she embarked on the wonderful though detailed job of planning all the elements of her day. The yacht manager promised a string quartet to accompany the cocktail party, arranged for the vows to be made above deck, and provided amazing food samplings.

In the end, Kara got her dream wedding on that boat, and her guests were thrilled to attend a celebration that was beyond the normal, everyday wedding package.

Wedding Day Reflections

Everything *about our yacht wedding was wonderful, except the boat traffic on the river. While we were exchanging our vows, other boats were ripping past us, and drunk people on those boats were calling out to us. Be sure to book a date and time that is not known for heavy boating use.*

—Sarah and James

Getting Married at Home

UNLESS your little brother has the backyard booked for one of his extreme wrestling get-togethers with his friends, chances are your search for a wedding location may begin and end at home. The at-home wedding can be a joy, as mentioned before, as your childhood home is transformed into the setting of a beautiful fairytale come to life. The yard where you played kickball now becomes a regal courtyard with silver serving bowls, marble pedestals displaying ornate floral pieces, and strolling violinists. The swimming pool can be filled with floating candles. Mom's prized rose bushes become the backdrop for your day (and they're free!). Best of all, you don't have to contend with a waiting list or a site fee.

Before you stop your search right here, thinking, *This sounds great! It's easy!* keep in mind that the at-home wedding can be every bit the ordeal as any big, involved wedding held at another site (and in some cases more so!). Depending upon the size and scope of your wedding, you may be dealing with a huge list of rentals, a tent, and any number of other headaches of which you may not yet be aware. Unless you're planning a small gathering of twenty to mill about your living room (which should be lovely as well), consider the following criteria and questions you'll have to answer (and act upon) should you choose to hold your wedding at home:

Is There Enough Room? If you'll be hosting 200 guests, does your home have room for all of them? Don't assume that half will be in the yard, as it may rain or be sweltering hot. One bride underestimated her need for space to accommodate guests, assuming that most would spend their time out by the pool, the buffet table, or the tented dance floor. To the bride's surprise, the guests flocked indoors for the air-conditioning and a football playoff game that was on television in the den. Avoid this by assessing space according to full capacity either indoors or out. When looking at outdoor space, ask if your backyard is big enough for a tent that will adequately cover your needed square footage. A good rental agent will come to your home; measure out your available space; calculate what size tent will fit; and advise you about the best placement of the bar, buffet, dance floor, and bandstand. One bride shared the story of an amazing rental professional who pointed out the best arrangements according to her existing landscaping, divots in the yard that might pose tripping threats, and potential puddle spots.

What Will You Need to Rent? Speaking of a good rental agent, you will certainly need to rent certain items (see the list presented later in this chapter), so do you have time to do the research, selections, and arranging that is necessary? Do rentals mean spending much more on your wedding?

Do You Have Enough Restrooms? This may not be the first thing that comes to mind, but many brides report that—as in crowded nightclubs—toilets do get stopped up. It's sad to see the father of the bride in his suit or tux, plunging away at an overflowing toilet. Another cringe-worthy issue is making sure all the bathrooms have toilet paper.

Is There Enough Seating? With correct measurements of tables and chairs, plus your accurate head count, you will need to make sure that everyone will be seated comfortably in the tent, out in the garden area, or indoors in your home. Do the math, map out a seating plan according to a well thought-out sketch of the room, and provide for all needed seating.

Will Any Permits Be Required? Will you need a permit for outdoor cooking, liquor, parking, or public gathering?

Is There Enough Parking Space Available? Beyond getting parking permits from the town, you should also advise neighbors of your upcoming event and let them know that your street will be lined with many cars and limos. Slip into their mailbox a simple note promising your consideration of their needs on that day, or let them know in person during an evening walkabout.

Who Will Set Up and Clean Up? It may make sense to depend on your family and friends for an afternoon set-up session—and a post-party or next-day cleanup session—but you may actually be adding to the stress of the event by putting extra obligation on them. They may say yes just to be nice, then resent having to spend their time doing physical labor. Unless you know your closest friends and relatives are truly up for the task, hire professional assistants for the job.

WHAT ABOUT DAMAGE TO YOUR HOME PROPERTY?

Red wine spilled on the cream-colored carpet, a broken knickknack, even a stomped-dead yard can ruin your event. (One bride reports that her father was livid when the lawn underneath the dance floor never quite came back to life after the wedding.) Take adequate measures to protect from damage: Cover delicate wood furniture with tablecloths, put away priceless antiques and china, remove the computer from the living room, and so on.

What About the Issue of Safety? Will you be worried about candles being knocked over in your home, small children needing supervision by the pool, uninvited guests gaining unnoticed access into your home? You can take care by assigning a close friend to watch out for trouble. Candles kept in safe containers, such as hurricane lamps, can prevent a thin pillar candle from being bumped into the curtains.

Who Will Serve Food and Beverages? Will you need to hire servers, or is buffet-style adequate for you? You don't want your parents walking around all night with a silver platter of croquettes.

How Will You Provide Music? Is there room for a band or DJ, or will you be better served by having your little brother be responsible for playing CD mixes all night? What about hiring a professional pianist to play on your family baby grand?

Is There Enough Closet Space for Coats? Will someone need to be hired or borrowed to help with that?

Do You Have Backup for Potential Power Failure? Will you need extra power in the form of generators in case there is a blackout or power surge. (It happens!)

Does Your Home Have Adequate Kitchen Facilities? Does the caterer have enough room in the refrigerator, pans that fit in your oven, enough power, and enough working space to do his or her job? (Have the caterer come for a "measuring and assessment" visit ahead of time.)

The beauty of having an at-home wedding is that everything is up to you. That's also the drawback. . . everything is up to you. Many brides report that they were smart to hire a wedding coordinator for this task, if even for the day.

General Site Criteria

No matter where you hold your wedding, whether it be at a traditional reception hall, an estate or mansion, or a museum, take the following criteria into consideration. These are the questions any smart bride will ask herself as she searches for the perfect location that offers all the advantages and avoids all the potential drawbacks. For best use of this list, make several photocopies of these pages, and use them as checklists for when you "interview" each site.

Wedding Mornings

Here are some atypical "watch-outs" I've heard with regards to at-home weddings:

- *Make sure there's enough room for your bridal gown.* One bride with a big, puffy gown couldn't fit through the crowd or in the bathroom!

- *Rent an ice-cube machine.* You don't want to run out of ice or keep filling ice trays all evening.

- *Offer only one kind of blender drink.* You don't want whoever's mixing drinks for the guests to be cleaning the blender every two minutes.

- *Invite your neighbors.* They'll never forgive you if they're not invited.

- *Lock the upstairs bedroom doors.* This keeps out potential snoops, thieves, and make-out artists. Do you really want someone reading your journal or getting intimate on your bed?

- *Hire someone to clean up immediately after the wedding.* One bride reports that her family can't relax when things are a mess. Because her mother couldn't wait until the next morning for the cleanup crew to move in, she did the cleanup work herself.

- *Get someone to take care of your pets for the day, away from your home.* Fido may be a friendly dog, but even the mildest of creatures can get overstimulated (or possibly stepped on) in such a crowd.

Site name:_____

Address: _____

Phone number:_____

E-mail or Web site:_____

Contact name: _____

Date visited: _____

_____ Is the capacity big enough?

_____ How many tables?

_____ Variety of table sizes? (six-seaters, eight-seaters, oval, round, long?)

_____ Number of chairs?

_____ Is there adequate parking? Onsite or nearby?

_____ Is parking free? If not, how much will it cost?

_____ IMPORTANT! Can the limousines fit into and negotiate the driveway?

_____ Is the reception site attractive? Note special features you like.

_____ Is the lighting adequate? Effective?

_____ Is the staff professional and willing to fulfill my wishes?

_____ Is their package all-inclusive?

_____ What (if any) extra fees are required, and what is their cost?

_____ For how many hours can the site be reserved as part of the standard package?

_____ What is the overtime fee?

_____ Is the dance floor big enough? How many guests can fit onto the dance floor at one time?

_____ Is there privacy?

_____ How many weddings will be held at the site on the same day?

_____ Is any dividing wall truly soundproof?

_____ Will I be allowed to bring in my own caterer and other vendors, or am I required to use theirs?

_____ Do they offer tastings of their chef's cuisine?

_____ Does their menu suit our wishes and needs?

_____ Do they offer special menu options for guests with special dietary needs?

_____ Do they provide a wedding cake as well? For what cost?

_____ Will they let me inspect their china, silverware, linens, and other essentials?

_____ Do they provide a selection of linens and china from which I can choose?

_____ Are the bathrooms clean and in good working order?

_____ Is there a coat room?

_____ Will there be a coat-check person?

_____ Is there a separate lounge for the bridal party pre-wedding?

_____ Do they have a liquor license?

_____ Will they allow me to bring in my own liquor if I so choose?

_____ Do they have a handicapped entrance? Is it adequate?

_____ Are there enough fire exits? Especially if your reception is in a downstairs room, ask about any fire or emergency escape routes for your guests.

_____ Do they offer a complete, well-written contract?

_____ Do they allow changes to the contract?

_____ Do they have liability insurance?

_____ Are permits needed?

_____ What are their restrictions—noise limits, dress codes, etc.?

_____ Do they have a cancellation/refund policy?

_____ Are they licensed for operation?

_____ Did they provide referrals? List names and contact information.

_____ Was I able to envision my dream wedding at this site?

Rentals

No matter what kind of wedding you're planning, or what location you choose, you may find you'll have to rent certain items. Most obviously, the outdoor wedding may require rental of a tent, chairs, tables, or other necessities. Even a traditional wedding may require that you rent chairs, linens, possibly ice-making or even bubble-blowing machines.

Check the sidebar to follow for a list of what you may need to rent, and then use the criteria provided to make the best choices in rentals.

Rental Options

- Tent
- Chuppah
- Tables (round or square, seating or buffet)
- Chairs
- Benches
- Linens
- Table skirts
- China
- Silverware
- Glassware, including crystal
- Serving dishes and serving silverware
- Silver platters
- Wine fountains
- Punch bowls
- Candelabra
- Silver tea and coffee servers
- Portable bars
- Pedestals
- Bridal arches
- Podiums

- High chairs and booster seats
- Ice-making machines
- Bubble-blowing machines
- Spotlights and decorative light machines
- Dance floors
- Band platforms
- Ramps
- Fountains
- Helium tank (As a money saver, you might get a helium tank from the rental place to blow up your own balloons for décor— if that is your chosen style. Yes, balloon blowup is time-consuming, and you may be better off just getting the balloons from a party supply store, but if you have willing volunteers, go for it. Renting the means to inflate your own balloons can save you money.)

Again, as you are starting at a late date, it may be hard to find a solid, professional rental agency with a good track record and affordable prices. Do not book a rental agency simply because it's the cheapest or most convenient one. You may think rentals are not an important aspect of your wedding planning, yet hundreds of brides could tell you horror stories about rickety tents collapsing, chipped or dirty china, malfunctioning wine fountains that sprayed guests with merlot, and so on. Make smart choices here; do your homework, and pay extra if you must. You should give these important elements the attention they deserve.

Say the Word

Don't worry about being a pest. (You couldn't possibly be as much of a pain as some brides are!) Wedding professionals are accustomed to brides who ask a lot of questions and make a lot of requests—it shows the pro that you're on top of your plans and should be respected. A spineless bride gets ripped off.

You should begin your search by first asking recently married friends from whom they rented. Do not simply go to the nearest rental store and fill out a checklist. Again, you want to make sure you choose a quality supplier with quality materials. Always check out the rental agency's status with the American Rental Association (800-334-2177) and skip the agency if it is not a member.

Make an appointment with the rental company manager and arrange to tour the store and view the goods.

While any good rental agent is going to offer a free on-site consultation to assess your rental needs, he or she should also welcome you into the rental store to get a good look at what your money will buy. Be sure the store is clean and organized, that their selections are well presented, and that they have a wide variety of options. The manager should allow you to take your time choosing your selections, and you should be allowed to view a fully constructed tent. If there is not one set up at the store, ask to be taken to a site when one of their tents is in place. A good manager will let you do this.

Be sure the rental place delivers and picks up after the event, and schedule precise times for delivery and retrieval. This should be confirmed several weeks before the wedding date, then again a week in advance, and yet again two days before the wedding. If you will be picking up and setting up your own items, be sure to schedule the precise time when you will be showing up for your order.

As you would with any professional, make sure the rental company offers a good contract. Be sure it includes not only the specifics of your wedding, such as time, date, and location (always include the location address on the contract or order form), but also a complete, itemized list of what you will be renting, including style numbers and colors. Double-check to make sure everything is included, and then sign the contract if it is to your liking.

One piece of advice from recent brides: Always look through the rental items before the wedding. If the boxes are shipped to your place a few days before the wedding—as they should be—assign someone to categorize everything in that shipment, make sure the shipment matches your order, and make sure all items are clean, in good condition, and there. Many brides who skipped this step were appalled to learn while setting up on the morning of the wedding (too late to do anything about it!) that some dishes were crusty with remnants of weddings past, that champagne glasses were missing, or that linens were the wrong color. Count chairs and tables—twice—and if you see any problems, call the rental company and stand your ground until they come running over with the correct items. (Mention that you know about the American Rental Association.)

Stress Relief

I know it's a headache, but you should assemble all tables and unfold all chairs when they are first delivered to be sure they are the correct size, style, and in good working order. Some rental tables get so flimsy after years of being opened and closed that they actually collapse or need reinforcement on the wedding day—not a welcome task for the groom, groomsmen, or fathers.

Arranging for high-quality rentals will take some thought and some action on your part. Selecting the right rental agency will help ensure that your wedding will look beautiful and run smoothly. The most plain of locations can be transformed into a magical realm. Your childhood home can become the ornate reception hall of your dreams. Any details you desire can be arranged through the hiring of the right rental agency, and the choice is up to you.

5

THE DESTINATION WEDDING

ESCAPING TO YOUR DREAM DAY

W E CALL IT the destination wedding, because "eloping" carries too much of that old-fashioned stigma associated with the bride and groom climbing out the window and down a ladder, suitcases in hand. The days of running away to marry are significantly over—despite what you may see on *The Jerry Springer Show*—and the destination wedding idea has taken over the concept of eloping. Nowadays brides and grooms are within their own realm of control, and they are traveling to distant places to tie the knot.

Within the industry, we see several different kinds of destination weddings, including these:

- *The Vacation Wedding*—the bride and groom decide to forego the traditional celebration at the banquet hall in their hometown and instead plan their nuptials for a unique destination such as a rainforest in Hawaii, with a spectacular waterfall as their backdrop.

- *The My Hometown/Your Hometown Wedding*—a bride and groom from two different areas of the country (or the world) hold one celebration in the bride's town and another in the groom's instead of shipping half the guests for miles.

♦ *The Last-Minute Getaway Wedding*—the bride and groom just want to be married. They don't want all the fuss, all the in-law involvement, and all the details and questions that go into planning a traditional wedding. The couple may be spontaneous, or may face a situation in which they need to be married *now* (but that's another book). The last-minute getaway wedding is the one you think of when couples run away to Vegas to marry. But put away your preconceptions about the Vegas wedding, because you're just as likely to find a well-planned spontaneous wedding with elements of class in Vegas as you are to find the cheesy five-minute chapel with Elvis at the keyboard.

Those are the primary categories of destination weddings, no matter how long the couple has to plan their event. Since you are limited in time, you will have to take into consideration the amount of work you want to put into each selection. A vacation wedding can take up to a year to plan—especially, for instance, when you are booking a lush Hawaiian resort at the height of tourist season. It may take longer if you're planning your wedding in a foreign country where the roots of your heritage are, and you're wrangling with red tape and permissions.

So do yourself a favor and respect your short amount of planning time. Know that destination weddings are very popular now, and that your late start may require your putting in extra time to find that perfect destination. Still, it can be done. Just read on to figure out what you want, what typically goes into planning it, and where you stand as far as being able to match your abilities to your dreams.

For some brides, the dream has always been a wedding on a Hawaiian beach at sunset. For others, the dream is an all-out wedding in a California vineyard, clear across the country from their Midwest home. In choosing the location, you are forming the foundation for how much will go into planning a destination wedding in a short amount of time. Lucky for you, the wedding industry is aware that not all brides are planning with a year or more to spare. The major resorts that you will consult for their getaway wedding packages will be able to supply you with complete information, although you might find that the best ones are booked and unavailable at the best times of year.

Many brides report that they were at first afraid to make the call to the wedding coordinator at a faraway resort. How could they be sure the wedding coordinator would do a good job? Is ordering everything over the phone a smart idea? Could they trust a stranger to arrange details as specified? However, these same brides came back to me and said that they couldn't have been happier. They did good research through simple phone and e-mail contacts, found reputable resorts with good track records in the destination wedding-planning arena, and the whole planning process was a breeze.

It's becoming common in the wedding world for resorts to attract engaged couples who not only honeymoon, but hold their weddings on the resort grounds as well. All-inclusive packages are becoming good buys—if you research well—and the resorts are hiring the best event planners around. So this is a very good time to check out the getaway wedding.

> ### Wedding Day Reflections
>
>
>
> The Four Seasons in Las Vegas had their act so together that it took little more than a few phone calls to arrange everything. We communicated by fax and e-mail, the coordinator asked me very detailed questions, I made my choices, and just a few days later we showed up in Vegas to find the wedding we had requested all laid out for us! It was amazing!
>
> —Jennifer

Is There a Good Time of Year for a Wedding?

UNFORTUNATELY, since we're talking about locations all over the world, answering this question is far more difficult than for familiar locations. For instance, the Caribbean has an off-season and an on-season, depending upon the weather. Vegas will mean relatively hot temperatures every day of the year. You'll have to research the particular destination you've chosen, via Web sites and calls to your local travel agent.

Popular Getaway Wedding Sites

- Hawaii
- The American Virgin Islands
- The British Virgin Islands
- The Caribbean
- Aruba
- Mexico
- Las Vegas
- Key West, Florida
- Napa Valley, California
- Paris
- London
- The French Riviera
- The Disney Resorts
- New York City
- Vermont (during high foliage season—great pictures!)
- Italy
- Greece
- South Pacific

Contact the Board of Tourism for any destination to ask about marriage requirements. (See the list of tourist associations listed in the Resources.)

The Guest List Does Matter

MANY short-time planners find that the fewer people they invite to a destination wedding, the easier it is. While the majority just take off on their own, some bring along a few close family members or their kids.

Their kids? Yes, the newest trend in the industry promotes having kids from previous marriage at the wedding and making them a part of the honeymoon as well. No, this isn't another *Springer* storyline. It's an example of how the wedding industry has changed to include the needs of the changing family structure. Now many resorts combine honeymoon packages with family packages, creating a personalized plan just for you. For instance, Maui Loves Kids has a wedding-planning coordinator who will plan your wedding for and with you, and when the ceremony is over, keep the kids busy with a long list of fun activities and day trips. Mom and Dad get to honeymoon the whole day away, and there is family bonding time left over. This kind of option can be perfect for the blending family.

If, however, you are sure you want to bring a crowd with you to the destination—as some couples do, even at the last minute—you now have a whole new list of considerations:

- *Have you given your guests enough time to make their travel plans?* Some may resent having to cancel an already-planned getaway because you snapped up the 4th of July weekend.

- *Can your guests afford last-minute travel tickets?* Sorry, but at this late date, if the guest is a close friend or relative and a "must show," you may have to pay for their travel and lodging. In fact, that's becoming a rule.

- *Can you get a block of rooms at the wedding location?* Especially at high travel season, you don't want your guests to stay at a one-star hotel while you're marrying and staying at a five-star. Consider their feelings and their need to be pampered.

- *What are your guests' travel requirements?* Will you be forcing everyone to get passports? What about those who are afraid to fly? (This may border on worrying about the ridiculous, but that's part of planning the perfect wedding.)

More Legalities

FOR any wedding, you will have to take the legalities into consideration, as in getting your state's required licenses and blood tests or physical exams. For a destination wedding, you will actually have to do twice the work. You'll have to research the current requirements of your destination—and I say current, because you cannot depend on Internet information or book information, but will have to call the state or country's board of marriage licensing for the most recent and applicable laws—and you'll have to make arrangements from where you are. Many brides report that this step was a lot of effort, requiring a great deal of correspondence, double-checking, and research. For any destination you will have to ask the following questions:

- What documents are needed for the filing of our marriage license?

- Can you supply us with a copy of the officiant's license to perform weddings (very important)?

- Is there a residency requirement? (Some locations require that you be present in the country for a specified number of days, to establish residency. Be sure to know this number of days so you can make your travel plans accordingly.)

- Are blood tests from our home state applicable there? If not, what is the time limit and time requirements for blood tests at your location?

- How many witnesses are needed, and what are the requirements for witnesses? (Some locations require that the witnesses have known both the bride and groom for a certain period of time. You can't just grab the taxi driver to serve as your witness!)

- Do you need proof of divorce?

- What kind of religious licensing do you require?

- Do you need a translator? (This is important, as many brides and grooms find that their marriage certificate is printed in a language they don't understand, and the ceremony is performed in a language they don't understand either.)

PATRICIA'S STORY

Patricia definitely took on too much when she attempted to plan her wedding in less than five months . . . in Peru. Most of her family was there, she reasoned, and she wanted to be married with family and friends in attendance. Although she had dual citizenship, her fiancé did not. All of the calls to the necessary agencies took weeks, delays were excruciating, and in the middle of all of her efforts were reports on the news and from her family in Peru about uprisings and violence in certain parts of the country.

While Patricia attempted to stick with her goal, it turned out that all her effort was not amounting to much. She was stressed-out, watching the local news like a hawk, fearing further violence at that location, snapping at the government officials and at her fiancé, and finally she just had to give up. She needed to accept that this particular destination wasn't going to work, no matter how hard she tried, within this short time span. Although the social strife in Peru wasn't her fault, all the red tape was maddening. She changed her plans and everything flowed together well. Some family members from Peru were able to attend her wedding, and she sent videotapes back with them for the rest of her loved ones to see.

Finding a Destination Wedding Planner

RESEARCHING a solid wedding planner is key if you will be depending upon this person to put together a legal, beautiful wedding that conforms to your expectations. Many of the best-known resorts all over the world have hired excellent wedding planners, and it is your job to research them as you would any other wedding professional. As always, ask for their licensing, membership in a professional planners association (such as the Association of Bridal Consultants), and a rundown of their experience.

Be sure to tell the planner that you are planning a distance wedding. After all, she may not know where you are calling from, and she will have a different approach for you when she takes into consideration your location. You may discuss plans to fax or e-mail more material.

Always work with one planner only. Some of the larger resorts have teams of planners who work on each wedding, and that makes for mix-ups. So be sure to ask to work specifically with the one planner you've chosen, get her name, and make her your wedding-planning partner.

Say the Word

Do not be afraid to ask too many questions, as a qualified planner is going to expect that the informed bride and groom are not inept but are instead well-versed in the steps needed to plan their wedding. If a planner gives you "attitude" and acts like you're wasting his or her time, move on to the next candidate. You want a good planner who will work well with you, and a friendly, understanding personality is going to make for a better working fit.

WORKING WITH THE PLANNER

Working with the wedding planner at a remote or faraway location is going to be similar to working with a wedding consultant near you, but you'll be doing a lot more corresponding. Too many brides take the easy road here in the interest of saving time, and they allow the planner to make the decisions for them. That's fine if you have less invested in the outcome of the wedding plans than most brides. But if you have a clear vision of what you want for your wedding, you will be best served by finding a way to share it with the planner.

- *Send pictures.* Many brides send pictures of the kinds of floral arrangements they want. To save time and money, have pictures scanned onto disk, and e-mail the images to your planner.

- *Ask for updates.* These can be e-mailed updates and confirmations of orders placed and plans made.

- *Be clear at the outset.* A good planner will respect your wishes.

- *Stand firm.* Don't be talked into anything you don't want.

- *Ask to be informed of any last-minute changes.* That way, there will be no surprises.

- *Get a good contract.* Be sure all plans are spelled out, including the names of the professionals the planner has hired, the exact location of the ceremony, and all other details.

- *Get all agreements in writing.* If a planner speaks of "verbal agreements" between herself and local professionals, run away! Verbal agreements are grounds for disaster.

- *Ask for a videotape of the destination.* This should include the location, the grounds, and a wedding in progress at that site.

- *Ask for their Web site and check it out.* Remember, though, that Web sites are designed to reflect the location in its best light.

- *Get a listing of all fees.* Be sure tips, local taxes, and hidden charges are included.

- *Get the planner's contact information.* Ask for personal and cell phone numbers and assurance that you can call when you need to. (Just be sure to keep time zones in mind, as one bride reports having woken her French planner up at 2:00 A.M.)

- *Remember that the planner is there to serve you, but she is not your personal slave.* Treat her with respect, honor her knowledge, and do not take your wedding frustrations out on her. Too many planners report that "flaky" brides drove them crazy.

- *Pay with your credit card, never in cash.* It's the only way to reserve and protect your reservations and plans.

Buying Time

Always ask for a press packet from resorts. The best wedding-planning departments of the major resorts always have a press packet with full-color photos of their work, more information than you could get out of them during an interview, and a better idea of what they offer to their clients. It's a great way to find out more about your prospective planner and the location.

Brides' Advice for Destination Weddings

- Don't give out your hotel room phone number to everyone. Just let one reliable person know what hotel you're at, and that you're to be called only in case of an emergency. Otherwise, the people who didn't get invited to the wedding will be calling with their well-wishes and driving you crazy.—Rebecca

- Research the customs of another country well. You don't want your wedding ruined because you're not allowed to go outside in your wedding dress, or your guests aren't allowed to gather in the town square.—Ursula

- Get a really good photographer. Spend extra time checking that option out. Don't just let the planner hire one. Get samples of his work, and make a good decision.—Lainie

- Choose a gown that travels well with you. My big, poofy gown got smashed in the garment bag compartment on the airplane, and it was all wrinkled when I wore it at my wedding. If I had known better, I would have chosen a simpler gown.—Nancy

- Make sure your guests with whom you are traveling know all about getting their passports in time.—Anya

- Carry your wedding rings on you. Don't put them in the suitcase or in a carry-on.—Renee

Remember that a destination wedding can be every bit as difficult to plan as an all-out wedding in your hometown. If you're limited by time, do a lot of research and make smart decisions with an eye toward what your limitations are. You may not have enough time to spend weeks on the phone with the U.S. Embassy in Kenya, and you may not have the patience to do anything more than make a few phone calls to a resort in Reno. It is all up to you, depending on what you want and what your resources are. Just be realistic, and don't take on any more than you can handle.

Money-Saving Advice for Destination Weddings

THERE's no guarantee that a destination wedding is going to save you money in the long run. What you might save on meals for 200 guests you may pay in airfare to get guests to and from your location. It's all relative, depending upon what you want.

Here, though, are some money-saving tips that can help you stretch out your budget and get more for your getaway dollars:

- ◆ *Pick the wedding package apart.* Figure out which elements of the standard wedding package you actually need, what they'd cost individually, and whether or not you can piece together a better deal on your own as just a guest of the resort, not a wedding guest.

- ◆ *Let the planner know that you want ways to save money.* Remember, this resort wants your repeat business, not just this one visit. They know that many couples like to re-visit their honeymoon spot years down the road, and they want you to come back again and again. That said, they may be more willing to give you a break on this visit. They also know, smart as they are, that brides and grooms are chatty, and that they refer the services they use to other engaged couples. So if you understand that the vendors want you to be happy, you won't be so afraid to ask for what you want.

Wedding Day Reflections

We had no idea there was a clause in our contract about paying by the scale of the trade rates. The company we used—which we admit now we rushed into booking and didn't check out very well— stated that we'd pay a certain amount, but the contract did say that the charge was subject to change according to what the dollar was worth. We tried to argue, but it was right there in black and white. What a nightmare!

—Eliza and Tom

♦ *Find out what hidden fees are.* Some destination packages sound like a great deal, but they are loaded with officiant fees, local taxes, gratuities, and other added expenses. Know your financial obligations in detail.

♦ *Get a written list of what's free.* Not to blame resorts for miscommunication, but having the details of what's included in writing will be helpful should you have to refute a charge that was promised to you gratis.

♦ *Stay within your budget.* Don't book at a location that's known for being extremely expensive to begin with.

♦ *Be sure the quoted amounts are stated and written in American currency!* Too many brides and grooms get ripped off when the deal hinges on what the currency rate is. If the dollar is not doing well internationally, you could wind up paying more if you've agreed to pay according to trade rates. For instance, the price of your location-grown flowers may sound wonderful, but when you convert the currency into American dollars, the amount is outrageous!

6

DRESSING THE BRIDE

Walking Down the Aisle in Style

Entire books have been written on how to find the perfect wedding gown for you, so we'll only touch on some of the basics. What's important here is finding the perfect wedding gown in only a few months, still allowing you plenty of time for selection, ordering, delivery, and fittings. Since ordering a designer gown can take months, you must make sure you tackle this project right away so you're not tearing your hair out over a late delivery—or worse, devastated that your gown will not arrive in time.

Buying a Gown Under Time Constraints

Brides who plan a wedding in less than six months usually find that they can choose a designer gown and have it delivered sooner than normal. But that is likely to cost more, unless you stumble upon some luck, such as locating a discontinued style that is ready to ship. Rush orders can add up to several hundred dollars to your bill, so if you have your heart set on a particular style, be ready to shell out some cash.

A better alternative is to use those beautiful pictures in the bridal magazines as simply style examples for the *types* of gown you would consider. Look at each picture for examples of beautiful necklines, bodices, trains, and so on. Then, go to your selected bridal store and see what they have to match your likes. With a limited planning time, you would be wise to keep an open mind, so that you are willing to consider a variety of styles. Do not be stubborn and demand a particular dress because you may not have time to get it. Of all the segments of your wedding, inflexibility in gown choice can hurt you most since the gown order is often the most lengthy process. Brides who do insist on ordering a designer gown must follow these rules:

1. *Check the delivery date.* If your wedding is five months away, and the gown will not be delivered for four months, choose another gown. You want to leave at least six weeks between receiving your gown and wearing it. This allows for the necessary alteration time, and provides the relief of knowing it is in your possession. Remember, brides not under time constraints typically order their gowns nine months in advance. So get yours right away.

2. *Get the delivery date confirmed.* Also make sure the contract says "time is of the essence." This means that the designer has to deliver your gown on time, or you get your money back. This will not help much at the last minute when your gown has not arrived,

Professionally Speaking

I n very rare cases, you will see an ad or hear of a bridal store that specializes in rush orders. Just be sure to check them out thoroughly. Eileen Claffey at Mary Lou's Bridals in Morristown, New Jersey, explained how her store has earned its reputation as the most reliable shop when time is short: "We've done plenty of rush weddings. While other stores can get a gown in six months, we can get it delivered in eight to twelve weeks. All we do is call the manufacturer, see whether the dress is in stock, and if it is, we have it shipped right away." No extra charges, no rush fee here, but you must check carefully to make sure a gown shop can provide this same high-quality service.

but at least you will be guaranteed a refund when you have to buy another dress off the rack.

3. *Be sure the sales clerk knows the date of your wedding and that you are concerned about receiving the gown in time.* A good clerk or manager will call you the minute it arrives. Tell the sales clerk that you must have the dress six weeks before the wedding date to allow for adequate fitting time. This ensures an earlier delivery date and less stress for you.

TRUNK SHOWS

As many brides report, you may be able to get a designer gown without having to order through a salon and wait five months. Several times a year, the major designers have trunk shows and sample sales, to which they come to unload their dresses, often at a discount. Usually, these gowns come in smaller sizes, such as 4, 6, and 8; but you will have access to designer gowns right away without the wait. Check the bridal designer Web sites listed in the back of this book for announcements of trunk shows and traveling sales.

> ### *Buying Time*
>
>
>
> W*hen ordering gowns online, check the source thoroughly. Be sure the company offers a guarantee for delivery in the stated amount of time and provides a refund guarantee as well.*

ORDERING OVER THE INTERNET

Many brides are ordering their gowns over the Internet, in an effort to save some time and money. Yes, many new companies promise fast delivery, designer knockoffs for just a few hundred dollars, and low prices; and yes, some brides have purchased amazing gowns through this process.

But before you jump into the technology wave of getting a wedding gown, keep this advice in mind:

♦ *Be sure the site offers a guaranteed delivery date.* Especially if you're hitting the Web to save yourself some time, be sure that you're guaranteed a quick delivery with a promise of refund if the date is not met.

♦ *Be sure the site is well-known.* Go with well-known designers' sites and avoid anything you haven't checked out thoroughly. Some newer fly-by-night rackets have turned up on the Internet, and brides are getting swindled.

♦ *Be sure to factor in shipping charges.* That great $500 dress may cost a lot more after you add in a hefty shipping charge, a rush fee, and insurance.

♦ *Be sure to factor in alteration charges.* This is one advantage that the bridal salons have over the Internet. No computer can do a great job of fitting your dress, and you may have to guess at a size. Not being able to try on a dress means taking a chance at size, and it also means finding an independent seamstress who may charge more for alterations.

Wedding Day Reflections

I *thought getting my gown over the Internet would be a great savings of time. I knew the style I wanted, they had it available in my size, and I could get it in a week. It turned out to be a nightmare, since the gown was poorly made, came a month late, and needed tons of alterations.*

—Marielle

♦ *Always check the site out with a professional association.* I spoke to a wedding consultant about an amazing Internet gown company, and was warned away from them. The consultant told me about their underhanded practices, their bad name in the industry, and brides' complaints.

♦ *Give plenty of time for returns and exchanges.* You've ordered clothes through catalogs and perhaps over the Internet before, and you know that a size 10 is not a size 10 in all worlds. So be sure to allow enough time for exchanges. In no other gown realm will you have to think about this option more.

While the Internet is a great place to go to research gowns and to get a great look at different styles and their availability, you're trading in that wonderful experience of twirling around in front of a great big mirror at a bridal salon. For many brides, this is a priceless experience, one they wouldn't trade in for all the money they could save on an Internet buy. Just take the necessary precautions and use your best judgment if you decide to take this route.

BUYING WITHOUT ORDERING

If you're pressed for time, you will not be able to buy a gown that has to be ordered and delivered. You may have to buy off the rack. It sounds like a sacrilege, and something to be avoided at all costs, but it may work out for you. Many brides do choose this option—not only due to lack of time. Even brides with a year's planning time may buy off the rack if they have found a stainless sample of a discontinued gown.

The one caveat regarding buying a sample is that many brides have tried that gown on before you. There may be lipstick stains in inconspicuous places, or the color may be slightly faded from time and wear. There may be some slightly loosened or torn seams. Luckily for you, these "drawbacks" equal discounts on the dress if you ask for them in the right way. Remember, the upside is that you get the beautiful dress of your choice right now, the bridal boutique manager gets to clear out the dress to make room for next year's models, and you get a discount. You can't lose.

Buying off the rack is a great choice for brides who are planning an informal wedding. Very often, you can find a beautiful white, off-white, or hued dress in department stores or outlets. Again, keep an open mind and let the dress find you. Informal weddings allow you a lot of leeway as far as the "rules" of wedding gowns, and you'll find that it is easier to buy and receive a gown when the formality is lessened.

You will, however, still have to have that dress tailored to you, so do not make the mistake of leaving this job to the last minute, thinking it's going to be one of the easiest. It isn't. While buying a dress and taking it home may be convenient, finding the right dress and the right seamstress to make it look perfect on you is complicated. Take no shortcuts. This is an *important* job.

Notes on Choosing the Right Gown

WHEREVER you're planning on getting it (and always get it from a reputable shop!), you'll need to choose the *right gown*. It has to fit not only the style and formality of your wedding, but it has to fit *you*. And I'm not just talking about fitting your body into it. It has to be your style. It has to be something you're comfortable in. It has to move with you, not overpower you, and accent your strengths and most beautiful features. It has to feel right, and you have to feel right wearing it.

Among the first factors you'll take into consideration, of course, is the formality. We can't avoid that one, so we'll deal with it first. For a formal wedding, you'll most likely go all out with a ball gown or a chic sheath dress. For a less formal wedding, you may still do the long-skirted gown, a ball gown, or a spaghetti-strapped long white dress delicately accented with pearls. For an informal wedding, the ball gown will be out of place, and you may choose a simple dress.

Yet, the rules of etiquette are bending for today's woman's individuality and willingness to make her own rules. Second-time brides are wearing white. Brides are wearing formal gowns to the ceremony and

---

Advantages of Simple Dress Styles

- Brides just look better wearing unadorned, classic, elegant styles. Too many beads and bangles will make you look like a chandelier. In a simpler dress, your face is the focal point (as it should be!).
- A simpler dress is easier to move around in. If your reception location will be somewhat crowded, or if you will be having an at-home wedding, you don't want to try to squeeze past people in your "poofy" gown.
- Bathroom breaks will not require three "assistants."
- They're less expensive.

Road-Testing a Wedding Gown

When trying on gowns, make sure you "test" each one. Too many brides just stand stiff-straight in front of a mirror, seeing only how the gown looks when they're at attention. For the best assessment of any dress, see how the dress moves when you're walking, dancing, sitting, and bending over. Check to see whether tall guests will be able to see right down the front of your bodice, and note whether the bodice cuts in when you're sitting down. Does a sheath dress make it impossible to walk? Sure, it may look great when you're standing still, but will you be "Morticia Addams-ing" down the aisle? Test each dress for the full range of movement, knowing that this extra time spent can save in alteration costs by avoiding the need to have waist seams taken out for better movement, and provide you with comfort and confidence overall.

changing into a more sexy white gown for the reception. In this day and age, anything goes. So don't limit yourself by what the etiquette rules say, or by what others say. You can have the dress you *want*.

The wedding industry may limit your quest somewhat, depending on your timing. Bridal shops are always stocking gowns for the next year's weddings. If your wedding is in the fall, you may have some trouble finding a suitable fall-weather gown if you're looking in the early summer. To avoid this problem, you can adjust your order according to what is available to you. Obviously, you won't go with a gown that looks too summery, but you may consider brocade gowns designed for the early summer or find some pretty leftover organza gowns in the fall.

To deal with the issue of coordinating timing, season, and the right fabric, go with the fabrics that work all year-round: silk, satin, tulle, and shantung. They will always be stocked. Designers are now showing beautiful crisp cotton blends that shimmer with blushed color and hold their shape well, so do not automatically pass up a dress because it is not silky.

Wedding Gown Alternatives

As mentioned earlier, your informal, beach, or home wedding may prevent you from getting a traditional, poofy ball gown. Recent brides who married with less than six months to plan reported that they turned to wedding gown alternatives that suited their style just fine. Number one in that category is the slip dress—perfect for the outdoor garden wedding or the beach wedding. You can find these anywhere, and they are most in stock in the middle of spring.

Don't pass up the prom gown rack. Prom gowns have gotten the royal treatment by dress designers these days, and some selections are gorgeous. Best of all, department stores stock a wide variety of these dresses in a wide range of sizes, so you do have a lot of options open. The only drawback: The industry has the prices up. Proms are bigger business than ever, and the buying audience will shell out several hundred dollars for a great gown. So choose well.

The younger set also dresses up formally for Christmas or holiday dances, winter formals, and other special events throughout the year. Department stores are almost always fully stocked, and they do offer more conservative styles in addition to the suggestive ones you may see displayed to catch shopper's eyes, so do not count out these departments if you are outside of prom season.

Penny-Wise

Prom gown designers are pulling out all the stops with their new, glamorous designs. Don't count such dresses out as wedding gown possibilities, judging them by their status as "prom gowns." Check some Web sites that you'll see mentioned in the newest prom gown issues of Seventeen and Teen magazines.

Antique stores also stock very high-quality gowns, as the desire to clean out the attic and sell old possessions hits everyone each spring. At several antique stores in Cape May, New Jersey, and Bucks County, Pennsylvania, I saw gorgeous champagne-white gowns with amazing histories, priced at a quarter of what retail glamour dresses were going for. The best part of these antique dresses is the detail. Back in the old days, dresses were embellished with delicate beading in intricate patterns. Dressmakers were master craft-workers, and their works of art are only now coming out of cedar chests around the country. Add to that goldmine the ready availability of beaded handbags, lace-up shoes, ornate wraps, and antique jewelry, and hairclips.

Don't count out secondhand stores, which are popping up in every city and town across the country. With the divorce rate soaring, many brides are handing their boxed and preserved wedding gowns over to a second-hand store for consignment, or even to a mission for a write-off. Don't scoff until you've looked. Many brides have found amazing gowns in the most unlikely places.

Buying Time

Tell the manager in what season your wedding will be held, and she will be able to direct you to their stock of suitable gowns. They may even have them on a sale rack (what luck!) or have some in the back room.

MARIA'S STORY

Maria had several thousand dollars budgeted for her gown. She had been visiting various shops and salons, trying to find the perfect gown, but nothing was clicking with her. On her way back from another disappointing outing, she was headed to Starbucks for a cup of coffee when she passed the local Goodwill store. A rather angry young woman was unloading boxes from her car and carrying them into the Goodwill. Maria stopped and offered to help, and in the ensuing discussion she learned that the woman had just gotten a divorce from her husband. She was

Gown-Shopping Smarts

In the interest of saving time and money, keep these rules in mind:

♦ *Know what styles look best on you.* You know what kind of neckline makes you look great, and you know what kind of bodice complements your shape. Tell the manager that you only want to see dresses with sweetheart necklines, for example.

♦ *Go gown shopping by yourself.* Too many opinions on the first visit can stretch out the process, as well-meaning relatives and friends may urge you to try other places or styles as well. Later on, you can bring a dependable advisor to give her opinion on the two or three styles you're considering.

♦ *Never order a gown without trying it on.* This includes catalog and online shopping. Always see the gown on first.

♦ *Don't refuse a dress because of how it looks on the hanger.* Dresses take on a new form when they're on the human body, and many, many brides swear that they fell in love with a gown they were reluctant to try on because it looked strange on the hanger.

now "clearing out" everything that reminded her of him, and one of those items was the perfectly preserved and boxed wedding gown and veil she had worn on her wedding day. Maria was amazed at the sordid story (I won't go into details!) and asked to see the dress.

It was lovely! Very simple, classic, with just the right touch of a pearl outline around the sweetheart neckline. Maria attempted to give the woman money for it, but the woman declined and told her to just take it. Now, luckily, Maria was not superstitious about wearing a gown from a failed marriage, and she was delighted to find a beautiful gown for free.

"You may not get a gown off the street like I did," Maria commented, "but brides-to-be should also know that many,

- *Never buy a gown that fits tightly to you or is a little smaller than you are now.* You may not lose the weight, and your weight may fluctuate. Always order a gown a little bit larger than you are. It can always be taken in.
- *Wear the exact undergarments you will wear on the wedding day when you're trying on your gown and getting fitted.* The style and fit of any bra is going to affect the fit of the gown, and the seamstress will need to make adjustments.
- *Wear the shoes you will wear on the wedding day, or shoes of the same height heel.* If you will be barefoot (as you might be for a beach wedding!), tell the seamstress.
- *Know how you will wear your hair—up or down.* Some necklines look better with loose, flowing curly hair, and others look best with an up-style. For the best vision of how your gown will look, wear your hair up or down—however you will have it on your wedding day—while trying on gowns. Or, bring a hair clip and adjust your hair to get a better look at what style works with the dresses you try.

many divorced women unload their gowns at places like Goodwill and missions and the like. They don't all make a big bonfire out of them. I never would have checked a Goodwill store, but I'm glad I know of a secret new source for amazing cast-offs."

———————————

Divorcees and brides who cancel their weddings at the last minute—as well as those poor souls whose fiancés back out—do unload their gowns at thrift shops. So don't count out these places.

As for dresses and gowns found at outlets and warehouses—yes, you may find a steal. However, many brides are fooled by the dress stocked in an outlet store that still has a price tag of $2,000. The

> **?**
>
> *My aunt has offered to alter my gown herself. She's made dresses for her daughters, and I appreciate the help with our expenses. Should I go for it?*
>
> Please don't attempt to save time and money by having a relative or friend do the fittings and alterations for you. Unless this person is a professional, this is too great a risk, as wedding gowns are not the average alteration task. Several brides have reported that their seams were falling apart during the wedding, and that they were tripping on loosely sewn hems all night.

crossing-out of a previous price—say $3,500—and the red-penciling of the lower $2,000 is the oldest trick in the book. The store may be getting you to think you're saving $1,500, but you're really spending a lot more than you might have at another location. Compare well.

I cannot leave out the option of period costume. Some brides swear by the idea of finding a "princess" gown at a costume rental store, and using that as a wedding dress. It may be a viable option, as wedding gown rental is becoming very popular.

If you're not the sentimental type who is going to save her wedding gown for her daughter, then by all means look into the rental agencies. The most current ones are impressive. They rent their gowns three times each, then donate them to charity. They offer a fairly wide variety, and often do the alterations themselves. Renting wedding gowns is a good option, as brides discover that many rental agencies actually stock big-name designer gowns that their own buyers find at designer trunk and sample sales in the city. You may be able to rent a Vera Wang for one-tenth the price you'd pay to buy one, and only you will know that the beautiful dress you have chosen so well is going back to the store in a few days.

Making Time for Fittings

IF you're really short on time, get your fittings right away. The seamstress needs at least a few weeks to fit your gown perfectly, and then you'll need a final fitting close to the wedding date to make any necessary adjustments to ensure that the dress accents you perfectly. Do not make the mistake of waiting until the last week, thinking that the seamstress can just sew up the sides and adjust the hem. A wedding gown takes an extraordinary amount of time to fit. It is not a pair of pants with a simple hem. The complicated panels and drapes mean the seamstress has to fashion the changes with painstaking detail, and you'll want to make sure you've allowed her enough time to do a great job.

Veils and Headpieces

IN most cases, the veil or headpiece is not ordered, but is instead chosen from a selection at the bridal store. As always, the type of veil you choose will depend upon the formality and whether or not you have been married before. Your seamstress will most likely bring you a selection of veils that go well with the gown you're considering. And while it may seem a savings of time to just buy what the seamstress says matches, it is always a good idea to shop around for a veil as an independent purchase. Other shops may have prettier, less expensive options. Or, if you're the do-it-yourself type, you might follow the current trend in which brides or their relatives make the veils using veil kits you can find in most craft shops.

The traditional veil, however, is being replaced by the jeweled hairpiece or tiara for a more dazzling, sophisticated look. Since this is happening more frequently, your options are wider. You are not limited to the bridal store's selections, then, as many major department stores and accessory stores carry faux-diamond and faux-pearl tiaras and headpieces.

Another great option is replacing the veil with a crown of flowers or blooms "woven" into an upswept hairstyle. Brides look beautiful

---

Buying Time

A*lways find out how busy a seamstress is, and make sure you visit her workshop. If her workspace is overcrowded with bagged gowns, and if she seems harried, choose another seamstress. Although the best in the area will be busy, you don't want to wind up with bad service or no service at all.*

when their hair is adorned with baby roses and other sweet-smelling blooms, and these individual buys do not cost much when ordered from a florist. If you are going with a wreath or crown of flowers, have the florist measure your head. It sounds like an obvious piece of advice, but too many brides have complained that the wreath was either too big or too small on the wedding day and that it took some work with pliers and extra wire to get a correct and flattering fit.

Whatever your choice of headpiece, always select a style that looks great with the neckline of your gown, and know ahead of time how you will wear your hair.

Penny-Wise

The make-it-yourself veil is a big trade item right now. In craft stores such as Michael's and Treasure Island, the selection of headbands, headpieces, veil material, trim material, and gentle appliqués is astounding. A beautiful veil can be made for just under $30, an amazing savings compared to a $200 price tag in a bridal store. If making a veil is beyond your time or capacities, ask a talented crafter friend to pitch in and make it her gift to you.

Shoes

THESE are an easy pick-up. Since your shoes will not have to be dyed, you will be able to take your pair home right away. If you'll be ordering many pairs of shoes—one for each of your attendants as well as your own—see whether you can negotiate a discount on the shoes. Many shoe stores offer this additional incentive to brides to entice wedding business.

Many short-time brides report that they are saving time and money—since they are spending so much extra on the rush portions of their weddings—by deciding to wear nice, white shoes that they already own. We all have a pair of strappy white heels in our closet that, if they are in good condition, can be an option. Many brides do this, especially when they plan to wear a long ball gown, or when their wedding is informal. So don't count out last summer's heels!

Accessories

As for accessories, many brides report that keeping jewelry simple is a wise choice. Simple pearls or diamonds will work. Overbearing jewelry may look great at the Oscars, but such a display on your wedding day, however, would overshadow you. Do you want guests ogling your fine jewelry, or do you want them to see your smile?

Today's jewelry businesses are thriving, as more artistry has come to the marketplace. Beyond what you'll find at the department store jewelry counters—again, pricey options—you can find many, many lines of pretty wedding-appropriate jewelry on the market. You'll find these in regular accessory stores, smaller jewelry stores, and even art shops in the trendier parts of your local town. Take some time to research what is out there, check out-of-the-way stores and gift markets, and choose elegantly.

For formal weddings, you and your attendants may be in elbow-length gloves. These can be found primarily at bridal shops, so you'd be smart to order them there for the speedy service of color-matching. Choose wisely, get a fabric that goes with the gowns, and order according to your bridesmaids' sizes. Order these at the time of the gown order, as they may take even longer to create than their gowns. Do not leave this to the last minute.

> ## *Penny-Wise*
>
>
>
> Be sure to tell your fiancé and your parents that you're scouting for wedding-day jewelry. They may prevent you from buying if they're planning to get you jewelry for a wedding-day present. This heads-up also opens up a dialogue so you can show them exactly what you like. While it may take away from the element of surprise, at least you'll be less likely to be stuck wearing a gaudy necklace your mother-in-law gave you when you bought a simple string of pearls for yourself.

Rings

THE most time-consuming part of getting your wedding bands is going to be in investigating, looking, trying on, and selecting. As in all wedding business, you'll need to make sure that you're going to a reputable jeweler who has a long history at its current location, a loyal customer base, and a good track record in solid service. Many brides choose to go to the regular jeweler their family has used for years, and those who don't have one typically rely on referrals from recently married friends. A mistake some brides make is going to an unknown or fly-by-night store, hoping to get a discount. Such stores are where the wedding ring nightmare stories come from, such as the jeweler who closed up shop after a week (taking hefty deposits with him), or sold the "$5,000 ring" that was really worth $1,000. So choose your jeweler carefully. Invest your time in this important decision.

Once you've found a good jeweler, familiarize yourself with ring lingo. The salesperson is going to ask you right off the bat what kind of rings you're looking for, and that question is geared toward "What kind of metal do you want?" You may think you know the difference between 24-karat and 14-karat, as in 24-karat is 100 percent gold and 14-karat is just over 50 percent gold, but did you know that the 14-karat is more durable than the more precious metal? If you have an active job, you may choose the less-expensive, more-durable 14-karat. Here are the general characteristics of ring metals:

> ## Buying Time
>
>
>
> You can find out all you need to know about rings, including finding a reputable dealer in your neighborhood and how to design your own wedding bands at www.adiamondisforever.com. You may not have time to design your own ring and have it custom-made, but this tool will save you time if you use it to see what kinds of ring styles are out there. This site also allows you to print out your plans for comparison-shopping.

- *Platinum* is strong, durable, and will last a lifetime. To avoid mistakes (and I'll call it a "mistake," rather than assume any reputable jeweler would attempt fraud), be sure the ring is stamped on the inside with either "PT" or "plat."

- *White gold* looks like platinum, but is far less expensive. White gold, however, is not very durable, sometimes chips easily, and is therefore more likely to split out of its setting.

- *Yellow gold* can be found in 14-karat, 18-karat, and 24-karat. Twenty-four-karat, you should know, is too soft for regular wear and tear. Fourteen-karat is more durable, as well as less expensive.

If you choose a platinum band, you can be assured that your wedding band will not be cheap. But here are a couple of tips to help you get more ring for your money:

- Compare the prices of individual rings vs. wedding band sets. In some cases, the individuals you choose will be cheaper than the more lavish sets.

- Don't go for the emotional purchase. Do not let a salesperson talk you into a splashier set of rings because you're influenced by comments such as "You deserve it!" or "Isn't your love worth it?"

Keep in mind that your rings should not only be sized to your fingers; they should be "comfort fitted" with a thin layer of gold around the inside. Ring guards are fine for regular jewelry, and they may mean less time in ordering your rings, but a ring guard is an encumbrance, and the space between the guard and the ring does get dirty.

> ## *Buying Time*
>
>
>
> According to the experts at Capital Diamond in Paramus, New Jersey, delivery of ordered rings will take only two to four weeks, depending upon the style and personalization you choose. Always ask the salesperson for the delivery date, and be sure the date they give you is written in your contract. For sanity's sake, get this job done months ahead of time, as you will not want to risk a delivery delay.

As for engraving, most processes take one or two days, tops. A busier ring shop in the height of wedding or holiday season may take a week. Again, find out what's expected and put it in writing.

Leave plenty of time to have your rings appraised at a site other than where you bought them, and purchase insurance on them. Then, find a very safe place for them, and keep them within sight until the wedding day.

7

THE BRIDESMAIDS' GOWNS

DRESSING THE WOMEN—
WITHOUT HUMILIATING THEM

As FAR AS your time goes, you can save yourself many hours by assuming control over choice of bridesmaids' gowns. Too many brides with lots of time on their hands turn this task into a major time-waster by bringing all their attendants to a bridal shop and turning them loose to "pick out what they want." Whenever you gather many egos, body shapes, and preferences, you're asking for a huge headache. Your time and your happiness will be well served if you start the process on your own.

Choosing the Bridesmaids' Dresses

You know the type of wedding you're planning, the formality, the style, and the location. You also know your bridesmaids' tastes, body shapes, and budgets. The best path to completion of this task begins with you doing some research by yourself.

♦ *Consider the formality.* Just as you did for your own gown, be sure your maids' gowns are going to fit in with the day. For a formal wedding, they should be in gowns or cocktail-length dresses.

For an informal, garden wedding, they should be in knee-length dresses. For a beach wedding, also consider slipdresses or sundresses for them.

♦ *Consider their tastes.* Every bride says she tries to get dresses her bridesmaids will wear again after the wedding, but this only seems to happen for attendants involved in informal or beach weddings. Even when brides choose the most gorgeous style of a formal bridesmaid's gown, few women will wear it again and again. There will be a better chance of this happening if you choose a very simple, elegant style. Avoid sexy, backless styles, as you may be burdening your heavier-chested maids with a bra dilemma.

Stress Relief

If your bridesmaids are far away, you can scan pictures and send them via e-mail, or you can send them the address to the designer's site (or sites) where you found the dresses.

♦ *Consider your bridesmaids' budgets.* You already may be asking a lot of them to change their plans to fit in your late-planned wedding. Some may be juggling demanding work or school schedules; some may have had to cancel other plans (albeit happily at this point) to be there for you. The worst thing you could do—and it has been done before—is to ask even more of them, thus draining their bank accounts on dresses, travel, lodging, gifts, showers, and so on. So try your best to choose a gown within a reasonable price range.

The smartest approach for the sake of your time is to choose three bridesmaid dress styles, and present them to your gathered bridesmaids. A good way to do this is at a bridesmaids' luncheon, where you place three pictures in front of them and let them discuss, deliberate, and come to a decision on their own.

A Rainbow Bridal Party?

In the same vein of individuality, some recent brides have gone with the "rainbow" effect. Their bridesmaids wear, with the bride's approval, different color dresses that complement one another. So some may be in blush pink and others in a complementary rose color, for instance. This again can allow you to take into account your bridesmaids' differing skin and hair tones. A platinum blonde may look washed-out in a pale-pink gown but brighter in the rose selection. Just the same, your olive-skinned friend may look better in the paler tone. Be open to the possibility of varying the look, which can indeed be lovely when done well. Varying the order won't require extra time, which is helpful at this point in the planning.

Do *not* bring them to the bridal salon to see the three that you've selected ahead of time, because the many other dresses in the shop will be like a distracting siren call to each of their differing opinions. Just present the three, give them time to check out the styles you've chosen, and provide a fabric swatch so that they can see what color they'd be wearing. "Then put on your protective headgear and watch them fight it out," says one bride with a joking smile. Yes, your maids may bicker over which style is best, but you will all come to a selection by the time coffee is served.

Here, again, is where the time crunch may actually serve you well. Simply tell your maids that you must have a decision right away because of the gown ordering or selection time. If you've done your preliminary selecting well, this process should not be too difficult. Do be sure to tell them the prices of these dresses, as that may be the determining factor. Not knowing the "bottom line" at this point may result in a not-too-sturdy decision.

Some brides are avoiding the whole debacle of finding one style that suits six different body types by having their maids wear differing styles of the same color dress. Your smaller maids can wear a narrower cut, your pregnant maid can wear an empire-waisted dress, and your larger maids can wear an A-line that suits their figures. Just be sure to order each of these gowns from the same place in the same dye lot, so that you do not also have differing shades of rose pink. This is a great time- and stress-saving option for which your bridesmaids will thank you. Every bridesmaid will love having a say in what she will wear, that she has the freedom to look her best on your wedding day, and that she might actually get to wear the dress again.

Fortunately, bridesmaids' dresses are no longer the hideous monstrosities they used to be. Gone are the neckline ruffles, the hoop skirts, the orange patterns, and the parasols. Designers have embraced this market as well, and created beautiful selections. (Some even work well as lovely second-time wedding gowns!) In short, your maids will have little to complain about if you take their needs and preferences into consideration and choose well for them.

The bridesmaids I've talked to ask—no, plead—that you make your wedding color choice with their dignity in mind. Orange may be your signature color, but please do not put your maids in orange dresses. Most bridesmaids ask, as well, that you avoid choosing patterned or floral dresses, pale colors, ruffles, too much lace, and big frilly bows. When asked what color they'd most love to wear, what color they'd wear again, bridesmaids mentioned black, dusty pinks, lavenders, and burgundies.

The Ordering Process

IF you will not be ordering your maids' gowns off the rack, you'll need to deal with a gown-ordering process similar to that for your wedding gown. To accomplish this feat, however, you will have to order several gowns in your maids' particular sizes. This is not as easy as it may sound. Designer styles may run either smaller or larger in size. A woman who wears a size 6 in regular clothes may wear a 4 in a designer style. And in another designer's world, she might need a size 8. So follow the Golden Rule in the wedding gown industry—just as you have to be measured for your gown, so must your bridesmaids for their dresses.

If your maids all live in the same town, you may choose to visit the salon together to be measured by an on-site seamstress. It may seem as though she's measuring every bit of you—arms, legs, everything—but she does know what she is doing. A well-measured gown or dress at this point can save you hours and hundreds of dollars in later fittings.

If your bridesmaids live all over the country, or the world, you'll have to take some extra steps. Again, simply having them tell you their dress size is not enough. Instruct them to have a legitimate seamstress (which they can find at most cleaners or in the Yellow Pages under "Alterations") take their measurements. She will write down their measurements on a standard sizing card, which they are to send you to be submitted with the order.

Once the seamstress or the salesperson has the size cards, she will place the order for your bridesmaids' gowns. As always, be sure to get

> ### *Buying Time*
>
>
>
> T he bridal shops may be a great place to look for bridesmaid dresses, but you'll find wide and diverse selections of appropriate bridesmaids' gowns in major department stores. Even better, the stores carry many of each style of gown, in a range of sizes. So if your bridal party is small enough, you may be able to pre-shop at Macy's formal department, choose three possibilities, then take your bridesmaids there to snap up all their gowns in one day.

Accommodating the Pregnant Bridesmaid

What becomes of the pregnant bridesmaid? If your wedding has been planned for only a few months out, chances are you already know whether one or more of your maids is expecting. How then do you handle the gown selection, ordering, and fittings? Be sure to choose a style that is flattering to pregnant women. A good way to do this is to cruise the maternity clothing sections of department stores and look at the formal dresses. See what kinds of waistlines are prominent (sorry for the pun!), as well as which neckline and skirt styles dominate.

Have your maid order her dress much larger than she needs it to be now, as you have no idea how large her body will be by the time of your wedding. Some women carry their pregnancies larger, smaller, higher, or lower than others, and a good fitting shortly before the wedding will help her make the most of her appearance on your wedding day.

Please keep her feelings in mind; be sensitive to the fact that she won't want to look awful in a dress that doesn't work for her shape, and that she deserves to feel beautiful that day as well.

If possible, go with her to her fittings, assure her that she looks lovely, and grab lunch afterwards. After all, as the bride, you need to make sure each bridesmaid is happy in her role as your attendant.

In addition, have her order her shoes a half size larger than she usually wears, as her feet are likely to swell. Of course, she can always take her shoes off at the reception—and probably will.

a good written contract and an itemized list of the order. A good bridal salon will have an order form that lists the bridesmaids' name, measured sizes, deposit amount, fitting information and prices, refund information, as well as your name, wedding date, and your contact information. Be sure the delivery date is on the contract, and get a copy of the contract for yourself.

Important: Always order the gowns from one shop. Do not allow your maids in a faraway state to order their own at a local shop. The gown you choose may come in just one designer style, but the individual gowns may be produced in several different locations. As a result, one bridesmaid's lavender dress may be a completely different, clashing shade from another's. Called "differing dye lots" in the industry, this applies to shoes as well.

> ### *Say the Word*
>
>
>
> For some of your bridesmaids, getting measured will be as "enjoyable" as trying on bathing suits—or as unpleasant as getting a root canal. Your heavier maids may prefer submitting their size cards in a sealed envelope. Without making a big deal out of it, you might simply tell them that's how it's being done.

Always order all like items from one place. Faraway bridesmaids can have their gowns shipped to them via Federal Express—insured, tracked, and with return receipt. Nearby brides can get the gowns from you themselves.

The Money Issue

SOME brides do pay for the bridesmaids' gowns themselves as gifts to their maids, but if this is not within your budget, you will have to be clear with your bridesmaids about the timing of payment. Let them know the amount of the deposit they will have to place when the dress is ordered and when the balance is due, or whether the whole amount is due up front. Also let them know what, if anything, the fittings will cost. (Some salons offer free alterations as part of their allure.)

Track each bridesmaid's status—current contact information, measurements, order, fittings, and payments—to be sure all of them stay on schedule (see the Bridesmaids' Dress Order Form in the "Helpful Forms" section in back of this book). Such an organized approach will not guarantee smooth sailing, of course. An unfortunate universal condition applies: There is a potential for problems when money and friendship mix. You'd like, for instance, to be sympathetic to your friend's financial struggles, but you're inwardly seething that she claims to be unable to pay the deposit on the gown yet boasts about her recent weekend in the Hamptons. Money sometimes causes friction so this may be a good job to hand over to your maid of honor. Let her be in charge of pressing for payment. You have too much to do to spend your time sending kind, but charged e-mails about late payments.

Buying Time

Federal Express (Fed Ex) is online at www.fedex.com and easy to reach by phone at 800-GO-FEDEX. You have to get an account number to access your shippings, but this is an easy way to track your parcels and to send them overnight—for a price. The Priority Mail system of the regular postal office is cheaper, so check them out as well at www.usps.com.

Fittings

FITTINGS do not have to be a group effort, unless you want them to be. Some brides and their attendants make a day of it, getting lunch and arranging other plans; others are way too busy to stand around while their maids are getting pinned and tucked. If you are short on time, allow your maids to take care of this task on their own. Just be sure to advise them to get their fittings done professionally, recommend your seamstress, remind them not to leave it until last minute, and let go of control on this one.

Choosing Shoes and Accessories

AGAIN, this is a one-day effort. Bring your maids to a pre-selected shoe store, show them a few styles of shoes, and let them make the selection. You might suggest the following:

- *Consider getting lower heels.* High heels may make your legs look great, but they will be worn for hours on the wedding day, and dancing may be difficult in them if you're not the type to remove your shoes for comfort. In addition, outdoor weddings usually mean that heels will be sinking in to moist ground. In this case, semi-flats are best. While ballerina slippers may be a pretty look for your bridesmaids, or for yourself, consider their impracticality in wet conditions and choose another delicate style.

- *Inform bridesmaids that they need wear these shoes only during the ceremony.* If you're having a beach wedding, remind your maids that the shoes may only be for the ceremony, and that they'll be barefoot for the beach bash.

- *Simpler is less expensive.* Avoid the embellishments. Let the dress be the main attraction.

- *Get shoes that are slightly loose, rather than slightly tight.* At the end of a long day of standing, feet will be swollen and shoes will not fit as well.

- *Try on the shoes at night.* After a long day of walking around at work or at home, your bridesmaids' feet will be naturally swollen to

> ### *Wedding Day Reflections*
>
>
>
> One of my bridesmaids was having a lot of trouble with money. She had just gotten divorced, her ex wasn't paying child support, and she was struggling. I really wanted her in my bridal party, so I offered to pay for her gown and shoes. We just promised not to let any of the other girls know. Deceptive, yes, but worth the outcome.
>
> —Jenny

some degree. Most bridal parties report that their shoes fit better on the wedding day when they applied this shopping trick.

♦ *Consider colors that go with almost everything.* Rather than dye the shoes, which can take a lot of time and may not be possible depending upon when your wedding will be, consider having your maids choose shoes in white, black, or the popular silver—colors that go with everything.

♦ *Allow your bridesmaids to make the choice.* After all, the shoes are for their feet, not yours. Your shoes do not have to match theirs as far as style.

With regard to accessories, overly adorned bridesmaids are distracting. Many brides like to give their bridesmaids simple, understated jewelry as gifts so they have some say in what their maids will be wearing on the wedding day.

Accessories are often lowly priced at standard accessory shops in the mall. There is no need to hit the fine jewelry counters at the department stores, unless you have the budget to do so. Some brides do say that they actually made their bridesmaids' jewelry (as customized jewelry is popular); but with less than six months to plan your wedding, you may not have the time or the patience to string beads for eight hours. So go with the available styles, choosing simple faux pearls or faux diamonds over color-coordinated stones.

Wedding Day Reflections

My best friend is a wonderful person, but I was so upset to see that on my wedding day, she had this big, clunky gold necklace on with her bridesmaid gown. I didn't have the heart—or the guts—to ask her to take it off, and I really let that bother me too much.

—Stacy

Outfits and Accessories for Flower Girls and Ring Bearers

THE child members of the bridal party do not take much effort to dress. The ring bearer can be fitted for a little rented tuxedo, as those are available at most men's shops. For a cheaper, more adorable look that suits an informal, outdoor, or beach wedding, just have him in a pair of black or white shorts and white button-down shirt with a little tie that matches the members of the male attendants. Keeping his attire simple will be a relief to his parents, and it is an easily made arrangement.

As for the flower girls, the selection can be as simple as you make it. Some bridal shops carry a wide range of flower-girl dresses, some to match the design and fabric of the bride's gown. However, these matched styles really do take advantage of brides' "Awwww, isn't that sweet?" mentality, and can cause them to make a decision that could mean significant expense. At one shop, I saw precious little linen flower-girl dresses that matched the wedding gown styles displayed in the store, and those flower-girl dresses were $450! So it may be wise to avoid the matching flower-girl dresses and take advantage of the trend for individual, suitable styles for kids. Having the children in white or off-white to match you makes for a nice look in your photos, as the kids do not get lost in a sea of color.

> ### *Buying Time*
>
>
>
> Buying off the rack for children is the best way to go, as you also do not have to wait for dresses to be ordered.

A better choice is to ask the flower girl's parents to accompany you to a standard children's clothing store. Many of these have sections of kids' fine dresses, and you can surely find a suitable style that is within the parents' budget.

A sash matching the wedding party's colors attached to the waist of a simple white party dress can work well for your flower girl, or she might wear a child's floral headpiece that could serve as the color match.

THE MEN'S WARDROBES

DRESSING IN STYLE—WITHOUT A HASSLE

Y OU MAY IMAGINE that ordering the men's tuxedos will be an easy task, but you will need to act far more in advance than you think. The best tuxedo shops, the ones with the greatest variety of styles and the best supply of clean, quality suits, have been booked a long time. You'll need to reserve your ushers' tuxes at least three months in advance, especially if your wedding will be during prom season, which is also high wedding season. Give yourself as much time as possible to be sure you can reserve the best in men's attire.

Be sure to include the groom in this process, as he will be wearing a tux himself. He may scoff and say, "I don't care." Yet in the end, most guys are as fashion-conscious as we are and they do remember the tuxes they wore to their proms (though they may have burned the pictures!).

Just explain to him that selecting a style will not take long, and that you simply want his input.

Choosing the Right Style for the Men

Just like you did for the women of the bridal party, you will have to make your selection of a tuxedo style that is suitable for the formality and style of your chosen wedding. For formal weddings, black tuxedos are the norm. For ultra-formal, you'll go with white tie and tails.

Be on the lookout now for a much wider selection of tuxedos. Now, the formal look also includes a very classy black shirt under a black tuxedo jacket and black tie. (The all-white look is reserved for prom-goers and little boys making their First Holy Communion.)

Visit several tux shops and ask to see not only their catalogs, but samples of their selections. Pictures may not capture the essence of the look, as they won't for bridesmaids' gowns, so you'll want to actually see and feel the tuxedos you're considering for your men. Again, here are some things to keep in mind:

- *Consider, of course, the formality.* For a formal wedding, the men will wear tuxedos with bow ties and perhaps vests or cummerbunds. For an informal wedding, the options are dark suits with matching shirts and ties. The best way to make appropriate choices and save time is to discuss with the tuxedo rental store manager your wedding plans and the look of your bridesmaids' gowns, the color, and even the location of the wedding. The manager will be able to point out the most popular selections and help you make an efficient decision.

- *Consider your ushers' budgets.* The more well-known designer suits such as Ralph Lauren will work for more than standard designs,

Buying Time

S*tart your research by checking out tuxedo options on the bridal Web sites listed in the Resources. At these sites, you can get a quick look at what styles are available, what seasonal choices are available, and at what prices. Some Web sites even tell you where you can find the tuxedo of your choice. This way, you'll be able to find what you want over the Internet, and your trip to the tuxedo rental shop will take less time.*

and you can find a great style at a lower price if you comparison-shop for more budget-conscious designer styles. Many
couples do take the time to think about their ushers' financial
constraints, including travel, college expenses, school expenses,
and so on in order to make the best choice according to budget. Again, the tuxedo rental agent can help you choose the best
style for any price.

- *Consider the location of the wedding.* If yours
  will be an outdoor wedding, you may
  not want your men in tuxedos at all.
  In fact, they will be uncomfortable in
  those tight collars and jackets. More
  on that later.

- *Consider their appearance.* Just as you took
  the women's sizes and shapes into account, you'll also have to think about
  the men's egos. What style of tux will
  flatter all of your men? A cummer-
  bund that will accentuate your rotund
  usher's waistline will only make him
  feel uncomfortable, for instance.

> ### Wedding Day Reflections
>
>
>
> My fiancée was surprised that
> I even wanted to do this job at all,
> but I know what colors look good
> on me. She wanted gray tuxes, but
> there is no way in hell that I'd
> ever be caught dead in a gray tux.
> And I'd never ask my buddies to
> wear the style she had picked out.
> So I just kind of took over the job,
> telling her she had much more
> important things to do.
>
> —Joseph, groom

Once you have chosen your desired style
of tux, either bring in the ushers for their sizing and orders, or—for faraway ushers—get
a copy of the brochure that holds a picture of the tux, and instruct
him to be measured for the appropriate size at a nearby tailor. Explain
that you need his cooperation for this important step.

What helps is that most men have been through the tux-ordering
process before, whether for other weddings or for proms or formals
in their past. So they may not need as much instruction and prod-
ding as you might think. You can save time by e-mailing them the
directions to the tux shop, recommending tailors in their area, and

reminding them to get the job done. It's also a smart idea to have the men e-mail you back when the job is done. Track each groomsman's status—current contact information, measurements, order, fittings, and payments—to be sure all of them stay on schedule (see sthe Tuxedo Rental Order Form in the "Helpful Forms" section in back of this book).

As always, get a copy of the itemized order and a copy of the signed contract with the pickup date clearly marked. Be sure to note when the fittings will be done, when the pickups can be accomplished, and when the tuxes need to be returned. Many ushers waste money because they did not know that the tuxes needed to be returned the day after the wedding. So clarify whether it's a next-day return or whether they've given you a cushion of a few days.

> ### Say the Word
>
>
>
> Many brides and grooms report that getting the men to the tailor is not as easy as getting the women there. Supplying the men with size cards that you can get from the tux shop, giving them instructions and a strict, ahead-of-time deadline date, and having the groom call to remind them to get this job done will spur them along.

When You're Going Without Tuxes

MANY weddings are going the informal route these days, and the tuxedo look does not fit into the more relaxed atmosphere. So, if your wedding will be a more downscaled affair, consider having your ushers in any of the following alternatives:

♦ *Suits.* Asking your men to wear all-black suits with white button-down shirts and black ties means that they will fit into a less-formal atmosphere, and that they will save on rentals. Just be sure to see the suits ahead of time. Ask them to wear their "wedding gear" to a pre-wedding party for the express purpose of getting checked out for their look. Hey, if you're saving them money in rental fees, they should willingly comply.

THE MEN'S WARDROBES   99

♦ *Black pants and white shirts with tie.* This is a fine look for an outdoor wedding. Just make sure their ties all match (you may choose to supply them), and that they have been instructed to wear either long sleeves or short sleeves. Again, ushers love this look, as it saves them money; and they do like to be more comfortable at outdoor weddings in the heat by not wearing a jacket. Plus, they do not have to carve time out of their schedules to get measured and ordered.

♦ *Khaki pants and white shirt with tie.* This is a wonderful outdoor or informal wedding look. You may think it is just too casual for any type of wedding, but in a group, the men look like a J Crew ad, and the unified look is striking. The wedding pictures, I'm told, are also more appropriate for display in a home than are stiff, posed portraits of the groom and his buddies in so-called "penguin suits."

Penny-Wise

Some brides report that they were able to get a discount on their father's tuxedo, but this usually only happens with a big tux rental order, such as a bridal party of ten or more men. But it can't hurt to ask. Remember, the wedding industry works on word-of-mouth referral. The tux shop will want you to rave to all your ushers about their helpful manager and great discount, so a manager may be willing to give you five-star service for your free advertising.

Shoes and Accessories for Men

You really should have all men in the wedding party wearing the same shoe style. Allowing each to wear his own shoes brings up the possibility of old and damaged shoes, shoes that aren't quite the right color, or shoes that aren't the right style. Tuxedo rental shops carry a wide variety of shoes for rent, which the men can reserve at the time they rent their tuxes.

For less formal events, the men can wear their own shoes, provided you get to check them out first. The men will probably complain and make good-natured jokes, which should subside when you remind them of the money they'll save.

As for accessories, choose wisely, as these accents can make or break the look for the men. Silk ties are the best choice, and the available variety is astounding.

Rental shops will have the ties and cummerbunds that are necessary for tuxedos. Make your selection wisely by spending some extra time looking at samples of each design. Years ago, tuxedo shops offered a dozen or so styles. Now you may find sixty to seventy. Be sure to choose a solid color that coordinates with the bridesmaids' gowns. Bring a swatch of the bridesmaids' fabric for correct matching. Do not try to match color from memory. This, too, should be done right away, so that the tux shop has time to ship in your choice. A reputable store will not allow you to leave this until the last minute anyway, so know the rules by which you're operating and take care of all details in one time-saving shot.

Notes for the Fathers

As a rule, the fathers should be dressed in formalwear that matches the ushers and the groom. They, too, should be in tuxedos if that is what the rest of the bridal party is wearing, and they should be included in any sizing and ordering trip in which the other men participate. If they are far away, they do the size card thing, too.

Cufflinks, shirt studs, and tie clips can be the groom's gift to the ushers, and indeed they should be to guarantee a unified look on the wedding day.

For the truly informal wedding, the men need no accessories.

9

PLANNING THE CEREMONY

FINALIZING THE DETAILS

IRONICALLY, WHILE THE ceremony itself is supposed to be the most important part of the wedding, it is also the simplest and typically the least time-consuming to plan. If you will be having a completely traditional, in-church wedding, you may choose to have your ceremony follow the prescribed outline the church uses for most weddings they do. You choose two or three readings, perhaps a song, and you're done. The vows are standard, all elements are in place for you, and the planning of the ceremony can be done in a matter of minutes.

However, the trend is moving away from the cookie-cutter ceremony. With more and more ceremonies going the nontraditional route—including the personalized and meaningful, with less emphasis on religious dogma—you may choose to handcraft your ceremony to suit your styles, tastes, and spirituality.

Here, you'll learn how to plan the elements of your ceremony in the least amount of time.

Following the Script

AT many churches and synagogues, you will receive a pamphlet of the prescribed order of wedding ceremonies, from processional through the vows, the recessional, and all elements in between. Always ask for a copy of their ceremony outline if one is not offered to you. Most churches and synagogues are aware that brides and grooms like to print out programs of their ceremony for their guests, and they will comply with this request. If they do not have a printed copy, ask them to dictate the steps to you.

Some religious establishments do not leave room for much individuality, so you will have to be sure to discuss all of your wishes with the officiant. With some good-natured diplomacy, you are likely to be able to incorporate your own touches to the ceremony.

Stress Relief

Some officiants you may see listed in the phone book and in full-color ads in local wedding guide magazines offer complete interfaith ceremonies. Check their credentials carefully to be sure that they are licensed to complete all ends of your religious ceremony. I have interviewed many brides who used such officiants with no complaints, and their marriages are indeed recognized in both faiths.

The Interfaith Wedding

IF you and your fiancé are of different faiths, and you plan to combine your religious elements for a ceremony that is not only pleasing to you but valid in each religion, you will have to take some extra steps. That will mean meeting with the officiants of both religions and working together to create a ceremony that works for all of you.

This may not seem worth the extra time and trouble, but is actually an easy and important step. Luckily, we live in a time where interfaith marriages are more common, and most houses of worship have had experience with this request before. Because you are not charting new territory, the steps may already be in place.

Choose your officiants well, explaining at the outset that this will be an interfaith wedding, and plan a meeting in which all parties will meet together to discuss the ceremony plans. Remember that you are the couple getting married, and make it clear that while you want to respect your individual faiths, you are determined to find a way to integrate the elements that you desire. You'll need to use a light touch here, and remember that this is not the time to try to boss around an officiant. A good officiant will respect that you are making an effort to include your faiths in your ceremony, and in present times, most will be willing to accommodate you.

The Non-Religious Ceremony

NOT all couples are connected to a religion or church—and some couples do face restrictions that will not allow them to marry in certain churches. For these reasons, more and more brides and grooms are choosing a non-religious ceremony. It may be a simple appearance before a justice of the peace, a captain of a ship, or any other non-affiliated professional who is licensed to perform marriage rites.

> ### *Buying Time*
>
>
>
> To save time, know which rituals of each faith you and your fiancé wish to include in the ceremony, and which aspects you do not. If you have your minds made up, you'll experience far less push and pull from concerned relatives or the officiants. Too many brides and grooms wind up having the ceremony their parents want, without any thought as to which religious beliefs or rituals are important to them.

If you plan to appear for a simple ceremony before a justice of the peace or a county judge, you must take some steps to arrange for the ceremony. Most judges need no more than a few weeks' notice to arrange a completely legal ceremony—but give them more, as you don't know when they have full dockets or will be on vacation.

In the case of the non-religious ceremony, you have all the freedom in the world to add whatever elements you like to your ceremony. So follow the tips you'll find in the rest of this chapter to create a specialized ceremony that speaks of your commitment to your fiancé.

Say the Word

This is also the time to let your officiants know where you will be holding the ceremony. Each wedding officiant has his or her own rules. For example, some priests or rabbis will not perform ceremonies in the outdoors or at a person's home. By making your preference clear at the beginning, you can save time by quickly eliminating a choice that will not work for you.

Music for the Ceremony

AGAIN, you may choose to go with whatever the church organist offers in her repertoire, or you may be more selective. We'll begin with the first step: Ask what kinds of musicians the ceremony site offers. Many churches and synagogues offer the following standard choices, often at an extra fee:

♦ Organist

♦ Choir

♦ Vocal soloist

♦ Pianist

You might opt for any of these choices, otherwise you are free to select your own musicians, as many brides do. At a recent wedding in East Hanover, New Jersey, bride Won Young Rim chose to have trumpeters as a part of her ceremony, which added a regal touch to her ceremony. It reminded her guests of a royal wedding, announcing to the world the significance of the day.

Other brides have used harpists, which is a lovely, elegant touch to the ceremony and even to the pre-wedding time when the guests are being escorted to their seats.

Vocal soloists are another fine choice, especially if you or your fiancé know the singer—and particularly when the performance is his or her contribution to your wedding.

As with all wedding professionals you use, interview and audition them so you will know what they will be providing. You want no surprises on your wedding day, so even if you have to carve a few hours

Music for Guest Seating Time

"Matrimonial Benediction" by Camille Saint-Saëns

"Jesu Joy of Man's Desiring" by Johann Sebastian Bach

"Air" (from *Watermusic*) by G. F. Handel

"The Four Seasons, Spring" by Antonio Vivaldi

"Flower Waltz" by Peter Tchaikovsky

"Benediction Nuptiale" by Saint-Saëns

"Suite in D" by Johann Sebastian Bach

"String Quartet Minuet no. 8" by Luigi Boccherini

"Minuet in D Major" by Wolfgang Amadeus Mozart

"Violin Concerto in A" by Franz Joseph Haydn

"Ave Maria" by Johann Sebastian Bach

Selections from George Winston

Selections from Enya

Selections of Natural Instrumental Music such as "The Natural
    Cello" or "The Natural Harp"

Selections from Andrea Boccelli

Selections from Sarah Brightman

out of your already-packed schedule, this decision should not be left to chance. Always make an appointment for an audition, bring your fiancé (and only your fiancé, as too many opinions will make any choice difficult), and sit back to listen to the performance.

When choosing your musicians, consider the following criteria:

♦ *What experience do they have?* Many musicians are registered with a professional association, which will allow you to check out their credentials.

♦ *What will they be wearing?* Specify whether you want them in a suit, dress, tuxedo, choir robes, or something else.

Music for the Processional

"Bridal Chorus" (from *Lohengrin*) by Richard Wagner (also known as "Here Comes the Bride")

"Rhapsody on a Theme" by Niccolò Paganini

"Ode to Joy" by Beethoven

"The Four Seasons" by Antonio Vivaldi

"Prince of Denmark's March: Trumpet Voluntary" by J. Clarke

"Canon in D Minor" by Johann Pachelbel

"Wedding March" from *The Marriage of Figaro* by Wolfgang Amadeus Mozart

---

♦ *How do they sound at the wedding site?* Have them audition in the church or synagogue or outdoors, wherever the wedding will be. Acoustics do count. At one seaside wedding, the choir's sound was swept away by the breeze and the sound of the surf. Even their microphones picked up the fuzzy sound of the wind blowing.

♦ *Are they familiar with the musical selection you have chosen?* Have any musician perform the songs you will want to hear. If they do not know your chosen song at this time, and the wedding is only a month away, find another performer.

♦ *Who recommends the musicians?* Get referrals from family and friends for quality professional musicians.

♦ *Have you considered music students?* If time requires, and if all the best professionals in your area are booked, consider approaching the music department of a local college or high school. These young people are often talented musicians, and will appreciate the venue and the resume material. Plus, you won't have to pay top dollar.

Most brides report that they hired or accepted several different kinds of musicians for their ceremony. They used a standard organist

Ceremony Performance Songs

"Ave Maria" by Johann Sebastian Bach

"Hallelujah Chorus" (from Handel's *Messiah*)

"Amazing Grace" by John Newton

"All I Ask of You" by Andrew Lloyd Webber

"Beautiful in My Eyes" by Joshua Kadison

"Can't Help Falling in Love" by Elvis Presley

"Can You Feel the Love Tonight?" by Elton John

"Endless Love" by Diana Ross

"Here and Now" by Luther Vandross

"I Cross My Heart" by George Strait

"I Only Have Eyes for You" by Art Garfunkel

"It Had to Be You" by Harry Connick, Jr.

"Just the Way You Are" by Billy Joel

"The Power of Love" by Celine Dion

"What a Wonderful World" by Louis Armstrong

"You Are So Beautiful" by Joe Cocker

"You're the Inspiration" by Chicago

or pianist for the processional, offering of the gifts in a Catholic ceremony, and communion parts, a soloist for the middle of the ceremony, and trumpeters for the recessional. If you don't have time to do all this arranging, as indeed you may not, choose one performer to provide all your wedding music. A classically trained pianist might be the best option.

MUSICAL SUGGESTIONS

Chances are, you do not have time to research many of the possible songs that might be played during your ceremony. And you may be so original that you'd rather not walk down the aisle to "Here Comes the Bride" (which, according to legend, started out as an old English drunken barroom song making fun of non-virgin brides). To save you the investigation time, I've collected lists of pieces you might consider for the various elements of your ceremony (see sidebars throughout this chapter).

The key to finding wedding music is to select what appeals to you, what speaks to your relationship, and what will enhance the type of wedding you're planning. As with every other part of your ceremony, you will have to inform the officiant of the music you'll be including. Some houses of worship have restrictions about secular music, and others do not allow any music in their ceremonies. For instance, "The Wedding Chorus" ("Here Comes the Bride") is banned in many houses of worship, as the composer was thought of as an anti-Semite in his time.

Readings

AGAIN, you may go with the readings that everyone goes with, taking your cue from the officiant. Catholic ceremonies, for example, use Corinthians 13 (". . . faith, hope, love . . . but the greatest of these is love.") as the standard reading for all wedding services. If

---

Music for the Recessional

"Wedding March" (from *A Midsummer Night's Dream*) by Felix Mendelssohn Bartoldy

"Bridal Chorus" from *Lohengrin* by Richard Wagner

"Hornpipe" (from *Watermusic*) by G. F. Handel

"The Four Seasons, Spring" by Antonio Vivaldi

For more informal recessionals, look to the contemporary songs listed above, or have some fun with "Good Lovin" by the Young Rascals; "Celebration" by Kool and the Gang; "Hot, Hot, Hot" by Buster Poindexter; "Walk This Way" by Aerosmith; or "Stand By Me" by Ben E. King. The idea is to begin the celebration right now, and your guests will love this let-loose musical pronouncement.

you're truly pressed for time and don't mind going by the book (or The Book, in this case!), then by all means go for the norm.

If you're planning to personalize your ceremony—whatever form it takes, from traditional religious to super-informal and non-religious—then you'll have to spend some time choosing more personalized readings.

Most brides and grooms choose a special loved one to perform the readings. It may be a parent, a member of the bridal party, a godparent, the person who introduced you to your fiancé, or even your boss. Make that decision ahead of time, and ask the person you've chosen whether he or she would consider doing the reading during your wedding.

Readings come in different forms, whether they be selections from a religious text, from a spiritual work such as Marianne Williamson's books, from ro-

Less Is More

Do not go overboard with the music selections during the ceremony. It may sound wonderful now to have three solos during the ceremony, but you may not want the ceremony to last so long. You will be nervous, your fiancé will be nervous, the weather may be hot, and your guests will have sat through ceremonies before. So for the best in ceremony planning—so you can get to "You may kiss the bride" sooner—consider choosing one or two solos.

mantic poetry such as Elizabeth Barrett Browning ("How do I love thee? Let me count the ways . . ."), or from personalized poetry that you or your fiancé have written.

Again, to save you time, here are parts of the more popular readings that you may choose to incorporate into your ceremony:

Love is patient and kind;
Love is not jealous or boastful;
It is not arrogant or rude.
Love does not insist on its own way;
It is not irritable or resentful;
It does not rejoice at wrong,

But rejoices in the right.
Love bears all things,
Believes all things,
Hopes all things,
Endures all things.
Love never ends.
—Corinthians 13:4—8a

Grow old along with me!
The best is yet to be,
The last of life, for which the first was made.
Our times are in his hand
Who saith, "A whole I planned,
Youth shows but half.
Trust God.
See all,
Nor be afraid!
—Robert Browning

My true love hath my heart and
    I have his;
By just exchange one for another given;
I hold his dear and mine he cannot miss;
There never was a better bargain driven;
My true love hath my heart and I have his.
My heart in me keeps him and me in one;
My heart in him his thoughts and senses guides;
He loves my heart for once it was his own;
I cherish his because in me it bides:
My true love hath my heart and I have his.
—Sir Phillip Sidney

How do I love thee? Let me count the ways.
I love thee to the depth and breadth and height
My soul can reach, when feeling out of sight.
For the ends of Being and ideal Grace.

I love thee to the level of every day's
Most quiet need, by sun and candlelight.
I love thee freely, as men strive for Right;
I love thee purely, as they turn from Praise.
I love thee with passion put to use
In my old griefs, and with my childhood's faith.

I love thee with a love I seemed
 to lose
With my lost saints,—I love thee
 with the breath,
Smiles, tears, of all my life,—and,
 if God choose,
I shall but love thee better after
 death.
—Elizabeth Barrett Browning

What greater thing is there for two
 human souls
than to feel that they are joined . . .
to strengthen each other . . .
to be at one with each other
in silent, unspeakable memories.
—George Eliot

Like everything which is not the
 involuntary result of fleeting
 emotion,
but the creation of time and will,
any marriage,
happy or unhappy,
is infinitely more interesting and
 significant
than any romance,
however passionate.
—W. H. Auden

> # Recommended Sources for Wedding Readings
>
>
>
> Poetry by John Browning, Elizabeth
> Barrett Browning, W. H. Auden,
> and others
> Selections from *The Invitation* by
> Oriah Mountain Dreamer
> Writings of Pema Chodron
> Writings of the Dalai Lama
> Writings of George Eliot
> Writings of Anne Morrow Lindbergh
> Writings of Sarah Ban Breathnach
> Writings of Maya Angelou
> Writings of Marianne Williamson
> Various poetry anthologies

It is never too late to be what you might have been,

—George Eliot

(I especially like this one for re-marriages and marriages late in life, as it gives a sense of hope for a happy marriage in the future.)

You can, of course, find plenty of romantic poetry to include in your ceremony readings, and your officiant can usually provide you with a detailed list of readings. So choose wisely, as the readings within your ceremony become a part of the bond you create on that day. They are as important as the vows, and they do impart messages to your guests.

Another idea is for you and the groom to give an informal speech about how you met, what you thought of each other, and special moments throughout your courtship. Such personal touches make a ceremony special. Remember, your guests may have been to dozens of weddings, which may all seem the same after a while. So make yours something to remember by adding personalized special touches to your ceremony. You'll be glad you took the time for this step.

Professionally Speaking

One of the most romantic weddings I've ever been to was one in which the bride and groom read letters that they had written to one another over the years. These were the words that were fresh from those bright, charged romantic days of the beginning of their love, and their passion came through. So if you and your fiancé wrote love letters, or even romantic e-mails, consider including selected portions of them as part of your ceremony. Just leave out the extra mushy or sexually explicit stuff!

—Sharon Naylor

The Vows

AGAIN, as some brides and grooms do, you can just agree with the officiant that you'll do the standard "love, honor, and cherish" routine. For many couples, this is easier, as they know they will be nervous, and that remembering such an important speech is probably asking too much of themselves. Add to that the fact that they're often petrified of writing their own vows.

When you boil the entire wedding process down, you'll find this step the very essence of it—the promise you're making to each other that binds you together forever. So the words are important.

If you're dead-set against repeating the vows that everyone else has taken for decades, you and your fiancé will have to make time to create your own vows. It's easy, and shouldn't take more than a couple of hours if you follow these rules:

- *Keep them short!* You are going to be nervous, and the less you have to say, the less chance you'll stumble over your words. Three to four sentences is fine.

- *Forget about memorizing.* Just arrange with the officiant to allow you to read from cards, or do the repeat-after-me process.

- *Work on the vows separately.* If you and your fiancé are sitting at a table together, there is going to be a lot of neck-craning and "What are you writing?" If done in separate rooms, you'll have a more personalized outcome.

- Agree to share your finished copies.

Those are the general rules of vow-writing, but let's get into the semantics. What exactly do you want to say? What are you promising to do? The word "obey" has been tossed out of even the most traditional of weddings. So you are free to create your own vows. The best are heartfelt, touching, honest, and tender. Some have funny moments that lighten the mood, which is perfectly in keeping with a humorous person's style. To get you started, grab a notebook and answer the following questions. Keep in mind that this is not a thesis you're working on. Don't put pressure on yourself to produce the best vows ever. You're competing with no one, and the best results often come from the first sweep at it.

- How did you feel when you first set eyes upon your partner?

- What was your first meeting like?

- How and when did you first fall in love with him (or her)?

Sample Vows

"I take you to be my husband, remaining ever faithful to you in every situation life can bring. You are my best friend, the first person I want to see in the morning, the last person I want to see at night. Of all my many blessings in life, you are the greatest one I have. I will always love you."

"The moment I met you, I knew you were the one. I always knew I wanted this moment to come, and I will carry in my heart forever the feeling I have right now: More love than anyone has a right to feel, gratitude, and a sense of peace at knowing that our lives will always be joined. We have been brought together, we have remained true to each other for all these years, and we have the brightest future ahead of us. I am proud to call you my wife/husband, and I devote myself to you for the rest of my life."

- ♦ When did you know you would be married?
- ♦ What does this person bring to your life?
- ♦ What will you always bring to your fiancé's life?
- ♦ What are you looking forward to sharing?

For brides who write their own vows, common themes are that their partners are their best friends, their soul mates, and their greatest

"I promise to love you, respect you, hold you at the top of my list of priorities, give thanks for you every day, and learn to appreciate all the little things you do. You make my life so much brighter. You make my world complete. I couldn't ask for a better partner than you, and I thank God that we are together now, and that we will be together always."

🎗

"When I told my friends, 'I'm going to marry that girl' they said I was crazy, that I was just head over heels right now and that rush would fade away. But that rush hasn't faded. I'm more crazy about you now than ever, and I can spot a good thing when I see it. When I saw you across that crowded room, it was like a spotlight was above you. You were the only thing I saw, like there was no one else in the world. And today, although I know there are lots of other people here, all I see is you. There's a spotlight on you right now. And just like on that day, I knew you were the person I would honor, respect, laugh with, joke with, share good and bad times with, bring into my own family, and love forever. I promise these things now and forever, with eternal loyalty."

blessings. They promise to love in good times and in bad, through all of life's unexpected twists and turns, and they promise loyalty and support.

The most wonderful aspect of writing your own vows is that you sound like you during the ceremony and your fiancé sounds like himself. Elements of your personalities are brought into the wedding itself, and your vows are truly your own.

If you have children and are joining two families, it's important that you have the kids participate in the vows as well. You may each take vows that make promises to be loyal and supportive and loving to

Say the Word

As with all other aspects of the wedding ceremony, run your vows by your officiant first, as he or she will typically like to have final say in this important matter.

the children, accepting them as your own. In some cases, the children are invited to share their thoughts, feelings, and promises as well. With the changing nature of weddings, all things are possible. So consider what you want, and take the time to create this portion of the wedding with complete control.

For more on writing your wedding vows, read Diane Warner's *Complete Book of Wedding Vows*. In it, she has listed appropriate vows for all sorts and styles of wedding ceremonies. (Also see sidebar, "Sample Vows" on page 114.)

10

PLANNING THE RECEPTION

MAKING YOUR PARTY UNFORGETTABLE

THE TASK OF planning your wedding reception can take a long time if you start with no clear idea of what you want. So many options are available—at any reception hall or through any caterer—that you could spin out by taking your first steps blindly. Many brides report that not having a list of what they want ahead of time cost them extra money, as they were easily swayed into impulse decisions and additional choices they did not need. By following this advice carefully, you'll save time and money, and will create the most memorable part of your wedding day with a minimum of hassle.

Step 1: Choosing a Style

JUST AS you chose a style to match the formality of your wedding day, the type of wedding you selected will affect your reception decisions. An ultraformal affair will always call for a lavish, several-course, seated dinner. An informal outdoor gathering might require just passed hors d'oeuvres or even a buffet. While it's true that former bounds of etiquette have loosened and that you can tailor your reception style to suit your tastes—such as having a sit-down dinner at an outdoor or beach wedding—you still ought to know what goes into each choice. At this short time, you'll want to base your decisions not only on ease, but on what works for your wishes.

Wedding Day Reflections

We tried to save a few bucks by having only five waiters for the cocktail party, and a lot of our guests complained that they were never offered certain things, or they just weren't offered food enough times. It got to the point where people were hoarding the snacks upon each waiter's visit because they didn't know when they'd see another waiter again.

—Tracy and Tom

THE SIT-DOWN DINNER

Everyone thinks of the sit-down dinner as mandatory for the formal wedding, and indeed it usually is. But you can have a formal sit-down dinner even at a small reception, perhaps in your home. You can rent the best linens, hire servers, and have the meal catered. Most brides find this their best option, as it gives guests the opportunity to sit back, relax, and be pampered by a gracious server. Since the sit-down dinner is the most common form of reception, we'll go into more detail about this option later in the chapter.

THE BUFFET

For some arrangements, the formal buffet is a wonderful idea. Many brides and grooms like to provide their guests with a wide, impressive range of appetizers and entrées, and they love the splashy presentation that a good caterer provides. For the best results, arrange to have buffet stations set around the room so your guests can easily access their chosen foods without standing in long lines.

PASSED HORS D'OEUVRES

Tuxedoed waiters will walk about the room offering your guests any number of delectable appetizers from silver platters. This is a terrific idea for cocktail parties or outdoor luncheons. Just be sure you have enough waiters to suit your guests' needs.

THE COMBINATION

If you're a bride and groom who wants it all (or you just can't make up your mind!), you can arrange with your caterer to have the buffet and passed hors d'oeuvres during the cocktail hour, and the seated dinner during the main part of the reception. This allows your guests many options, and you don't have to make a definitive choice.

The good news is that today's freedom in wedding reception protocol opens nearly all options, so you can create a reception with any and all elements you wish. Remember, most people have been to dozens of weddings and will appreciate something a bit different than what they've experienced many times before. As far as style, only your taste and budget limit your options.

Step 2: Choosing Your Caterer

IF you'll be holding your reception at a banquet facility, you may not have much choice about the caterer you'll use. Some brides are content with using the hall's main caterer and prefer not making a big deal about bringing in another caterer to do the job. In this short planning time, that option may work fine for you. But if you're holding your wedding at home or at another location that doesn't supply its own caterer, you will have to interview and choose a catering service based on the following criteria:

- They have had professional training, such as at a culinary institute
- They belong to a professional association
- They have worked numerous weddings before yours
- They have worked your kind of wedding before (whether outdoor, at-home, or another style)
- They can provide the kinds of food and service you wish to have at your reception

- They are willing to discuss your ideas

- They seem eager to please you

- You have a friendly rapport with them

- They have a limit on the number of weddings they will be catering around your wedding time

- They bring their own cooking equipment to the site

- They have their own assistants and staff

- They are organized

- They provide a solid contract with all details outlined

- They offer a full refund and cancellation clause in their contract

- They offer a sample tasting at your request

- They have insurance

Catering Tips

Even if you're short on time and cash and can't find a caterer, don't assign the food prep to Grandma. Instead, look for a well-trained culinary student at a nearby culinary institute whom you might hire for a fraction of the cost of a professional caterer. The students are amazingly well-trained by the late stages of their schooling, and they'll appreciate having the credit for their resume.

It is important that you research caterers well. For this important element of the wedding (guests remember food the most!) be sure you choose the best caterer you can get. Ask friends for referrals—and not just friends who have had weddings. Because caterers work all kinds of events, you might even ask a friend who is involved in his or her corporation's planning of special events. You can also find referrals through other wedding professionals, but always ask for a tasting so you can be sure of a caterer's quality.

Convenient Catering

Have the caterer or banquet hall manager fax you a copy of their menu selections. This way, you and your fiancé can go over the list, make your selections in your spare time—not under the watchful eye of a caterer who may not want to hear how much you hate scallops—and go to your interview with your choices circled. By all means, avoid asking others what they think about the menu. Too many opinions lead you to confusion and wasted time, and mean that you'll be stuck trying to please those you asked. (You might even get stuck with those dreaded scallops!)

Step 3: Meeting with the Caterer

As mentioned before, know what you want. You'll save hours of listening to a caterer or banquet hall manager's sales pitch if you can say right off the bat: "We want a cocktail hour with buffet stations and a sit-down dinner for 100." The caterer will appreciate your decision-making abilities as well as your respect for his or her time. Yes, caterers want to make the arrangements with you, but they are busy people, too. Have your general decisions made so that the process is easier for everyone—especially if you've slipped into their schedule on short notice.

Some things to keep in mind when choosing your menu selections:

- ♦ *What is your budget?* Be realistic about what you can and cannot afford. Simply explain to the caterer that you're limited to a certain amount of money and want to get the best reception that your budgeted amount can buy. Caterers have planned weddings to fit all kinds of budgets; trust that your caterer can create wonders with the affordable selections. Don't be afraid to ask caterers to note the most affordable selections on the faxed menu, and clearly state that you want excellent choices.

♦ *Do you have a variety of choices?* Make sure you provide a wide range of options from which your guests can choose.

♦ *Do you meet your guests' special dietary needs?* If you have several vegetarian cousins, for instance, you ought to include several non-meat options. Diabetics will appreciate a dessert option that they can enjoy.

♦ *Are you ordering too much food?* Make it clear to the caterer that you don't want an overabundance of food. Some weddings are so awash with food offerings that guests are overwhelmed, and most of the food doesn't get eaten.

♦ *What happens to the leftovers?* We're not suggesting you bring along plastic containers and dole out stuffed salmon to your relatives. Some catering halls will deliver leftovers to women's shelters, hospitals, and other organizations at your request.

♦ *Do you like the selections?* Many brides and grooms choose the foods they love. Some add a personal touch by serving wedding guests the same menu they enjoyed on their first date. Guests love hearing that touch of the romantic.

♦ *If you are having a theme wedding, does the food reflect the theme?* For instance, if you're having a Hawaiian luau on the beach, can the caterer prepare a wonderful mahi mahi dish or lobster salad?

♦ *Will the food hold up in the weather?* If you're having an outdoor wedding on a hot day, will the creamy salads require a constant ice bath to remain edible? On hot days, lighter fare is recommended. Be sure to tell the caterer what weather conditions you expect.

You can get ideas by looking at menus, such as the samples on the next few pages, provided with permission of Jerome Louie of The Bernards Inn in Bernardsville, New Jersey.

The Traditional Formal Dinner

THIS is the extravagant dinner where you'll find food stations all around. All of the following is included in this package:

BEVERAGE SERVICE

This is a five-hour premium open bar
where you'll choose from the following:

Champagne, Wine, Premium Liquors: Absolut, Bacardi, Beefeater, Canadian Club, Crown Royal, Dewar's, Old Grand Dad, Johnny Walker Red, Jack Daniels, Seagram's 7

Domestic and Imported Beer: Budweiser, Coors Light, Amstel Light, Heineken

Assorted Soft Drinks

An Assortment of Non-Alcoholic Beers and Wines

THE COCKTAIL HOUR

Upon your arrival, your guests will be greeted
by our servers offering Chilled Champagne.

THE WINE BAR

Your guests will enjoy this elaborate display of imported
and domestic wines especially selected by our wine director.

APPETIZERS

Your selection of six of the following butlered hors d'oeuvres:

Mushroom Duxelles

Proscuitto

Wrapped Asparagus

Tomato and Zucchini Tarts

Asparagus Mousse

Phyllo Triangle with Feta Cheese and Leeks

Mozzarella & Plum Tomato Tarts

Gourmet Pizza

Grilled Chicken & Pineapple Skewers with Coconut Honey Glaze

Salmon Mousse on Black Bread

Miniature Crab Cakes with a Red Pepper Coulis

Alsatian Tans

Cocktail Franks en Croute

Tenderloin of Beef on Herb-Toasted Crouton

Beef Wontons

Jumbo Chilled Shrimp
Unlimited shrimp passed butler style
with a tangy cocktail sauce and lemon

Baby Rack of Lamb
Tender rack of lamb passed butler style

COCKTAIL DISPLAYS
Beautifully arranged tables to include the following:

*An Elaborate Assortment of Fine International and Domestic Cheeses:
Brie, Camembert, Cheddar, Gouda, Montrachet, Port Salut, Saga
Blue and Havarti with flatbreads; Specialty Biscuits, Baguettes, and
Fresh Seasonal Fruit; and Fresh Garden Crudites*

PASTA STATION
Please select two of the following:

*Penne Pasta with Fresh Tomatoes, Prosciutto,
and Pepper Vodka Sauce*

Pesto Agnolotti with Portobello Mushrooms

*Bow-Tie Pasta with Fresh Seasonal Vegetables
and a Basil Olive Oil*

Cavatelli with Broccoli in a Lemon Herb Beurre Blanc

*Fusilli with Smoked Salmon and
Wild Mushrooms in a White Wine Sauce*

CAPTAIN'S STATION
Please select two of the following:

Traditional Antipasto
*Grilled eggplant and zucchini, roasted red and
yellow peppers, marinated artichokes, prosciutto,
Genoa salami, mozzarella cheese,
tomatoes, and calamata olives*

Swordfish en Brochette
*Marinated swordfish and vegetables,
grilled on skewer, served over toasted couscous*

Sushi Presentation
*Authentic Japanese preparation:
California roll; cucumber roll; tuna sushi;
Shrimp sushi with pickled ginger, wasabi and soy sauce
($15.00 additional per guest)*

Shrimp and Scallop Fricassee
*Small shrimp and bay scallops sautéed
in a brandied lobster cream sauce*

Beef Burgundy
A classic French presentation of boeuf bourguignonne

Coq Au Vin
Seared boneless breast of chicken and red wine

Chilled Seafood Display
Iced jumbo shrimp, crab claws, bluepoint and
chesapeake oysters, littleneck and cherrystone clams
shucked to order
($15.00 additional per guest)

Chicken and Vegetable Stir-Fry
Tender strips of chicken and crisp vegetables
in a pineapple and sesame glaze

Shrimp Creole
Sauteed shrimp, clams and andouille sausage
with onions and tomatoes, served over saffron rice

CHEF'S CARVING STATION
Please select one of the following:

Prime Beef Tenderloin Rubbed with Crushed Garlic

Baked Black Forest Ham with Pineapple Chutney

Herb Roasted Turkey with Cranberry-Orange Relish

The Semiformal Wedding Dinner

CHAMPAGNE TOAST
First Course
Please select one of the following:

Appetizers
Leek and Potato Soup

Lobster Bisque

Baby Spinach Salad with Applewood Smoked Bacon Vinaigrette

Beggar's Purse of Coach Farms Goat Cheese over Grilled Vegetables

Wild Mushroom in Puff Pastry, Crêpe Mushroom Sauce

*Watercress and Endive Salad with Pears, Toasted Hazelnuts,
Roquefort tossed in a Sherry Wine Vinaigrette*

Grilled Portobello Mushroom and Asparagus

Intermezzo
Served in an elegant chilled glass

Pink Champagne Sorbet

Lemon Sorbet

Pear Sorbet

Entrée
A duet presentation to include:

*Roasted Chateaubriand served with a Rich Madeira
Wine Sauce and Sautéed Atlantic Salmon*

*Whole Grain Mustard and Dill Beurre Blanc with Chef's
signature presentation of fresh seasonal vegetables and potato*

May substitute chicken on duct plate.

Tableside choice of two entrées available
at a $10.00 per person supplement charge.

The Wedding Cake
Prepared on-premise by our pastry chef.
A variety of selections and styles custom-designed
for your very special occasion to be served with the following:

*A Selection of White and Dark Chocolate Dipped
Strawberries and assorted Chocolate Truffles*

COFFEE SERVICE
Freshly Brewed Regular and Decaffeinated Coffee,
Espresso and a selection of Fine Teas

COMPLETE CORDIAL SERVICE
Amaretto, Baileys, Frangelico, Creme de Menthe,
Kahlua, Sambuca, and Ports

Inclusive in All Packages

A separate ballroom for your cocktail hour

A maître d' and manager to host your affair

All premium bar beverages, including
wine service through dinner

Bartending fees

Chef's carving fees

Wedding cake accompanied by chocolate
strawberries and truffles, prepared by our pastry chef

A selection of linens and candles

Recommendation list for all associated services,
i.e., musicians, photographers, florists

Direction maps for your guests

Complimentary overnight guest room for the
bride & groom (minimum of 75 guests required),
to include a welcome basket with champagne

Special hotel rates for overnight guests

Personalized reservation cards

Coat room attendants

Optional Services

Special entrée selections or portions available for children

Special vegetarian or dietary plate

Entrée plates for musicians and photographers

Ceremony labor fee additional $4.00 per person

Valet parking $500.00

Setting Up the Bar

ARRANGING for beverages is one of the trickiest parts of planning a reception. If drink charges are not part of a complete package—such as in the sample menu shown on the previous pages—many brides and grooms are taken aback by the quoted prices of per-person drink charges, feeling the amounts are too high. An open bar may be customary, but the prices may be astronomical. While I would not suggest offering a cash bar, as that option is still considered tacky and insulting to your guests, you might work out an arrangement with the caterer or bar service for a more affordable and appropriate bar menu. According to banquet managers, arranging a bar arrangement takes very little time. Most couples choose from one of three basic bar packages: the everything-goes top-shelf menu; the limited selection of house brands; and the very limited selection of wine, beer, and soft drinks. Your manager will undoubtedly be able to discuss with you the items on each list, so that you can choose a package that suits your event's style.

By far the most common way to save on your bar tab is to offer a limited selection of available drinks. You may, for instance, offer only a few kinds of domestic wines, beers, juices, and soft drinks rather than include all top-shelf selections. Again, your caterer is probably accustomed to this request, and can easily accommodate your needs.

When making your list of beverage selections, be sure to provide an ample variety. For instance, you might want to choose some of the following:

> *Stress Relief*
>
>
>
> I*f you know you're inviting a younger set, such as a group of rowdy, college-aged kids, you might want to express your concerns to the manager. Explain that while you want your guests to have a good time, you don't want any sloppy-drunk antics. So stronger drinks, such as straight shots, tequila, or Long Island Iced Teas, should not be on the menu.*

- *Wines:* Whites and reds, including chardonnay, chablis, merlot, and petit blanc

- *Beers:* Domestic regular, light, and lager

- *Soft drinks:* Regular, diet, and non-caffeinated

- *Juices:* Cranberry, orange, grapefruit, and pineapple are most common at weddings.

- *Liquors:* Limited top-shelf names, unless you have a favorite. Consider vodka, rum, gin, and after-dinner liqueurs such as Grand Marnier and cognac.

Your wine selection will depend upon the types of food you'll be serving at the reception. While offering several different kinds of wines—as in white, red, Bordeaux, and so on—is a good idea, choosing the right wine for the meal conveys attention to detail. Any wine steward at a top-quality liquor store can help you select the right brands of wine, or you might research them yourself on the Internet.

To get you started, the following general primer specifies which types of wines go with each kind of food:

- *Light white whites,* such as pinot blancs, zinfandels, muscadets, and reislings, go with salads, cheeses, clams, light fish, salads, and pasta with oil dressings.

- *Rich white wines,* such as sauvignon blancs and California chardonnays, go with chicken, salmon, lobster, pasta with cream sauces, and creamy cheeses such as Brie.

- *Light red wines,* such as chiantis, merlots, and Beaujolais, go with chicken, pasta with meat sauces, and hard cheeses.

- *Rich red wines,* such as Bordeaux, California merlot, and cabernet sauvignon, go with beef, veal, pork, and other heavier dishes.

This list is just to give you an idea of the types of wines you'll be researching. Wine ratings do change from week to week on Web sites and at stores, but there is no reason to keep changing your decision. A quality-rated vintage will be fine for your party.

If you have the money, you may choose to make champagne available all night long, but more money-crunched brides and grooms arrange with the bar manager to provide one round to all guests for the champagne toast. Ask what vintage of champagne the manager offers, and if you're given a selection, don't just choose the prettiest name. Take some time and check out the various selections at a local gourmet wine and cheese store. They often have little review labels under each bottle that provide the ratings and descriptions of the champagne as listed in connoisseur magazines.

Buying Time

For *more in-depth information on wines and champagnes, as well as ratings and recommendations, check out* Wine Spectator *at www.winespectator.com.*

What's for Dessert?

No wedding would be complete without a magnificent wedding cake. This focal point of the reception is often proudly displayed in the front of the room for all your guests to see. Wedding cake design has undergone a tremendous change in the past few years, so your options include far more than the standard cake of yesteryear. Now, you can help design a work of art that will not only be beautiful, but delicious as well. Here is some advice to help you with the cake-ordering process:

- *Order early.* Most cake bakers prefer a few months' notice of your order, especially around the busy wedding seasons of June, July, and August. You can place a rush order with a month's notice, but you may have to pay extra. Many bakeries are limited in the number of cakes they can turn out within a specific amount of time so they have to draw the line somewhere. If the baker will be staying overtime to create yours, you should expect to pay adequate compensation.

- *Decide ahead of time what kind of cake you want.* Do you want the standard three-tiered cake with columns separating each tier? Do you want staggered tiers, where the layers are off-center and form a sort of icing-covered sculpture? Have a general idea of how you want your cake to look, then sit down with your baker to decide on the particulars. Many brides tackle this job by bringing to the meeting a picture of their ideal wedding cake. Perhaps you've seen a beautiful picture of a fondant-covered cake with pearl-blue swiss dots and a sugar-cream ribbon bow. Bring it to your baker and ask for a reproduction. Not only is this the most direct way to get what you want, but it will save lots of time for the baker.

- *Provide an accurate count of the number of guests you expect.* Even though not all guests will eat cake at the reception, you'll want to have plenty for those who do.

- *Describe the formality of your wedding.* The baker will need to add the appropriate décor to the cake.

- *Discuss the weather conditions you expect to face.* Many sugar-icing cakes have melted in the sun and slid off the table. Butter cream is a good selection for hot weather.

- *Make arrangements for delivery.* This may be standard, but you'll want to make sure the baker can do it and that he knows where and when to deliver the masterpiece.

Lovely on the Outside . . .
Delicious on the Inside

The very famous Sylvia Weinstock's cake-decorating company in New York City— where many celebrity and high-profile clients purchase their wedding cakes—offers a wide variety of cake flavors, including the following:

CAKE FLAVORS

- Yellow
- Chocolate
- Lemon
- Almond
- Hazelnut
- Carrot
- Coconut
- White
- Banana
- Fruitcake

The company's filling flavors are equally diverse and mouthwatering:

FILLING FLAVORS

- Chocolate mousse (very popular!)
- Vanilla butter
- Lemon
- Raspberry
- Strawberry
- Apricot
- Peach
- Banana
- Cannoli cream
- Cappuccino mousse

Your options are wide open, and while many bakeries may not be able to provide a list as extensive as Ms. Weinstock's, you at least know what options are out there. Be sure to ask what's available when you're shopping for cakes.

Now, for the cake details.

You can choose either an icing-covered cake or a cake topped with rolled fondant. Rolled fondant, which looks something like a sheet of white or pastel-colored wax, is the kind you most often see on the covers of wedding magazines. This type of frosting can make a wedding cake look like a jeweled gift box; however, it is more expensive since it takes a skilled hand to create the look.

As for cake flavor, you are no longer limited to the regular white cake with strawberry filling. The cake business is getting much more creative than that, offering amazing flavors that your guests will love. In addition, bakers are allowing brides and grooms to select different inner flavors for each tier of the cake. That provides more variety for guests, and usually doesn't cost extra.

For cake toppers, skip the little plastic bride and groom. That fad is so out that you may not even be able to find those knick-knacks anyway. A popular touch is fresh flowers arranged in a drape or design across your cake. Talk to your florist about which kinds of flowers you can have on your cake, and make arrangements for her to do the decorating of the cake on the wedding day, on-site. Most florists have decorated with fresh flowers before, so you're not asking for anything unrealistic.

The cake is not the only dessert option available for your reception. Weddings of all kinds—from the most formal to the most informal—feature an array of desserts to tempt all sweet-tooth types. Some popular ideas are Napoleons, chocolate mousse, bananas flambé, cheesecake, cannoli, éclairs, chocolate-dipped fruits, assorted pastries, and ice-cream sundaes for the kids. Your caterer may recom-

> ## *Wedding Day Reflections*
>
>
>
> *We knew we wanted a cake filled with cannoli cream, but the bakery did not offer cannoli cream as a wedding cake option. Knowing that they are an Italian bakery, and do a lot of cannoli cream for other desserts, we simply asked if they would make this a special order. The baker was happy to do it for us, and we returned after the wedding to tell him that our guests loved their cake. A few weeks later, they added cannoli filling to their wedding cake options list.*
>
> —Stephanie and Ben

mend a selection of desserts, so keep your options in mind, and choose well. Remember that while you may think your guests will be too stuffed after that cocktail hour and entrée, there's always room for dessert!

The Extras

A part of the reception hall's package may be the use of color-coordinated linens and the ordering of imprinted napkins and matchbooks. Be sure to ask the manager—or the rental agent, if you're not using a reception hall—what colors are available, and never order linens without seeing a color sample. The manager's idea of rose pink may be different from your idea, and from the tone of your bridesmaids' dresses. Ask to see a swatch or a sample of the actual tablecloth, and be sure to specify what extras you'll be ordering.

Do not forget to order enough napkins, as well as tablecloths for the guest tables, buffet table, gift table, and cake table. Your manager ought to have this information ready, but if you're in charge of your own home or location wedding, you'll need to think like a pro and provide for all of your linen needs at one time.

Professionally Speaking

Always be sure your florist is going to wash the flowers and that there are no pesticides remaining on the flowers. We pull the blooms off the stem right before the reception, then wash and dry them thoroughly before arranging them on the cake.

—Angela Lanzafame, The Potted Geranium, East Hanover, New Jersey

---

The Seating Chart

For some brides and grooms, nothing causes more headaches during the reception planning than making up the seating chart. Family dynamics may be such that everyone has someone with whom they can't be seated. Someone owes someone else money, someone's not on speaking terms with someone else, and this one's new wife will be there. It can be enough to give you a migraine.

Some less-organized brides report that creating their seating arrangements took weeks, and I can tell you why. They asked for too many opinions. Yes, knowing that Uncle Isaac can't sit with Uncle Bob may be helpful, but for the sake of time, these people will simply have to get over themselves and sit at a large round table without talking for a few hours. Case closed.

If you're lucky, your tables may seem to form themselves—your first cousins sit at one, your second cousins sit at another, for example. Or you might group people by age range, putting the younger set right by the dance floor so they don't knock older guests over as they rush to dance to their favorite songs.

Penny-Wise

Y ou may be able to knock some off your price tag if you skip the printed napkins and matchbooks. They aren't necessities if they come at a price; but if they're free, why not?

Start the process with the givens. The bride and groom will sit at the main table. You may choose to have a long table for the whole bridal party, but that trend is fading as more and more couples opt for their own private table. Bridal parties, too, are often thankful for this arrangement, as their coupled maids and ushers can sit with their non-wedding-party dates during the event.

The bride's parents and closest relatives are at one of the closest tables to the main table, and the groom's parents and closest relatives are at the closest table on the other side. Everyone else gets arranged. Your banquet hall manager should be able to tell you about the availability of larger or smaller tables—as should your rental manager if you'll be renting tables—so check to see whether a table for ten can be set next to a table for six. It may not look uniform, but it may work better than arranging all the guests in groups of equal size.

Planning the Entertainment

THE music is also what your guests will remember of your big day. They may love the chateaubriand, but if the music is too loud or too explicit, they may lose their appetites.

Seating Arrangement Warnings

Here are some notes of caution from brides and grooms who learned the hard way.

Do not put all the kids at one table. It will be complete chaos. If you invite kids under age thirteen to the reception, have them sit with their parents.

—Elizabeth and Luke

Be sure older relatives can access their tables. It was very difficult for my aunt to get her walker through the crowded chairs and tables to get out to the bathroom.

—Emily and Chris

If your relatives are the type to complain about "Why am I at table 7 when Aunt Ruth is at table 5?," just skip the whole numbering thing and give your tables names like Joy and Forever and Promise.

—Ann and Jared

Don't think you're saving time by not having a seating chart. We thought it would be fine if people just grabbed a table where they wanted to sit during our reception, but it was a nightmare. People were jamming sixteen to a small table so they could all be together. Chairs were everywhere, and some couples had to sit alone.

—Patrice and Randall

Let the groom's mom arrange her side of the family's seating arrangements. She'll feel like she had something to do, and you don't have to worry about who those unknown people are.

—Leslie and Michael

CHOOSING THE ENTERTAINER

At this late stage in the game, finding a high-quality band or DJ to play at your wedding is likely to be time-intensive. The best and most reasonably priced groups probably have been booked for a year (if not years), and you'll be counting on lucky breaks if your wedding is to fit into their schedule. Start your search by asking for referrals. If you loved the band that played at your friend's wedding, ask her for their card and include them in your interview process.

Again, don't automatically select the band or DJ with the largest ad in the Yellow Pages. Although that may mean that the band does a good business, they may simply charge a lot and have a substantial pool of PR money. Just include the names in your search list.

> ### *Stress Relief*
>
>
>
> D*o not book a band because you heard them a year ago and loved them. Band members change, DJ companies hire new talent, and ways of doing business may be different now. Always interview them according to what they offer now. This is no time to risk bad quality for the sake of saving time.*

Save time by calling around *on weekdays* to see whether the band or DJ is even available on your wedding day. Getting into particulars will do no good if they're not even in the running, so a simple "Do you have any openings on September 4th?" will do.

The entertainment manager will require some information from you before you can get all the information you'll need from him. In addition to your wedding date, he'll also need to know where it will be. Bands and DJs will need good power sources and platforms on which to perform, and some do not do outdoor weddings. So again, providing all this information up front can save you time.

Let them know your budget. Have a realistic figure ahead of time. Asking recently married friends what they paid would be rude, but you can politely ask what cost range they saw when they were planning their weddings. Work with bands and DJs who can offer you their standard price, not ones who say, "Well, come on in and we'll work something out." That may be code for "Come in, we'll see how young and naïve and desperate you are, and then we'll gauge our prices to that."

As you interview for availability, make sure the entertainer performs the kinds of music you want. Ask for a repertoire, and be sure they play a wide enough range of songs to please your guests. Your younger guests may like dancing to the Top 40 songs, while your older guests may prefer the Big Band sound. Accommodate your guests and the dance floor will always be filled.

It may seem like you'll save time by asking for a tape or a video of their performance. But when you add in shipping time, viewing time, and the fact that what you see on a carefully produced tape may not be what you get, this may not be the best use of your efforts. Always interview and audition the bands and DJs first. Ask whether you can see them in action at another event, if possible. You may be able to stick your head in the door to watch them perform at a wedding or corporate party. Look around. Are the guests dancing? Do they seem to be enjoying the music? How's the sound? What is the band wearing? Is their equipment in good shape?

Professionally Speaking

A sad fact in the events industry is that many unscrupulous vendors do take advantage of some customers. One wedding service company director recommends that couples, especially young brides and grooms in their early twenties, bring an older, more established relative along for the initial business visit as a sort of intimidation factor (his words, not mine!). This, of course, is your choice.

When auditioning, give each band or DJ enough time to set up, play several songs, and talk to you afterward. An hour will give you time to check your reactions to the music, and see what kind of interaction the entertainer has with you. You may not want a DJ who talks too much, and you'll have to assess the DJ's personal style. If he's too "over-the-top," asking him to tone it down will do no good. Just choose another DJ whose style is more suitable to your event and your crowd.

Again, don't have too many people involved in the DJ decision. Most brides and grooms say that checking out bands makes a good outing for themselves and their maid of honor and best man.

PLANNING THE SONG LIST

When you choose an entertainer based on performance, style, value, and the quality of the contract, you'll have to do some planning with the performer. Submit your list of favorite songs, along with your wishes for your first dance and any other special dances. Not all brides are dancing with their fathers to "Daddy's Little Girl," and not all grooms are dancing with their mothers to "Son of Mine." Instead, some couples are choosing special dance songs for their bridal party, their parents, their grandparents, or the longest-married couple in the room.

You'll be able to see a list of the songs your entertainer can provide; and if you're up to the task, you can choose the selections you want to hear on your wedding day. I've seen the song lists, veritable phonebook-sized collections of every song ever written and performed. It would probably take more time than you have available to go through every one and create a by-the-book song list for your DJ to play, so you would be smart to just ask for *types* of songs to be played. Aside from the standard Top 40 and Big Band tunes, you might also ask for a good mix of the following, depending on what your crowd is like:

+ Classical (for dinnertime)

+ Easy listening

+ Rhythm and blues

+ Jazz

+ Motown

+ Country

+ Cajun/Zydeco

Wedding Day Reflections

We dropped in to see our prospective band play at another wedding, and we heard so much feedback from their speakers—screechy noise that sends chills up your spine—that we ran out of there and did not hire them.

—Carol and Ryan

Timeless Tunes

Some of the most popular songs requested today:

BRIDE AND GROOM'S FIRST SONG

"Kiss to Build a Dream On," Louis Armstrong

"Night and Day," Ella Fitzgerald

"Someone to Watch over Me," Johnny Hodges

"What a Wonderful World," Louis Armstrong

"What Are You Doing the Rest of Your Life?" Abbey Lincoln

"Always and Forever," Heatwave

"The First Time Ever I Saw Your Face," Roberta Flack

"When a Man Loves a Woman," Percy Sledge

"You Bring Me Joy," Anita Baker

"You Send Me," Sam Cooke

"Wonderful Tonight," Eric Clapton

Please Note: "I Will Always Love You," sung by Whitney Houston, is actually a song about breaking up. Listen carefully to the words of the song you choose.

- Big Band/Swing
- '70s music
- '80s music
- Line dances
- Salsa/Latin
- Gospel

Penny-Wise

— $ —

As in other aspects of the event-planning business, you may have to pay extra for late-stage booking of a band or DJ. Find out whether they charge additional fees for late bookings, and how much extra you'll have to pay. Actually, a true professional will be willing to waive the late fee, but don't be surprised if you cannot find an entertainer who has such a big heart.

- Dance/Club
- Broadway
- Christian
- Calypso
- Reggae
- Mariachi
- Steel drum
- Tango
- Samba
- Cumbia
- Bachata
- Merengue
- Ethnic: Jewish, Klezmer, Greek, Arabic, Italian, Irish, German, Polish, Ukrainian, Asian, Portuguese, Scottish, Spanish, Celtic, and others

NANCY AND DEREK'S STORY

I actually had a lot of fun planning the music for Nancy and Derek's wedding. Nancy had been to plenty of cookie-cutter receptions, and she and Derek didn't want the same songs played for their guests. They wanted their reception to be special. So she and I talked about music "phases," wherein the DJ would switch from song type to song type in blocks throughout the night.

The couple knew they had a lot of older guests who would not be staying until late in the night. So they started the night off with music that would appeal to the older guests—Big Band music from the '40s. Nancy had found a CD in a record store

For the Party

Some of the most popular general party songs requested today:

"Ain't Too Proud to Beg," Temptations

"Brown Eyed Girl," Van Morrison

"Build Me Up Buttercup," Foundations

"Conga," Miami Sound Machine

"Devil with the Blue Dress," Mitch Ryder (perfect if your maids are in blue!)

"I Saw Her Standing There," Beatles

"Let's Twist Again," Chubby Checker

"Louie Louie," Kingsmen

"Love Shack," B52s

"Mack the Knife," Bobby Darin

"Stand by Me," Ben E. King/John Lennon

"Unforgettable," Nat King Cole and Natalie Cole

"What I Like About You," Romantics

called "Stagedoor Canteen," and she asked the DJ to play four or five songs from that. The older guests hit the dance floor, doing the Lindy and the Peabody (ask your great-aunts and uncles about those!), and the younger guests were so impressed they joined right in. Nancy said her great-aunts were glowing, happy to be the center of attention and once again trying out their dance moves. "My Aunt Anne was amazing!" Nancy said, "and afterwards, she thanked me so much for giving her a few songs to dance to."

After a round of applause for the golden era crowd, Nancy had the music switch to her ethnic roots. All of the Italian music was played, and then again an entire set of the crowd got to hear their favorites and dance the Tarantella. After that, the couple had the DJ move on to jazz for the dessert portion of the reception, and then to Top 40 for the younger guests who stayed into the night.

"It really didn't take much effort," Nancy shares, "and it was more fun for us to know that our guests had a great time dancing to the music that was more for them than for us. We heard our favorites, but we gave our guests a great time. And we had a great time because of that."

Wedding Day Reflections

Brides and grooms are having a lot of fun with their reception entertainment. When Jill Althouse of Lititz, Pennsylvania, married Mark Wood, the DJ played a recording of Jill's college friends singing a karaoke tune. The crowd loved it, the bride was radiant, and it was one of the most memorable parts of the night.

WHAT DON'T YOU WANT?

Speaking up about what you *don't* want to hear is also very important. For instance, you won't want to hear a song that reminds you of someone else. Your recently divorced sister won't appreciate hearing her wedding song. So take a few minutes to think of songs that shouldn't be played, and notify the entertainer about them.

Also tell the entertainer what other elements you don't want, such as flashing lights, certain line dances (If you hear The Chicken Dance one more time you'll scream, right?), the Dollar Dance, perhaps even the bouquet and garter toss. Some brides and grooms are skipping these last two, breaking with tradition and the meanings of these old rites.

MAKING YOUR OWN MUSIC

If you cannot find an entertainer, and your wedding is of a suitable style, you might put together your own music collection to be played at the reception. This, of course, might mean asking a friend to help create music mixes for you, and assigning a friend to keep watch over the music system during the night; but it can be done if that's your only option.

Many brides report that the grooms love to take on this task, creating great, personalized CDs. Best of all, the couple gets to keep that music selection to play whenever they want a reminder of their big night.

Yes, putting together your own music is a time-consuming job, but it's an option that gives you total control over the songs played, quality of the songs played, and a huge savings in price.

I'll Drink to That!

IT used to be that the best man was the only one who would give a toast at the reception. Sometimes the bride's parents would stand up and give a little speech. Now, speeches and toasts at a reception are all the rage, and everyone's getting into the act.

I've included this topic in this book because you and your fiancé may choose to propose a little toast to each other or to your families. Again, just as you did while writing your vows, don't stress too much over your speech. It's not your dissertation. Just put together a short little sentiment, and share your feelings with others in the room.

You might also invite others ahead of time to share a few words, such as:

We don't want to have to hover over the machine all night. How can we predict what kind of music will be needed at certain points in the reception?

If you go this route, be sure to create just two different kinds of CDs. One should be dancing music, and the other should be more mellow instrumental music suitable for playing when the guests are eating their meals. Ask someone to make the switch when the time is right, so you don't have to do it.

- ◆ The person or people who are responsible for your meeting

- ◆ Your closest childhood friend

- ◆ Your maid of honor

- ◆ Your godparents

Buying Time

As far as writing out the place cards, you can save time by putting couples on one card, rather than each name on individual cards. It will take your guests less time to find their cards as well. Etiquette does state that place cards be handwritten, but many brides and grooms are using computer cards printed in a decorative font.

- The longest-married couple, who can provide advice for a long and happy marriage

Another special addition to the reception, as many elated brides and grooms can tell you, is the performing of a special song. In some cases, the groom will grab the mike and serenade his sweetheart with a special tune, or the bride and groom can sing a duet together. It's a special touch that should be arranged with the entertainers ahead of time. And be sure those video cameras are rolling!

11

THE FLOWERS

CHOOSING THE PERFECT ARRANGEMENTS

Y OU'RE PROBABLY TIRED of hearing this, but this is another job you will have to tackle right away. Especially during high wedding season, the best florists will be booked solid. And if you're planning your wedding for anywhere near Valentine's Day or Mother's Day, you're in deep trouble. Finding a florist who is not over-committed at this time is likely to take a lot of work; many florists actually hire part-time assistants to help out with their high demand for arrangements.

Yet no matter what time of year you're planning for, you will still face a jammed floral industry. The best florists are booked a year in advance, and many limit the number of weddings they'll do in any one weekend. So give yourself at least a few weeks to call around and check for availability.

It's almost certain that the floral manager you speak to at the outset will find it tough to squeeze you into his or her schedule. You may get a big sigh and the unwelcome news that the florist can do it for extra money—a *lot* of extra money. Hey, supply and demand is what this business is all about; and when you consider how labor-intensive the florist's job is, it is no wonder that they charge extra to take on more work. After all, they may be hiring extra assistants or delivery personnel at that time. So don't be surprised if you're facing higher prices than usual. This is one area where lack of planning time will cost you.

Choosing a Florist

As always, begin with referrals. Ask recently married friends who did their floral arrangements, and whether or not they would recommend them. Don't take your approval of the floral arrangements you saw at the wedding as proof of a job well done. Many brides keep to themselves the fact that their floral designer was a prima donna or difficult about payment schedules and delivery. Or you may not have heard that the boutonnieres were originally delivered to the wrong address. So ask a lot of questions and gather a list of highly recommended floral designers.

You can check the Yellow Pages or the Internet for florists near you, but you're working with the unknown. Subject them to even more scrutiny than you would a florist you or your family has been working with for years.

Be sure any florist is a member of professional associations and has a blemish-free record with the Better Business Bureau. Ask your other wedding professionals what they've heard about this florist. The wedding industry, being a word-of-mouth community, is quite gossipy. If a company has a wicked reputation, you'll hear about it. Watch out, though, for professionals who recommend in a gushy way another florist with whom they've worked for years. They may be using a business tactic wherein one professional gets a kickback for referring another. Always go for quality, taking into consideration reputation and track record.

Buying Time

To save time, plan your initial consultation with floral designers for weekday nights if possible. This way, you'll avoid the logjam of other brides who come in on their available weekends to book the florist two years in advance. Your time is precious, so take advantage of the florists' slower business times for the best service and availability.

Make sure that you immediately inform the manager that you're searching for a florist to work your short-time wedding. State the date.

If the shop isn't going to be able to work your wedding, you'll find out in five seconds. If they are available, ask when would be a good time for a sit-down session with the designer. The better designers will have enough experience in the wedding-planning field to know that a solid consultation may take a half-hour to an hour. Choose a time when the florist is not too busy.

Before you go to your first consultation, however, you can save a lot of time and be much more efficient if you have all the necessary wedding information. Designers who

Say the Word

Be diplomatic and respectful of florists' time. They love that. They've dealt with too many pushy, demanding, center of the universe brides in their day, and a kind bride is a welcome change.

have all the details they need can be far more helpful. Angela Lanza-fame of The Potted Geranium in East Hanover, New Jersey, suggests that before brides come in, they should have made all these major and detailed decisions:

♦ *Know your exact date.* Florists cannot guarantee service if you have three dates picked out, but nothing booked. Have a solid date, the ceremony and reception sites already reserved, and all major decisions made. The florist needs to know exactly when you'll need this major part of your wedding décor.

♦ *Know the formality of your wedding.* The florist needs to know whether your wedding will be ultraformal, formal, semiformal, informal, or specialty. These different styles, or even themes, will dictate the design of your floral pieces, from the bouquets to the centerpieces. More formal arrangements will be suitable to a formal wedding, and if your wedding is informal, the flowers will have to reflect that as well.

♦ *Know the setting of your wedding.* The florist will need to know whether you're having a church wedding with altar décor, a synagogue wedding with a floral motif for the chuppah, an outdoor wedding with a floral arch, and beyond. You'll have to approximate the size and describe the layout of the sites at this time, as the florist will need to know the scope of the job she or he is being asked to do. At a later point, when and if you hire the florist, he or she can visit the sites with you, discuss ideas, and sketch out a décor plan for the locations you've chosen.

- *Know the size of your wedding.* How many guests will you have? Twenty? Two hundred? The designer must know approximately how many centerpieces you're considering. Because each centerpiece can take an hour to put together, the florist will need to know how much time the job requires.

- *Know the size of your bridal party.* Be sure you have asked all of your bridesmaids and they have accepted. You will save lots of time if your florist knows you have six maids and six ushers, as well as two flower girls who will need floral wreaths for their hair.

- *Know what your gown looks like.* Certain types of bouquets will complement the cut of your gown. The designer knows what looks prettiest when held in front of a sheath dress as opposed to a full skirt. Unbeknownst to you, the designer is also sizing you up. Depending upon your height and weight, he or she will be imagining which kind of bouquet will accent your shape and size.

- *Know what your bridesmaids' gowns look like.* Show a picture to the designer so he or she can see the style of your maids' dresses. The same rules apply for your maids as for you.

- *Know your colors.* While this piece of information is not vital at this booking stage, the florist will benefit from knowing your color scheme when booking and at a later date. Bring the florist swatches from the bridesmaids' gowns to show what motif you like. Often the color of the swatch will suggest to the

Questions to Ask Florists

As a good consumer, ask each florist you interview the following questions:

How many weddings are you working that weekend?

Have you done this kind of wedding before? (Specify whether outdoor, at-home, location, or other.)

How long have you been in business?

How many weddings have you done?

May I see pictures or reviews of your work?

Can you work within my budget?

Will you be arranging my flowers, or will a trained member of your staff or an assistant?

Can I rent other items from you, such as aisle runners, a chuppah, columns, or pedestals?

What is your delivery fee?

Do you have insurance?

Do you offer a cancellation or refund policy?

floral designer a few varieties of flowers that may coordinate well in a bouquet or matching centerpiece. The designer will then have a chance to consider which kinds of flowers to order, if not import, for your wedding.

♦ *Know what you want.* If you envision a wedding featuring a sea of flowers, tell the designer that you have a lot of plans and that this will be a big job. If you value simplicity and have in mind only a few small touches of floral color, mention that. You can also help tremendously as far as respecting everyone's time by bringing with you a few pictures of what you like.

Buying Time

Visit the florist's shop on a Friday morning, when the staff is likely to be busily putting the finishing touches on the floral order for a Saturday wedding. Ask if you can peek at their work and their workspace; this will allow you to assess whether they're doing the job to a high enough standard for you. This only takes a few moments, and is well worth the time in terms of your investment.

With all this information in mind, a florist can accurately assess your needs and you can accurately assess whether or not you've chosen the right florist for the job. As in all aspects of your planning process, remember that you are the bride and the professionals should be willing to meet your vision for your wedding—within reason.

A significant factor in your decision of which florist you hire will be the florist's personality. Is this person willing to take time to discuss your needs and ideas? Does she have loftier visions for your wedding, telling you to "leave it all up to her?" Does he try to push you into additional purchases? Is she calm and patient with you? Is he understanding of your decision-making capabilities? Is she friendly and warm? Does he seem to be a true professional—responsible, pleasant, organized? Do you trust her?

See how you feel when you're in the flower shop. Is the place beautifully arranged? Is it clean? Or is the staff rushing around frantically while impatient customers are turning red as they experience the delays and disorganization? That's a sign that the florist is overbooked and unable to cope with customers' needs. A busy shop is a good sign, showing that the florist has a great reputation and invites customer loyalty and good business. A chaotic shop, where no one is being served well, is a warning to get out of there.

Notice whether the shop has a wide array of flowers available in a glass case. How do those flowers look? Are they fresh and healthy, or seemingly old and past their prime? You can get a good feel for the quality of the florist's supplier by checking the available stock. They'll often have arrangements in the refrigerated display case as well. Check them out for style and beauty.

Yes, your choice of florist is a big decision, as the flowers may be one of the most important aspects of your wedding day. The bouquets and centerpieces, décor, and special touches, create the ambience of your celebration. At no other time in your life are you likely to be surrounded by such a celebration of who you are and who you're becoming. So be sure to hire the best designer you can afford, and make the choices you truly envision.

Before You Choose Your Flowers

BEFORE you start tearing into *Modern Bride,* ripping out photos of bouquets and centerpieces you love, first acquaint yourself with the flower industry. As you probably know, not all flowers are priced the same at all times of the year. Flowers have an in-season and an off-season, just like weddings do, and will be much more affordable during their in season. Domestically grown flowers will be much less expensive than imported ones, such as the popular stephanotis flown in from Hawaii.

Talk openly with your designer about your wishes for your floral order, and be flexible about what's possible and what's not possible. The designer will respect your budget and your tastes, and she may be able to guide you to the most economical—but still beautiful—choices.

POPULAR INEXPENSIVE FLOWERS

- ◆ Carnations

- ◆ Chrysanthemums

- ◆ Daffodils

- Domestic orchids

- Baby's breath

POPULAR MODERATELY PRICED FLOWERS

- Daisies

- Heather

- Roses

- Tulips (in season)

- Ivy

- Lilacs

- Violets

- Irises

POPULAR EXPENSIVE FLOWERS

- Bird of Paradise

- Gardenia

- Lily

- Lily of the valley

- Imported orchid

- Amaryllis

- Orange blossom

- Stephanotis

Another factor for the superstitious bride—or the bride who enjoys inserting personalized meaning into her day—is the fact that many flowers have symbolic meanings. The Afton Florist in Florham Park, New Jersey, provides some samples from the book *Le Language des Fleurs,* Lady Mary Wortley Montagu (1917):

Flower	Meaning
Amaryllis	Beautiful
Baby's breath	Innocence
Calla lily	Beauty
Camellia	Loveliness
Carnation	Innocence, pure love
Chrysanthemum	(red) love; (white) truth
Daffodil	You're the only one
Daisy	Innocence, loyal love, purity
Freesia	Innocence
Gardenia	You're lovely
Gerbera daisy	Beauty
Heather	(white) wishes will come true; (lavender) admiration
Holly	Foresight
Iris	Faith
Ivy	Wedded love, fidelity, friendship, affection
Lilac	Innocence
Lilac	Truth
Lily of the valley	Sweetness, you've made my life complete
Lily	(white) purity; (tiger) wealth, pride
Orange blossom	First marriage (Etiquette states that if this is your second+ marriage, you may not use orange blossoms at your wedding.)
Orchid	Love, beauty
Rose	(white) innocence and purity
Tulip	Perfect love
Violet	Faithful

Flowers with Negative Meaning

If you're at all superstitious, you might want to avoid these flowers that have negative meanings:

Flower	Meaning
Begonia	Beware
Yellow Carnation	Rejection
Orange Lily	Hatred
Marigold	Cruelty
Yellow Rose	Jealousy
Snapdragon	Deception

With a bit of planning, you might have your floral arrangements speak of your love and loyalty to one another (or you could give your dreaded mother-in-law an orange lily corsage!)

Making Your Selections

ONCE you know what kinds of flowers you're interested in—whether for price, availability, meaning, or just general love of the bloom— it's time to create your individual pieces. With the help of the floral designer, you'll sit down and specify exactly what you want your bouquets, centerpieces, and other floral touches to look like.

BRIDE'S BOUQUET

Your bouquet is going to make quite a statement as you walk down the aisle, so be sure that it is *you*. In today's wedding atmosphere, you have a lot more freedom about the kinds of flowers you choose for your bouquet. No longer do you have to stick to all-white, all roses or stephanotis. Now, more and more floral designers are going with different types and colors of flowers. Brides are asking for more flair to their bouquets, with a little added color. So ask for those red roses or those little purple flowers.

Another wonderful change in today's bouquet style is that they are much smaller than you may have seen in years past. The choice is yours: you can choose a more delicate style over the long, cascading bouquet. You can decide not to be hidden behind a wall of rosebuds and baby's breath, and you don't want to lug around a ten-pound bouquet during the ceremony. Another popular option is the *Biedermeier* style, which is a rounded ball of flowers. Most brides report it to be the most flattering accent to any shape or dress style. It also works well for most levels of formality.

> ### Say the Word
>
>
>
> When I asked for a Biedermeier *bouquet, the designer was quite impressed that I knew my stuff. It showed her that I had done some research, and I knew what I wanted. As a result, she respected me more as a client, and we could communicate much more clearly about my wedding preferences.*
>
> —Sandra

BRIDESMAIDS' BOUQUETS

These, of course, should match the style of your bouquet, contain colors that coordinate with their gowns, and be a little smaller than your bouquet. The maid of honor may get a significant flower or extra blooms to set her apart. Again, smaller is better here, as your maids will want to show off those amazing gowns you found.

FLOWER-GIRL FLOWERS

Flower girls don't need bouquets. Tiny, charming nosegays or pomanders are fine for the little ones, but many brides go with the basket of rose petals and pray that the petals get scattered without an attention-getting tantrum.

Timeless Bouquets

Other types of bride's bouquets that are still popular include:

- *The Nosegay*—a small, round gathering of flowers that are tied together with ribbon or lace. Most often, nosegays have been used as the throwaway bouquet, but brides can use that small, delicate style for their own bouquets as well.

- *The Hand-Tied*—a tight cluster of different types of flowers, tied tightly at the stems with wire and ribbon.

- *The Cascade*—a long arrangement of flowers.

- *The Pomander*—usually used for flower girls, but brides are carrying these small, perfectly round balls of flowers with a ribbon loop attached for carrying.

BOUTONNIERES

The men's boutonnieres should be small and simple, perhaps a single rose or stephanotis, something that goes with the flowers in your bouquet. You may choose to have the groom wear a white flower while the ushers wear a shaded color, depending upon their wardrobe for the day. Don't forget boutonnieres for the fathers, grandfathers, godfathers, and other special male guests!

CORSAGES

Most moms and grandmothers with whom I spoke said they really wanted some say in this decision, as they had personal preferences. Some didn't like traditional pin-on corsages; some hated wrist-worn ones ("This is not the prom!" complained one); and all stated that they wanted a smaller corsage. So take some time to ask the important women in your life what they want for corsages. It's okay if the moms have different styles, depending upon their tastes.

CENTERPIECES

There are some drawbacks to big, overflowing floral centerpieces. Smaller arrangements allow your guests to actually see each other across the table. Plus, everyone wants an unobstructed view of you, no matter where you are in the room. So talk small with your designer.

ROOM DÉCOR

If you have a sufficient budget, you may choose floral arrangements for your ceremony site, altars, the guest book sign-in table, buffet tables, or the gift table. Some brides even place floral pieces in the restrooms at the reception. And don't forget that floral doesn't just mean flowers. It also means greenery, which can be arranged in garlands and

Centerpiece Options

Some brides with limited cash flow are opting to omit the floral centerpiece. Pillar candles are all the rage now, with flower-petals strewn on the table around the base. It's an inexpensive option, considering that some floral centerpieces cost $150 each, while you can get a pillar candle for $8 to $15. One budget-conscious couple skipped the floral centerpiece look and went for the magic of light, choosing small candle-holding lanterns they found at a Christmas shop. Other brides and grooms with beach weddings or sea themes have used small fishbowls featuring ninety-nine-cent live goldfish in brilliant colors from white to bright orange.

green plant arrangements for a tropical look. Talk with your designer about the options that are open to you. Some floral designers do lighting décor as well, so if you want strings of white lights, your designer may be able to provide this for you.

Penny-Wise

If you want those strings of white lights, but don't want to pay a fortune for them, ask your friends and family a few months ahead of time if you can borrow their holiday strings for use at your wedding. Be sure you specify that you want the simple, small bulbs that are standard, and promise that you'll label the strings by owner and return them after the wedding.

OTHER FLOWERS TO ORDER

Don't forget to order any extras you'll need, such as rose petals for the flower girls to scatter, loose flowers you'll want to wear in your hair, special floral arrangements for the ceremony site, flowers to decorate the cake, flowers for the chuppah, or pew décor.

VERONICA'S STORY

One of the most impressive wedding memories I've kept was a young bride's use of flowers to remember her deceased mother. Veronica had lost her mother to breast cancer three years before her wedding, and while she had healed from the loss in her everyday life, she knew she would feel a momentous sense of grief on her wedding day without her mom there.

Her wedding was held on a yacht on the Hudson River, overlooking the New York and New Jersey skylines, and just as the sun set on her reception, the guests were gathered on the port side of the ship for a remembrance moment. Veronica spoke for a minute about what her mother's love meant to her and how she knew she would be a good wife because of the example her mother had set. Veronica then tossed several long-stemmed white roses into the river in remembrance of her mother.

It was not a somber moment. Veronica was filled with joy at having been raised with the love and lessons of a woman as wonderful as her mother, and the guests were put at ease by the ges-

Eat the Flowers!

Many brides are going with edible flowers for their cakes, punch bowls—even napkin rings. They are a simple acquisition, and you only have to ask for them. Types of edible flowers available include:

- Borage (a blue flower)
- Calendula (yellow, orange, cream-colored)
- Lavender (purple)
- Marigold (orange, yellow)
- Nasturtium (red, orange, yellow)
- Pansy (yellow, purple)
- Rose (most colors)
- Squash blossom (yellow)
- Tulip (most colors)
- Violet (white, purple)

Ask your florist about edible flowers and your plans for them. Some flowers can be sugar-coated and candied with instructions found in the book *The Edible Flower Garden* by Rosalind Creasy. Because your florist is unlikely to do this task for you, you might consider doing it yourself as a side effort, or have a friend do it.

ture. Veronica knew that some were bound to make sentimental comments to her, such as "Your mother would be so proud!" and she did not want to be reduced to tears each time. So she handled the situation with ease and grace, and she loved having her mother be a part of her wedding day—through the flowers that she loved so much.

Your Flower and Décor Shopping List

To save time, and to provide a complete picture of your floral needs, here is a list of flower types you might want to order. Have this list on hand when you place your order so you don't forget any. This not only saves you time; it saves your florist the frustration of constantly getting phone calls from you about "Just one more thing. . . ."

For the Bride

_____ Your bouquet

_____ Flowers for your hair

For the Bride's Attendants

_____ Maid/matron of honor's bouquet

_____ Bridesmaids' bouquets

_____ Flower girls' bouquets or nosegays

_____ Rose petals for flower girls

_____ Flowers for the bridesmaids' hair

For the Groom and Groomsmen

_____ Groom's boutonniere

_____ Best man's boutonniere

_____ Ushers' boutonnieres

_____ Ring bearers' boutonnieres

For Special Guests

_____ Bride's mother's corsage

_____ Bride's grandmothers' corsages

_____ Groom's mother's corsage

_____ Groom's grandmothers' corsages

_____ Corsages for godparents

_____ Corsages for readers, candle-lighters, performers, wedding coordinator, other special female guests

_____ Boutonnieres for readers, candle-lighters, performers, other special male guests

_____ Flowers for new step-children
_____ Memory flowers

For the Ceremony Site
_____ Pew bows
_____ Altar décor
_____ Candles
_____ Floral arch
_____ Chuppah
_____ Aisle runner
_____ Floral arrangements for outside the church or synagogue, such as handrail décor or door wreaths
_____ Floral arrangements on pedestals
_____ Floral arrangements on windowsills
_____ Flowers on guest book signing table
_____ Greenery garlands

For the Reception
_____ Centerpieces for head table
_____ Centerpieces for all guests' tables
_____ Centerpieces for buffet tables
_____ Centerpieces for gift tables
_____ Centerpieces for guest book table
_____ Centerpieces for name card table
_____ Centerpieces for favors table
_____ Centerpieces for bar
_____ Flowers to decorate the cake
_____ Flowers to "sprinkle" around candle centerpieces
_____ Flowers for the getaway car
_____ Flowers for toasting flute stems
_____ Flowers for cake knife handle
_____ Throwaway bouquet
_____ Other flowers

Post-Wedding Flowers (optional)

_____ Flowers to be delivered to both sets of parents the day after the wedding

_____ Flowers placed in guests' hotel rooms

_____ Memorial grave wreaths to be placed on graves of departed loved ones

_____ Rose petals to sprinkle on the wedding night bed (optional!)

Get More for Your Wedding Budget

SINCE you are planning in less than six months, you are facing the daunting challenge of having to pay more for many items and services. Nowhere is this more true that in the flower section of your budget. This means you're going to have to find ways to get more blooms for your buck. Consider the following money-saving options:

- *Consider getting sprays for your arrangements.* Floral sprays have several flowers per stem, and are generally less expensive than single-stem flowers. Using sprays makes it look like you've included more flowers.

- *Use larger flowers for centerpieces and decorative arrangements.* Inexpensive, large, in-season flowers will make a better impression from a distance than smaller, expensive flowers.

- *Consider purchasing inexpensive topiaries.* This idea comes from Leah Ingram, author of *Your Wedding Your Way,* who suggests you get inexpensive topiaries from The Home Depot. The topiary look is a classy one, and the prices are quite manageable compared to topiaries found at a florist shop or nursery.

- *Just use flowers for your bouquets, boutonnieres, and corsages.* Pew bows can be made of inexpensive tulle, centerpieces can be candles, favors or framed photos, and the throwaway bouquet can sit behind the guest book.

Save Time with Your Flowers, Too

One of the biggest time drains when placing your flowers is demanding flowers that are out of season or difficult to get during a particular time of year. Marilyn Waga of Belle Fleur Florists in New York City says that you need to have a clear conversation with your florist at the outset of your ordering process. Tell your florist what types of flowers you envision for your wedding and listen to his or her advice about availability of those particular kinds of flowers. "Trust your florist," she says. "We will always make our best efforts to get what you want, although it may take some extra time and effort. But you can save time by having an alternative selection ready in case we just can't get the flowers you want when you want them." That said, providing a back-up list will save time and effort for both you and your florist.

Some of Waga's advice about what's available only at certain times of the year:

♦ Good news! Roses are available in full colors all year-round

♦ The colors of the flowers determine what's in season and what's out of season

♦ Bulbs—such as daffodils, tulips, and hyacinths—can be found in the spring

♦ Peonies are only available in the spring

♦ Flowering cherry blossoms and dogwoods are only available in the spring

Waga says that your regional location has a great deal to do with which flowers are available at the time you hold your wedding, and weather factors have a lot to do with what the flower market will look like. So save some time during your hunt for the perfect flowers, and trust your floral designer to advise you about easily-obtained flowers. The process goes much more quickly when you're dealing with what's readily available.

- *Don't order a floral swag for around the cake table.* Ask for a fabric swag instead.

- *Don't get centerpieces for the head table.* The maids' bouquets can be set out on the table in front of their seats for the same effect.

- *Use silk rather than real flowers.* If you don't mind silk flowers, check craft shops for sales of high-quality, attractive silk flowers. For extra savings (including time!) hire one of the craft store workers to make your centerpieces for you.

- *Skip putting flowers on the backs of each guest's chair.* It sounds like a great idea and looks great in pictures, but provides relatively little show for the expense.

- *Skip decorating the getaway car.*

- *Depend on natural surroundings for your décor.* Carefully assess your ceremony and reception locations. If they're naturally beautiful, if they have a great view overlooking the city or a mountain range, you may not have to decorate them with a garden of flowers.

Do It Yourself?

Lots of brides love the do-it-yourself approach to weddings, and some areas of the planning suit themselves to the crafter. Flowers is seldom one of them.

BARBARA'S STORY

I knew my friend Barb was in deep trouble when she came to me with a too-rosy glow to her face and said she had decided to do her wedding flowers herself. Her wedding was just five months away, she hadn't planned anything fully, she worked an 80-hour workweek, and to my knowledge, she had never taken a class in floral design. But she insisted it would be a snap; she'd seen how to do it in a magazine.

Needless to say, Barb nearly had a nervous breakdown the day before her wedding when she couldn't get the bouquets to come out the same size, and her centerpieces were wilting. For every point raised in her blood pressure, she saved a few hundred dollars, but was it worth it?

Yes, you may have a handful of friends and family who can help, but this job is best left to the professionals. After all, floral design is an art. People train for many years to perfect the styles and to learn the correct coordination and presentation of flowers and greenery. Certain blooms stay fresh for a day, others get thirty-six hours before drooping. No magazine in the world can give you the years of experience required to pull off the floral design for an entire wedding.

Plus, at this late time in planning, you will be busy right up until the last minute before your wedding, and you simply will not have time to spend days on a task that a professional could do in less time with far better results. There is an important factor to keep in mind during this process: your sanity.

My best advice is to avoid the do-it-yourself route with the flowers. You can better express your creativity someplace else in your wedding.

12

PHOTOGRAPHY AND VIDEOGRAPHY

Capturing Your Everlasting Moments

Certainly you'll want to capture the images and expressions of your big day forever in photographs and perhaps on videotape. After all, your wedding day is one of the most important of your life, and you are going to look drop-dead gorgeous in that gown. Since photography and videography is an important part of all weddings, and is an involved process, it can crunch up a lot of wedding budgets. In some parts of the country, photographers charge up to $10,000 (if not more) for wedding albums with illustrious, celebrity-filled credits and magazine layouts. Some professionals charge substantial fees for their assistants, and provide packages filled with extras that may seem necessary at first glance.

While this category may present you with some challenges, you can handle them well by heeding the advice you'll find here. I've spoken to many photographers and videographers about weddings planned on short notice, who all assured me (this is the good news!) that they've done lots of weddings with just a few months' notice. While the industry standard is four to six months' notice, they do get calls for weddings planned three months and even one month out.

If they have the spot open on their calendar, they will take on your wedding photography and treat you like any long-time-reserved bride.

Most reputable ones do *not* charge extra fees for booking weddings in the near future, and all responded that brides and grooms in your position can get excellent arrangements for their photos and videos. You're going to get advice that other brides don't have right now, so in that sense you're at an advantage.

For the sake of clarity, let's discuss the photographer and the videographer separately.

The Photographer

WHEN you hire a photographer, you're not just hiring the person who will create your portraits and albums; you're choosing someone who will choreograph your day. No, he or she won't lead the line dances (at least I hope not!), but will take charge of where you go and what you do for portions of the day. He or she will whisk you away after the ceremony for the required photos, and how speedy and well organized that job is done will determine how soon you can get to your reception. The photographer's work style will be a part of your wedding, and his or her personality will make or break your day. So, in essence, you're also choosing *the right person* to be an integral part of the entire process.

We'll start off with the basics at this point. With just a few months to go, you'll first have to call around to get referrals. Ask family and friends who they used, ask to see some of their pictures, and get a list of names. Many photographers work for studios at which several different people work. While your friend may have gotten the best photographer that studio had, you may be stuck with a newly hired and untested photographer who is the only one available for that date. Do not hire solely on the basis of the company's reputation, but hire on the basis of the individual photographer who will actually do the work. Again, this calls for an interview, which should be done with the utmost care.

Always make appointments to visit the studio. While simply asking them to send samples or visiting the company's Web site may seem like ways to save time, actually stopping in at their workplace is a better idea. This way, you'll be able to see more of their work in person, and can check out a variety of shots and portrait sizes, album styles, and backdrops for in-studio sittings. In addition, you'll be able to look at how they run their business. Are negatives strewn all over the place? Large envelopes stacked in piles on desks? Does the place look unorganized? Is the photographer overloaded with work? Is the studio disheveled? Stopping in and checking the place out is the best way to get this information.

Ask about their equipment: How new is it? What kind of film do they use? Be sure they have the best equipment available, and have plenty of experience using it. Digital photography is the latest technology, and is considered the highest quality by many photographers. There are, however, some photographers who believe that digital does not always produce the best image, and there is some talk in the photography world about digital shots fading slightly over time. So ask your photographer to see actual photos taken with digital cameras, and some taken with other high-quality cameras. Include the standard 35-millimeter in that compare-contrast as well, as you may find that the quality of those shots are every bit as lovely with the right framing, lighting, and lens effects. The difference in price may be astounding, well worth the extra few minutes it takes to look at the few categories of photos.

Digital is also a more expensive option right now. Most photographers say they have to charge up to double the price for each 8 × 10 taken, as the technology is so much more costly. So consider whether you want the best of both worlds for a price, or if you're willing to ask the photographer to use a more standard technology for your shots.

Make sure, too, that they can take the kinds of pictures you want. Some may not have certain filters you'd like to use, such as star filters that make all the lights in a picture look like little starbursts.

Ask about black and white photographs as well. Many brides and grooms are now getting at least some pictures in black and white.

Wedding Day Reflections

We thought that getting all our wedding photos in black and white was an amazing idea. The décor at our apartment is black and white, so we wanted to get portraits that we could display. While ours worked for us, we didn't quite think about our parents and bridal parties. Their décor didn't match, and they didn't want to hang black and whites with their color photos. So our pictures aren't out with the rest of the families'. Plus, if we ever change our décor, we can't put our wedding photo out in the future. We wish we'd had a few rolls taken in color.

—Rebecca and Stephen

Cindi Dixon of Silver Studios in Lancaster, Pennsylvania, is a wedding and portrait photographer who specializes in black and white wedding portraits. When asked about the trend of developing color photographs as black and whites, Cindi says while that is possible, you won't get as perfect an image as you would using black and white film. So she takes pictures using both kinds of film. The black and whites within her portfolio are amazing. Something about the shades and the contrasts makes everyone look better in black and white. Done well, some black and white photos are a great addition to any wedding package.

With those important questions covered, ask the following standard questions of all the photographers you'll be interviewing for this very important job:

♦ What kinds of packages do you offer?

♦ Is there a budget package, and what is included in it?

♦ How many hours of work are included in your basic package?

♦ What does overtime cost?

♦ Who will be taking our pictures? Can we get that person's credits list and resume?

♦ Do you have any other weddings planned for that day?

♦ How many weddings will you be working that weekend?

- Will you be working with an assistant? Multiple assistants?

- Do you use ladders and spotlights? (Many brides found these distracting during the ceremony.)

- Do you have backup cameras?

- How many rolls of film will you shoot?

- What time will you arrive before the ceremony?

- How long does completing the post-ceremony pictures take?

- How many weeks will it take before we get the photos back?

- How long do you keep the negatives?

- Where do you keep the negatives? (Be sure it's a safe place—not the studio basement!)

- Do you digitize the negatives?

- Do you have insurance?

- What is your payment schedule?

- What kind of refund/cancellation policy do you have?

Those are the basic questions, but you can tailor your interview questions to suit your event. You may want to ask the photographer whether he or she has worked an outdoor wedding before. Indeed, that's an important one, as photographers should be well-versed in working with changing light and shadows. Be sure to hire a pro who has lots of experience in the kind of wedding you're planning.

As with most wedding professionals, membership in a professional association is a major plus. While most photographers are well-trained, membership in the following organizations means that they have good contacts within the industry, a source of information on the most recent technology, and good training. While membership is not a necessity, ask your photographer whether he or she belongs to one of the following organizations:

- ◆ WPPI—Wedding Portrait Photographers International
- ◆ PPA—Professional Photographers of America
- ◆ BBB—Better Business Bureau

Professionally Speaking

At the very beginning, I try to get a sense of what the bride and groom want. In my area, I get a lot of sophisticated brides who know exactly what they're looking for, and I've taken some for pictures at various landmarks in the city. It's all very individual, depending upon the bride's tastes, and I work to make sure both our visions work together well.

—Terry Slotkin, Terise Slotkin Photography, New York City

Most photographers, as mentioned before, will not be frightened of a close wedding date. After all, they aren't in the same position as florists or caterers, who have to prepare hundreds of items ahead of time. Photographers simply have to grab their equipment and supplies and go. Still, make sure you allow enough time for a good conversation with your photographer to discuss this important issue: what *you* want.

As in all areas of your wedding, you'll need to come into the consultation knowing what you do and do not want. You don't have much time to drag your feet, or even to pick and choose between styles. Your photographer has been in these consultations before, and he or she will guide you. But if you can make solid decisions rather than waffle over shots in an enormous photo album for hours, you will make everyone's job easier.

Just like the florist, the photographer will size you up when you walk in for your consultation. Only this time, more of the assessment will depend on personalities. Good photographers know that their performance depends upon the needs and wishes of the bride and groom. To truly know that, they need to establish good communication with you, and find out what your style is. Some brides know exactly what they want. Others are open to suggestion. Others, some professionals have told me, are obviously under the oppressive influence of their parents' desires. Photographers can spot a wavering mind at fifty paces.

So this initial "interview" is meant to set your mind at ease, find out what you like, what you've envisioned for your wedding pictures, and what your personal style is.

Most photographers agree that brides and grooms of today want photographs that are not the standard wedding photos of old. They've seen a lot of advertisements, a lot of artistry in the media, amazing color shots in bridal magazines, and celebrity wedding photos. They don't want the stiffly posed line-up shots that were standard in their mothers' and grandmothers' day. They want the glamour shots, the beautiful settings, the perfect arrangements, pictures that speak of who they are and who is important to them. Good photographers will ask you all about the styles you like and what you've seen; they will also provide you with samples of the kind of work they do.

> ### Buying Time
>
>
>
> When you come to the first meeting with your photographer, bring photos that you've taken from any kind of magazine (it doesn't have to be wedding-focused). Show him or her any image that strikes you, that hits home with what you like so the professional can determine at a quick glance what pictures you love.

Photographers will also notice how nervous you are. They'll see right away whether you're overwhelmed, frightened by all the major decisions, or even if you're a people-pleaser. Wedding professionals are generally frustrated when a bride and groom come in with no knowledge of what they want, and just say "Just do whatever." Those customers are often the ones who produce the most trouble for wedding photographers. When the pictures are done (and the stress is off), the couple may be disappointed that they don't have the kinds of pictures they want—even though they are at fault for not specifying their preferences. So don't be a headache, and don't give yourself a headache later on by not stating what you want and working with your professional photographer to create it. It is your day, your photo package, and you'll be living with these pictures forever. So speak up!

Wedding Day Reflections

I fully admit it: I was intimidated by my photographer. He was so artsy, so "I have a vision for you," and he told us all these things he wanted to do with our photos. I can't say that he pushed us— we could have said no—but we didn't want to rock the boat. Big mistake. We spent a long time before our reception trying to stage these odd action shots, waiting for the light to be perfect, and it was really frustrating. All we had to do was stand up for what we wanted. If we could do it over again, we would.

—Fran and Brian

As mentioned before, the photographer can tell when there is a definite parental influence to the decisions, often by cueing in on pushy parents who come for the visit, looking even more intently at the sample albums than the bride does. Most photographers know how to handle this situation. It's a given that parents who are paying for the wedding want to create a beautiful day for their child, but they also want to make a statement about themselves. They want to impress the guests, show their status, have the wedding they didn't have when they were younger. In many cases, they want pictures they feel are suitable for their own display and collection and dispersion to relatives. It isn't that they don't trust their engaged kids to choose suitable pictures. It's just that this is the one aspect of their child's wedding that will be lasting in their lives, and they want to make sure they get a say in it.

If your parents or the groom's parents have anything to do with the planning of your wedding, for the sake of diplomacy it's wise to ask what kind of picture they'd like for their own collection. Your offering is a wonderful gesture, one the parents will appreciate at this planning time. Just be sure to set a boundary. Ask what kind of *picture* they want to have—not *pictures,* or you'll get a list of required shots. That would put you in the difficult position of either having to say no or putting yourself through an agonizing wedding-day pose-down to suit their needs, and you'll wish you hadn't been so kind in the first place. So take this step with your eyes open.

Wedding photographers use the word "document" a lot these days. What they are documenting is your individuality. Knowing that every bride and groom is different from other couples, and that each individual has his or her own style and history, photographers set out to create an individual look. The best vendors will capture those priceless moments that you couldn't predict ahead of time. While they may not know the members of your family, they can tell who has a special role in your life and to what the crowd is reacting. So when your little nieces are dancing with you on the dance floor, the photographer will be flashing away. When your favorite uncle sings "Fly Me to the Moon" to the two of you, the photographer will be there. He'll capture the look in your eyes as you're watching your groom talk with your parents. She'll catch you hugging your sister. He'll get that shot of the two of you walking off into the sunset. A good photographer knows how to capture the essence of your day.

Of course, for the best outcome, the photographer will need a lot of information from you. Beyond the obvious date and time, you'll need to provide this information:

Professionally Speaking

I *did one wedding where the bride's mother already had a married older daughter, whose wedding portrait was displayed in the mother's home. That portrait was a classic, outdoor profile portrait, full-length, and she wanted one just like it of her second daughter so that the portraits would match. So I assured her that I would take that kind of portrait in addition to the less posed ones the daughter wanted. With a little cooperation and a few sketches, I was able to meet the mom's needs without overriding the daughter.*

—Cindi Dixon, Silver Studios, Lancaster, Pennsylvania

♦ *The locations.* Of course, you'll provide the name, address, and directions to the wedding site and reception site, but you may want to stop off at a garden, lake, gazebo, home, or other site for the post-ceremony pictures. Be sure to tell the photographer where you want to go, so that he or she can prepare for any necessary traveling. It's important to be honest and fair from the outset, as you don't want to book a photographer then break the news that he or she will be traveling for an hour to take pictures down at the beach. The photographer may charge you extra, as different wedding packages specify the number of locations you'll be using.

♦ *The formality.* Most pros will wear a suit or tuxedo, but you should inform your photographer if yours is to be an informal wedding so the person doesn't arrive overdressed. Tell the photographer if it's an outdoor wedding, so that he or she can dress appropriately.

♦ *The size.* Give a number of how many guests you expect so the photographer can approximate how much film is needed to capture the event.

♦ *A list of special shots you want taken.* You will be distracted on the wedding day, dancing and greeting your guests. Give your photographer a checklist of photos to ensure you get that shot of you with your Uncle Augie before he leaves.

♦ *Whether or not you want table shots.* If you're going to provide those throwaway cameras, let the guests take candids of each other. Photographers know this practice is common, so don't feel as though you have to hide it. You will save money in the long run by telling your photographer to focus the limited shots on you and the bridal party.

Stress Relief

Photographers are wonderful peace regulators. With the right information, they can avoid unpleasant situations. There is a special place in heaven for pros who know just what to say to fussy kids to get them to smile for the wedding pictures.

♦ *What other shots you don't want.* If you don't want lineup shots, tell your photographer. The same goes for posed pictures of sides of the family. With mixed families and strained relationships, someone may have to be awkwardly left out.

◆ *Whether there are any tensions within your family.* Many brides and grooms are upset that their brother is bringing his new girl-friend to the wedding when he isn't divorced from his wife yet. If everyone loves the wife and hates the girlfriend, the photographer needs to be informed to avoid this tension.

◆ *When you want the majority of the photos taken.* You can arrange to have all your group photos taken during the cocktail party, instead of having to step out during the dancing to get those shots done.

Putting together your wedding package is actually quite simple. You'll be able to view completed sample albums and choose the collections you like. You'll see several differ-ent styles of portraits in different sizes, and you'll be able to pick the number of shots you want.

Most brides and grooms report being happier with a selection of different sizes of photos. All 8 × 10s, for instance, would cost more than a selection of 5 × 7s and even 3 × 5s. Before you make your choices, ask the photog-rapher whether you'll be allowed to keep your proofs. The best pho-tographers allow this, giving you perhaps hundreds of photos to keep for framing and handing to your friends. If this is possible, you'll be able to order fewer photos in your package.

Consider how many albums you're going to order. You may want to just get one for the two of you, and two smaller ones for your parents. Some brides and grooms report that they wasted a lot of money by ordering albums for everyone from their bridal parties to their grandparents.

> ## Professionally Speaking
>
>
>
> The trend right now is for couples to meet before the wedding ceremony to get all their posed shots out of the way. These couples are not worried about bad luck in seeing each other before the wed-ding, and say that getting the staged photos done is a relief so they can relax and enjoy the rest of the day.
> —Terry Slotkin, Terise Slotkin Photography, New York City

Questions for the Photographer

When planning your package with the photographer, you'll need to ask some extra questions besides the obvious. Of course you'll ask about packages, time of service, overtime, album costs, but you should also look at the photographer's price plan with some other more detailed questions in mind:

- ◆ Can we get a breakdown of the prices of each type of photo?

- ◆ How much are reprints?

- ◆ How much are special framings and mountings?

- ◆ When will the photos be done and available?

- ◆ How long will it take to have the albums and portraits made?

If you opt to enclose a small wedding photo with each thank-you card you send, carefully count the number you'll need so you don't order too many. Brides who lack forethought order according to their individual headcount, forgetting that many thank-you notes will go to couples, so take time to get the real count. Some brides go all out by enclosing personalized shots with each thank-you card, such as pictures of the recipient with the bride and groom. While this kind of personalized attention is wonderful, it takes a lot of time, and requires that individual portraits be taken at the reception. You may have neither the time nor the inclination to prepare for this, so this idea may be best left to brides who have an unlimited budget for all the extra shots.

HARRIET AND MARTIN'S STORY

Harriet had a wonderful idea for her informal wedding. They set up a kind of photo booth for the guests to go in and take their own individual pictures. Without any arranging from the couple, and while the photographer was free to take the required shots during the day, the guests went into the photo booth—where a camera was already set up for shots at the right distance and focus—and they took a series of fun, candid shots. The guests loved it, and the photos came out great. Harriet and Martin sent some of these photos to their guests afterwards, in addition to their formal wedding photo.

Your Wedding Photo Checklist

HERE is a list of the most common photos taken at weddings. Use this list to check off what you want, make notes about what you don't want, and show it to your photographer to save some time and to create your unique package.

> ### Penny-Wise
>
>
>
> Save lots of money by making the albums for your parents and anyone else on your list. After the wedding, when the stress is off, take some of your proofs and candids when you get copies from your guests, and make more personal albums. You might choose to include photocopied poetry, graphics, and a personal note in each one. Some brides have used wedding-themed stickers in these small albums as well.

Pre-Ceremony

_____ Bride at salon getting hair done

_____ Bridesmaids at bridal brunch

_____ Bride getting dressed

_____ Maid of honor pinning on veil

_____ Bride in gown

_____ Bride with mother

_____ Bride with father

_____ Bride with mother and father

_____ Bride with siblings

_____ Bride with maid/matron of honor

_____ Bride with bridesmaids

_____ Bride with flower girls

_____ Bride with all female attendants

_____ Groom and ushers getting ready at their location

_____ Groom in tux

_____ Groom with mother

_____ Groom with father

_____ Groom with mother and father

_____ Groom with siblings

_____ Groom with best man

_____ Groom with ushers or groomsmen

_____ Groom with all male attendants

_____ Departure to ceremony

During the Ceremony

_____ Guests arriving at the church

_____ Groom waiting with best man

_____ Ushers seating guests

_____ Guest book attendant

_____ Musicians performing

_____ Bride and father getting out of the limo

_____ Bride and her attendants entering the ceremony site

_____ Bride having her veil put over her face by maid of honor

_____ Grandparents being seated

_____ Groom's parents being seated

_____ Mother of the bride being seated

_____ Groom and ushers taking their place for the ceremony

_____ Attendants coming down the aisle

_____ Flower girl

_____ Ring bearer

_____ Bride and father coming down the aisle

_____ Bride and groom's first hello

_____ The exchange of vows

_____ Lighting of the unity candle

_____ Exchange of the rings

_____ Musicians or readers

_____ Bride and groom's first kiss as husband and wife

_____ Bride and groom coming up the aisle

_____ Bride and groom's first moments alone after the ceremony

_____ The receiving line

After the Ceremony

_____ Bride and groom

_____ Bride and groom with both sets of parents

_____ Bride and groom with separate sets of parents

_____ Bride and groom with female attendants

_____ Bride and groom with male attendants

_____ Bride and groom with child attendants

_____ Bride and groom with siblings

_____ Bride and groom with grandparents

_____ Bride and groom with the person/people who introduced them

_____ Champagne toast

_____ Bride and groom getting into limo

_____ Bride and groom in limo

During the Reception

_____ Bride and groom arriving at the reception

_____ Group shots of the bridal party outside the reception site, such as on
the grounds, by fountains, lakes, or greenery

_____ Bride and groom entering the reception site

_____ Bridal party in the bridal suite

_____ Guests mingling at the cocktail party

_____ The buffet tables

The Not-So-Common Shots

Some shots are no longer taken at weddings, either because they are "out of date" or most brides and grooms agree that they are "cheesy." Such shots may include:

- Ushers lifting the bride up

- The arms-entwined champagne drink

- The kiss leaned over the cake

- Table shots

- A silhouette of the bride and groom

- A picture of the bride and groom printed over sheet music of your wedding song

Be sure to communicate with your photographer if you don't want these or any other common shots.

_____ Ice sculptures

_____ The wedding cake

_____ Bridal party being announced into the room

_____ Bride and groom being announced into the room

_____ The head table

_____ The parents' tables

_____ The first dance

_____ Bride and her father dancing

_____ Groom and his mother dancing

_____ Guests dancing

_____ Best man's toast

_____ Others' toasts

Ways to Save Money on Photographs

♦ *Hire the photographer for only the ceremony and the beginning of the reception.* Many brides and grooms cut their cakes early so the photographer can leave soon afterward.

♦ *Order fewer album photos.* If you can keep your proofs, limit the number of photos you order for your albums.

♦ *Get some photos in black and white.* These are often less expensive, as well as very effective.

♦ *Develop the pictures on your own.* Arrange to have the photographer give you the rolls of film afterwards, and take them to the developer yourself. This sounds strange, but many brides and grooms are going for this money-saving option.

♦ *Limit the number of pictures.* Tell the photographer how many rolls of film he or she should take.

♦ *Skip the throwaway cameras.* If you have a lot of guests, you'll be paying to develop many film rolls, some of which may not have been taken completely. Plus, few of the candid shots may turn out.

_____ Bride and groom cutting the cake
_____ Bride tossing the bouquet
_____ Slipping off of the garter
_____ Groom tossing the garter
_____ Bride and groom with people who caught the bouquet and garter
_____ Party shots
_____ Bride and groom leaving the reception
_____ Other shots:

After the wedding, when the photos come back, be sure just you and your groom pick the photos for your own album. Your parents can go through the proofs and pick their own, if they wish, but you should be in charge of which pictures you choose.

In the end, your effort will be worthwhile, as you will have gorgeous shots to display and cherish forever.

The Videographer

IF you want your day captured on video, you'll again have to do some legwork to find a videographer who is available on your day, who has the credentials and talent to do a good job, and who meets all your wishes for the best production of a moving image.

You may follow the hiring advice mentioned in the photographer's section, remembering that a videographer should be hired as an individual. Photographers often mention that their studio has videographers on staff, and suggest that you hire one of theirs, perhaps at a discount. I generally warn brides away from this, as videographers also should be chosen on their individual merit. Like your photographer, your videographer should be a good personal fit. And the equipment does matter—not just for sight, but for sound and effect.

CHECKING THEIR EQUIPMENT

As you call around to research availability and package prices, it helps to know the videography lingo. Steve Blahitka of Back East Productions in East Hanover, New Jersey, says that the most important decision you'll make regards the pairing of good equipment with good film stock. With the advances in technology, digital cameras produce the highest-quality images and are much smaller and less cumbersome than camera models of the past. For these reasons, most of the best videographers use digital cameras.

Depending upon what kind of video result you want, you would be wise to ask about multiple cameras. The videographer, after all, can't be in all places at the same time, so you may decide to go with a two- or three-camera set-up. The best videographers will set up a camera in the alcove or balcony of the site, test it, get it rolling, and then take the required footage on the main level of the ceremony. Afterwards, all the footage will be edited together with wonderful transitions and different views. Although having multiple cameras is more expensive due to the extra film use, effort, and editing afterwards, this choice is highly popular.

As far as film stock, you have a choice. It is possible to get very high-quality images on a less-expensive type of film stock, such as high-8, VHS, or even beta. Prices will vary depending upon the film stock you choose.

You may have heard talk about digital videotapes fading over time. Any videotape will fade over time, especially if you view it a lot. So don't worry about future fading; be sure that the video looks great right now. Even if a superior-quality tape does lose some of its crystal-clear quality in ten years, it will still be better than a poor-quality tape taken right now.

Another equipment option is lighting. Find out what the videographer does for lighting—whether his cameras adjust to light, or whether spotlights will be necessary. Spotlights can be a major distraction during all parts of the wedding. In fact, many brides and grooms report that their church officiant took one look at the spotlight being set up and said "no way" to the glare of the lights, so the videographer couldn't adequately capture the vows.

> ### *Professionally Speaking*
>
>
>
> Y*ou don't have to get the best quality film stock for the best quality image. With a good digital camera, you can get a superior image with VHS film.*
>
> —Steve Blahitka, Back East Productions, East Hanover, New Jersey

KAREN AND JEFF'S STORY

The lighting was the only detail that Karen and Jeff didn't check out with the videographer. They meticulously researched him, asked about all details of their business arrangement, but did not know enough about his industry to know that their reception would be flood-lighted with a blinding spotlight the videographer would turn on and off during the video-worthy parts of the night.

Their reception site was beautiful, filled with candles and delicate lighting specially planned by a designer, but every time the videographer flicked on his bright lights in the small room, the guests shielded their eyes. All the images of Karen and Jeff's reception showed people squinting or covering their eyes. The ushers even put on their sunglasses. The couple wished they'd known about this major distraction beforehand.

Unless you want a silent videotape, you'll also have to concern yourself with the sound. Videographers know about attaching microphones to the groom before the ceremony so that all the vows can be heard and recorded. Often this involves a small microphone that can't be seen against the groom's clothes. Ask to see the mike and make sure it's not a big, obvious one. And stay away from videographers who use handheld mikes.

Since sound is a key part of the video, test their sample videos for sound as well. Some brides report that their wedding videos had an annoying clicking that the videographer explained was the tape advancing. Be sure that the sound is clear and doesn't have any feedback or echo. Investing your time in checking video quality—as busy as you are right now—will pay off.

Say the Word

Because videographers need light to shoot, you should ask about their lighting systems before you hire a videographer. Explain that you've seen really intrusive lighting before, and ask what can be done about that. A good videographer will understand. It is also vitally important that you let the videographer know what kind of light conditions he or she will be working in. If you plan an outdoor wedding during the day, the videographer knows that he or she doesn't need the extra lights. If you'll be in a small, enclosed room, he or she will know that the spotlight is required. Good communication here will reward you with the best arrangement.

Again, ask if he or she will be using ladders to get those higher-up shots. If you'll have to compete with the sound of rickety ladders being set up or carted all over, simply tell your videographer that you don't want that distraction during the day.

PLAN FOR A STYLE OF RECORDING

Many videographers tape weddings like a documentary, following the whole path of the day. In a documentary, you might have old footage, background scenes, interviews, candid captures, and official footage. Just spell out what you want, combining your vision with the artistry of the videographer. Ask for romantic shots, if you want them. Ask for specific interviews of special people in your life. In the past, videographers have taken it upon themselves to go from table to table asking each guest to say a few words to the camera as a message to the two of you. This often comes out awkward, as some guests may be camera-shy, drunk, or simply babble on for a long time. If you don't want this potential waste of film, tell the videographer that interviews aren't your style, and that you'd prefer footage of the dancing.

> # Don't Risk Losing Your Moment
>
>
>
> Be sure the videographer plans to test the microphones before the wedding, and that he or she has backups in case one set doesn't work. At one beautiful wedding, the microphones did not work, and the video came out with the bride and groom mouthing their words. The vows—the most important part of the ceremony—were not audible on the tape.

CHECK OUT THE SPECIAL EFFECTS

Brides and grooms are moving away from the special effects fad, not wanting to pay extra for dancing bunnies to hop across the screen in the wedding footage. I've seen wedding tapes filled to the extreme with eye-boggling special effects, such as strobing (in which the footage gets jumpy and disorienting) and even tennis players bounding across the screen (in that case, neither the bride nor the groom

Say the Word

Get a list of the special effects your videographer offers, and specify exactly which ones you want. Do not leave the choice to the videographer, as you may not agree with what he or she puts in, or may find it overkill. Also ask to see sample videotapes of their effects-heavy weddings and their non-effects tapes. See the difference, and judge for yourselves what you want.

played tennis, so the addition was baffling!). Good videographers will have a wealth of special effects to offer; be firm about what you want.

One special effect that most brides and grooms go for is the montage of baby pictures and shots of their growing-up years that begins their tape. Many couples find this a wonderful addition to their wedding tape, definitely worth the extra expense. If you do choose this option, gather your old baby photos and provide them to the videographer ahead of time. Remember, though, that incorporating old home movie reels or videotapes will require extra editing work for the videographer, and will add to the cost, depending on how many pictures you provide supply.

Making the Right Decision

You'll have to verify that the videographer is the right person for you. As with the photographer, make sure you have good rapport, that this person is willing to hear your ideas, and that he or she makes you feel at ease. You must be able to trust the videographer, like his or her style, and know that this is someone you'll want to have around on the wedding day. If you find someone pushy and demanding at this point, you may not want to be led around by the nose on your big day. Get a good feel for how this person sets you at ease. Again, explain any delicate family situations, and go over what your family wants for the videotapes. Communicate all, and you'll promote the best conditions for creating a lovely videotape of your wedding.

Questions for the Videographer

In addition to the questions you asked the photographer, ask your videographer these:

- What kind of equipment do you use?
- What kind of film stock do you offer?
- In what format will you provide the final tape?
- Can you use multiple cameras, and what will that cost?
- What are the details of each package you offer?
- Can we customize a package?
- Do you place a microphone on the groom? Who else wears a microphone?
- What music do you have available for use on the tape?
- Can we give you our own song list to use for background music?
- Can we give you our own music CDs to use?
- Can we get the baby footage montage?
- What kind of tapes do you use for the final product? (Be sure they copy onto high-quality tapes, not cheap ones.)
- What will you be wearing?
- Will you be using an assistant?
- Do you have backup equipment?
- Will you be using ladders?
- Do you have reliable transportation?
- Will we be expected to pay for your travel?
- Do you have insurance?
- Do you have a refund/cancellation clause in your contract?

DOING IT YOURSELF

Many brides and grooms say they skipped hiring a professional video-grapher in an effort to save time or money. They asked a family friend to do the taping for them, and were happy with the results. The lighting may not have been perfect, and some shots may not have been caught, but for them, the savings were worthwhile.

> *Wedding Day Reflections*
>
>
>
> We know our friend meant well, but he got drunk during the recep-tion, and the second half of our wedding tape was shaky, blurry, and kind of goofy. So while we saved money having him tape for us, we weren't happy with the outcome.
>
> —Carolyn and James

You may not agree. For every couple that was happy with this arrangement, another couple was disappointed. Their happy-to-oblige guest may eventually get worn out from the great responsibility during the day and night. Important shots may be missed when the guest goes to the restroom, the bar, or outside for a smoke.

Another factor to think about when asking a friend to tape for you is that you're asking this person to work during your wedding. He or she may not be able to dance with the spouse they came with, he may not get to enjoy himself, or she may be exhausted during the evening. If you do choose this option, be sure to take your friend out to dinner after you get back from the honeymoon, give him or her a bottle of champagne, and otherwise treat this person like gold. This friend has done a momentous task for you, and should be well rewarded.

MAKING COPIES OF THE VIDEO

If your video came out amazing and you want to make copies for everyone, don't cut corners by making your own duplicates. Brides and grooms who have done this have not only produced low-quality, grainy copies, but many have damaged their priceless master tape in the process. While asking the videographer to do it for you may add to your expense, the copying should really be done by a pro.

Ways to Save Money on Videography

+ *Hire the videographer for only the ceremony and the beginning of the reception.* Cut your cake early so that he or she can leave.

+ *Get a simple package.* Select one that doesn't require a lot of hours.

+ *Use amateur footage for pre-ceremony videos.* Don't have the rehearsal and morning of the wedding taped professionally. You can have your own footage edited in if necessary.

+ *Don't order special effects.*

+ *Get the raw footage tapes, instead of the specially edited ones.* You may have to fast-forward through a half hour of cocktail party milling to get to the good stuff, but it will be worth the savings.

+ *Use lower quality film stock with a good camera.*

+ *Make fewer copies.* Rather than give everyone under the sun a copy, let others view your copy.

Videography is an important issue for brides with short planning time. If your wedding is just a few months away, and some of your guests won't be able to attend, making copies of your wedding video for loved ones who are unable to make it—especially grandparents and best friends—is a good idea. A well-made copy in a pretty video-tape slipcover can be an arms-open gift that says, "We wish you could have been there."

13

TRANSPORTATION AND LODGING

THE PERFECT ARRIVAL AND SURROUNDINGS

EVEN THE BEST-LAID plans for your ceremony and reception will do no good if you and your guests can't get to these events. While most brides and grooms are only concerned with making a grand entrance or exit in a shiny, white limousine or classic car, taking reliability, service, and value into consideration is necessary as well. The transportation you choose for yourself—and honored guests!—on your wedding day can become a make-or-break situation. Be sure you hire the right company, the right cars, and the right packages for your wedding needs.

Booking in Time

SINCE your time is limited, you may face a challenge in finding an available limo or classic car. Since many weddings are booked a year ahead of time, and since many brides book a line of limos for their use, the best companies may not have any cars available, or may not have your first choice of cars available. So do some initial calling to find out which companies near you have good, quality cars open for your use.

Knowing that limos are booked for more reasons than weddings —such as business use, formal events, proms, and even funerals—you should tackle this job immediately. Still, most limo companies representatives to whom I spoke said that they can arrange transportation packages with just a few weeks' notice. The bride and groom may have to be flexible on what they'll actually use, but the company can usually accommodate them.

The First Steps

I'LL say it again: This type of company also needs to be checked out thoroughly. In addition to obtaining referrals from family and friends, check the company's rating with the Better Business Bureau and the National Limousine Association (www.nla.com). Any complaints or grievances will be listed there.

NATASHA AND GREG'S STORY

The limo company Natasha and Greg were considering had an impressive lineup of cars, good prices, and even a list of celebrity clientele. They seemed perfect. But when Natasha called around to check on the company, she ran across a complaint about rude drivers the company hired. When she dug further, she learned that a bride and groom had lost track of time during their reception and were an hour late coming out to take their limo to the airport hotel. The driver, instead of understanding that they were having such a great time, was in a complete rage that they forgot to make their departure according to *his* schedule. He took turns too quickly, jammed on the brakes, and pounded on the steering wheel. The bride and groom were shocked and frightened, not wanting to die on their wedding night.

The bride called her father in tears from the honeymoon suite, told him what happened, and her father put a complaint in with the Better Business Bureau. Now, few other brides and grooms will have to start off their married life with the limo ride from hell.

You may have heard lots of nightmare stories about limos that broke down, drivers who got lost and did not show up to pick up the bride, even drivers who showed up wearing out-of-fashion suits and strange hats. In the world of weddings, these stories make the rounds, and sometimes with good reason. Problems do happen on wedding days, and when you're dealing with cars, traffic, and complicated scheduling, there's plenty of room for mishaps. But you can cut down on your chances of transportation nightmares by doing your homework, carving time out of your schedule to research your transportation options thoroughly so you can make the best decisions possible.

After you've gathered your list of transportation companies that come highly referred and have clean records with their organizations, do a little pre-work before you start making calls. Have the following pieces of information handy for the most efficient planning process and the greatest savings of time:

> ### Buying Time
>
>
>
> *If you just want the best service in a standard style of car, save yourself time by calling the nearest four- or five-star hotel and asking their concierge which limousine company they depend on for the needs of their most-valued clients. Because these ritzy hotels are not going to hire substandard professionals, you will certainly get a list of the best-name companies in the area. Of course, they may be more expensive options, but you will get the service and reliability you pay for.*

- *The date of the wedding.* Obviously, the limo company will need to know which date you have picked. This could work to your advantage if you've planned a Friday night wedding, as a greater variety of cars are likely to be available at a lower price. Time and location will also have to be mentioned, as they will factor into the manager's figuring of the availability of the car you're considering.

- *The bridal party and family members who you'll want to ride in limos.* Rather than guess at the number of limos you'll need, know exactly how many bridesmaids and ushers, parents and grandparents you want chauffeured around in style. The manager will help you figure out how to accommodate the various numbers of people who need to be transported in each group. For instance, if you have twelve bridal party members, you'll need a twelve-seater limo. With four parents and four grandparents on your list, the company's eight-seater will be booked.

Professionally Speaking

In many cases, brides and grooms overestimate how many cars they'll need. I've been in business a long time, and have on several occasions saved couples money by showing them they only need three limos when they thought they needed four. A good limousine director will give you that straight advice.

—Robert Bannon, America's Best Limousines, New Jersey

♦ *The times and places the cars will be needed.* This will take some planning, as you'll need to know when and where pick-ups and drop-offs will be required. For most standard weddings, limos pick up the bride and bridesmaids at one place and take them to the church. They also pick up the groom and his ushers and take them to the church. Everyone will be driven from the ceremony site to the reception. But you may choose to fill your package hours with extra stops, such as at a park on the way to the reception to take scenic photos. You may want the limo to take you to the beauty salon in the morning. You may want the grandparents picked up at home. Clarifying all these details early is important, so the manager can tell you whether he has time in his booking schedule for the arrangements you need.

♦ *Your wedding budget.* Never walk into a limo place desperate to book whatever car is available, giving a clear-cut sign that you'll pay anything. Be firm about your budget, even though you may feel you're asking a lot for this last-minute booking. A true professional will respect your boundaries, honor your budget, and work with what you have to get what you want.

- *Your preferred style.* Again, saying "I don't know" or "Whatever" will waste your time and send the message that you don't care what you get. If you want the traditional white stretch limo, say you do. If you're envisioning a more elegant classic car such as an antique Bentley, request that. Have pictures of what you've seen in ads, and ask whether the company can put you in something original and attention-getting.

- *The details of your day.* You can't book a package if you have no idea what the step-by-step events of your day will be. So be able to provide a list of how long the day will be, what is happening when, where you need to be, and the level of formality you plan. By being able to provide a clear image of the day, you're enabling the limo manager to customize your package for the best savings to you.

Penny-Wise

If you have booked rooms for your guests at a hotel, ask the hotel manager whether you can arrange to have their shuttle bus transport your guests to and from the ceremony, reception, and the hotel. Most hotel managers consider this a standard service, and may even provide it free if your block of rooms is large enough. If it's going to cost you, compare prices with other minibus companies for the best rates.

- *All your transportation needs.* This goes beyond your own car and those for your bridal party and parents. Will guests have to get from their hotel to the ceremony and reception sites? Can the company give you rates for a party bus or vans that can take guests where they need to go? Many brides report that they hired party buses for their bridal parties as well as for their hotel-bound guests, saying that getting the minibus rather than four limos saved them money, and that the bridal party loved the festive, free atmosphere on the bus.

It's Not Just Limos Anymore

YOU'RE probably seeing more and more shiny white Rolls Royces out in front of churches these days, and indeed the variation on the limo is becoming all the rage. Limos are and will continue to be the number one choice of brides and grooms, but many couples are looking into the classic car and the customized auto to make a bold statement.

Some cars you might want to ask about:

- Bentley
- Rolls Royce
- Excalibur
- Classic convertibles
- Jaguar
- Mercedes
- Stretch Humvee
- Stretch Navigator
- Lexus
- Sedans
- Minivans (perfect for decorating—something you might not get to do with another type of car).

Wedding Day Reflections

We *found that not only did the Bentley make a better picture, but it was more available at the limo places. Everyone else was booking limos, so we went for the classic car. It did cost a little more, but we made up for that by only using it for part of the day.*

—Kelly and Todd

So for the best booking task, be sure you have an idea of what you want. If you know you want that Rolls, save time by looking for just that when you call around.

Since you have limited booking time, staying flexible enough to consider what's available is wise. All the white limos may be booked, so you may have to go with black or silver. You might find these less expensive than the white ones, so good luck may show through a disappointing situation.

The Interview Process

ONE of the best pieces of advice is to always go to the limo company for the interview. Some less reputable companies will offer to bring a limo to your house for your inspection. While that may seem a kind and generous offer, it often means that the company has something to hide. Either they do not have a well-established office, or have no office at all. I ran into one supposed professional who owned three limos that he parked behind his house. He ran the business out of his home and did not have the skills or staff to handle a wedding well.

Professionally Speaking

One thing you should keep in mind is that the limousine is the only type of vehicle in which, by law, you can drink alcohol. You can book the other types of cars, but you may not be able to have that champagne toast in them.

—Robert Bannon, America's Best Limousines

So when you plan your interviews, ask to come in for a sit-down with the manager. Calling around may save time, but you will have to look at the cars anyway. So reserve a few days for this process, take the groom along, and for your best self-interest, take along someone who knows cars.

Upon the first visit, check out the storefront. Is it attractive? Clean? Well-kept?

Is the office organized and well-staffed? Does the receptionist have good phone skills? Are they getting a lot of calls and taking a lot of reservations?

The manager should be willing to answer all of your questions. Here's a list of the questions you have to ask to fully assess the company's service:

- ◆ What types of cars do you offer?

- ◆ What are your prices for each type of car?

♦ What is the standard time limit? (For most companies, three hours is standard.)

♦ Is there a minimum time limit?

♦ What does overtime cost?

♦ Are there extra charges for stopping at different locations?

♦ Do you have backup cars available in case ours breaks down?

♦ How many weddings are you doing that weekend?

♦ Is there another wedding booked for earlier in the day?

♦ Will you need that car for another wedding later that day?

♦ Can we decorate the car we've chosen?

♦ What will the driver be wearing?

♦ What is the deposit and payment schedule?

♦ Do you have insurance?

♦ Do you have a refund/cancellation policy?

> ### Say the Word
>
> Always ask whether the drivers will have not only a cell phone, but two-way radios as well. Cell phones are great for communication, but they don't always find service in some areas. A two-way radio in the car is a mark of true professionalism, as drivers can always stay in touch with their home base.

If the answers you get suit your needs and tastes, then look at the cars. If they look old or out of style, move on. If they're scratched, dented, or have peeling paint, move on. The manager can promise you that the cars are going in for repair next week, but if they're not in good condition right now, choose another agency. These cars, remember, are the company's lifeblood. They need to be perfectly kept at all times, so take their condition as an indication of the type of company you're dealing with.

They all may look perfect and spotless on the outside—and indeed all the cars should be cleaned and waxed at all times—but you'll need to see the *inside* of the cars to make your best decisions. Ask to step inside and check the cars out. A reputable dealer will let you do this as part of standard customer service. If he balks or says he doesn't have the keys, there's most likely some kind of problem and you should walk away.

Once inside the car, make sure the seats are in good repair. Are they comfortable, or are springs evident through the seats? Are there patched tears in the upholstery? Stains?

Is the car stocked with glasses, champagne flutes, an ice bucket?

Very important: Is there enough room for your gown and veil? Limos typically have plenty of room, but if you're booking a classic Bentley or Rolls, you may find the backseat a little cramped. Some brides report that their gowns got smashed and wrinkled during a short ride, especially on a hot day.

> ## Say the Word
>
>
>
> Ask the manager for a non-smoking car so you can be sure you won't be climbing into a car that smells of cigarette smoke or the lingering effects of the cigar-puffing bachelor party.

Ask the company representative to turn the car on so you can be sure everything is in working order. You may not need the television set, the VCR, or the refrigerator, but the windows and sunroof should be functional.

It may not be possible to book a specific car by license plate number, but you can ask. Different companies have different policies, and some may be willing to let you reserve the car you've looked at.

It's also important at this stage to let the manager know where the car will be required to go. Some limousines could not traverse a country road with winding twists. A stretch Navigator could not easily make the narrow turns to get down one-way Hoboken streets. Be sure to describe the terrain the car will be expected to handle.

Making the Deal

OKAY, you've checked the company, and see a glowing record. You've checked the cars, and find them in tip-top shape. Now it's time to piece together your wedding-day package so that you get the right kind of service at the right price.

Say the Word

Take the issue of directions into your own hands. Even if the manager says, "Don't worry, we'll find it," offer to call in or fax the exact directions to all wedding day sites. You can send them the map you're sending to your guests, or you can use a map provided by the banquet hall manager. Taking this step will remove your worrying about lost cars.

TIME

Most car packages are standard at three hours. Brides and grooms typically use these three hours for all transportation up to the drop-off at the reception, at which point the limos are gone. I would suggest adding some extra time onto your package, just to be safe. It usually winds up being less expensive to increase reserved time than to rack up overtime during the wedding day. Remember, the limousine company may have another appointment the evening of your wedding—such as taking someone to the airport—and you may be out of luck when the plan doesn't go your way, or when you're slapped with a hefty overcharge fee.

NUMBER OF CARS

As Robert Bannon said, you may not need as many cars as you think you do. Limousines come in sizes that seat six, eight, ten, or twelve, so you may need only two when you thought you needed four. Work with the manager to arrange for the number of cars you'll need to book.

THE SCHEDULE

Have an organized pick-up/drop-off list ready for the manager to record. He's done this before, so he'll be able to guide you about which information he needs. Be sure you can provide exact street addresses and times.

WHO'S DRIVING?

Arrange for the booking of a particular driver. Ask for their best and most experienced. Find out how long the driver's been working with them, and make sure he or she's done plenty of weddings beforehand.

WHAT'S FREE IN THE PACKAGE?

Most reputable limo companies will provide complimentary champagne, soft drinks, bottled water, ice, and snacks inside the cars on the wedding day. Some companies will roll out a red carpet leading to the door of the car after the ceremony, and they will have a champagne stand, chilled champagne, and crystal glasses for the bride and groom to enjoy a toast before they climb into the car. Ask what's free, and don't be afraid to delete what you don't want of those free items. The company may be very excited about the fact that their car has a wedding horn that plays music when the driver beeps, but you may not want that kind of blaring announcement.

Say the Word

Be sure a "time is of the essence" clause is included in your transportation contract. This clause states that the vendor must be on time, or you will have the right to a partial refund or a change to your final payment.

GET THE COMPANY'S INFORMATION

You may have the company's business card, but make sure you get the driver's cell-phone number and their 24-hour number in case you need to call the office on the wedding day. You won't want to get an answering machine if the cars are missing right before the ceremony.

GET IT ALL IN WRITING

No verbal agreements. Get everything in a standard contract with all details spelled out, right down to the itemized schedule of who's being picked up when. Check the contract out carefully, be sure the car you want is identified in the list, and that all other details are covered.

The Horse and Carriage Ride

Horse and carriage rides are a favorite of many brides and grooms. For some, it offered a relaxed ride alone, a romantic break in the middle of the hectic schedule, and a chance to be the center of attention along the road to the reception. If you do choose to go this route, call reputable companies, ask for an interview and to view the carriage and the horse, and make all arrangements appropriately. That means being honest about the conditions and the length of the trip between the ceremony and reception, as you don't want the poor horse to trot on the shoulder of an interstate, or have to pull you for a long ride. A trip of a couple of short blocks is best for this option, and be sure to plan for alternate transportation in case of rain.

CONFIRM YOUR RESERVATIONS

As with everything else, confirm a month ahead of time, then two weeks ahead of time, then again right before the wedding. Don't worry about being a nuisance. These companies get hundreds of confirmation calls a week. They're used to it.

GETTING OTHERS TO HELP OUT

You might have friends or family who own classic cars. Should they offer you a ride on your wedding day, you might choose to take them up on it. Just be sure the car is in fine running order and your driver is reliable. If despite your Uncle Charley's good intentions, you know he might get sloshed during the reception, be sure to hire a driver. Or you might accept a dependable friend's offer to drive you around in his convertible, and have more freedom to decorate with a "Just Married" sign.

Bride's Projected Transportation Needs (Sample List)

Limos

+ Bride and father to ceremony
+ Bridesmaids to ceremony
+ Groom and ushers to ceremony
+ Bride's mother and grandmother to ceremony
+ Groom's family to ceremony
+ Bride and groom to pictures site
+ Bridal party to pictures site
+ Bride's and groom's parents and grandparents to reception site
+ Bride and groom to reception site
+ Bridal party to reception site

Other Cars

+ Guests from hotel to ceremony site
+ Guests from ceremony site to reception site
+ Guests from reception site back to hotel

Lodging

IF any guests will be coming from out of town, it's a good idea to arrange lodging for them at a nearby hotel. In many cases, the reception may be held at a banquet hall that is part of a large hotel, and the block of rooms you need may become part of your wedding package. This works out well for guests, and for you, as transportation after the reception is not a problem. Guests also have the freedom to run up to their room at any time during the night to check on kids, make phone calls, or attend to any number of other tasks.

Buying Time

If booking a block of rooms is not within your effort level right now, simply provide your guests with a list of hotels that they can contact for their own booking. Provide the hotel's reservations phone number—which may be different from the 800-number you get out of the phone book—as well as mention of the price and the hotel's distance from the reception site. The manager can help you with that part.

If you're booking a block of rooms, know in advance how many rooms you'll need. Ask the hotel manager whether you can book more rooms than you'll need, then cancel out remainders when you get your final headcount. In many cases, a manager may let you reserve a realistic number of rooms on a credit card, and cancel with just a few hours' notice at no charge. During the busy wedding season when all rooms are at a premium, however, it's likely that you'll have to pay for any rooms you've reserved, even if they wind up unused.

Be sure to assess the hotel according to your guests' needs. Ask the manager for the availability of what your guests require, and then make your selections according to this list:

- Cost of rooms
- Availability of connected rooms
- Availability of suites
- Availability of efficiencies
- Air-conditioning and/or heat
- Complimentary breakfast for guests (saves you a bundle!)
- Coffeemakers in the rooms
- Smoking or non-smoking rooms

- Cots or cribs

- Lower-floor rooms for those who don't like heights

- Handicapped access

- Game rooms

- Pools and Jacuzzis

- Nearby shopping and sightseeing

- Free shuttles to and from the airport

- Free shuttles to and from the wedding

BABYSITTING

One issue that almost always crops up during weddings is the need for babysitters.
Guests who come from out of town will almost certainly bring their kids, and if those
little ones are not invited to the wedding, you
may be called upon to find a reliable babysitter in the area. Brides complain about this
issue a lot. As if they don't have enough to do,
now they have to hire a babysitter willing to
watch six toddlers for six hours?!

> ### Penny-Wise
>
>
>
> *Paying for babysitters is not your job. The parents brought the kids into town, so they should take care of this expense. Don't try to be the pleaser and offer to pay for sitters.*

Some hotels have babysitting services, but
you would be much better off skipping that.
After all, you have no idea who these babysitters are. Some brides
report calling on a nearby neighbor; others checked with their church
to find a suitable referral. Perhaps the best and most reliable action is
to call the local high school, ask for a referral of their most upstanding
students, and arrange for those students to contact you about a possible babysitting job. In the case of more than three kids—or two
extremely active ones—you might want to hire more than one sitter
to handle the task.

Helpful Advice Regarding Wedding Night Lodging

Many brides and grooms to whom I spoke had plenty of input on this, so I'll let them tell you what they learned:

If you're leaving for the honeymoon the next day, get a room by the airport. It may be exhausting taking a long ride the night of the wedding, but it's better than having to get up at 5:00 A.M. to get to the airport and take that flight.

—Trina and Dennis

If you're going to get a room at the hotel where the reception is, don't tell anyone which room you're in. Our friends were calling us and knocking on the door all night.

—Samantha and Nicholas

Don't bother with booking the ultra-deluxe honeymoon suite for the wedding night. You'll be so tired and so ready for bed that you won't care that the room has a wet bar, a Jacuzzi, or a great view.

—Sally and Paul

Just save a few bucks and go back to your place.

—Mary and Allen

How to Save on Lodging Costs

HOTEL rooms can cost a few hundred dollars a night, especially at nicer hotels. You can save money by taking the following steps:

- Book a block of rooms, and ask for a discount.

- See whether you can get your wedding night room for free if you're booking a lot of other rooms.

- Check discount Web sites like priceline.com.

- Limit how long your guests will be staying by telling them they're booked for one or two nights.

- Negotiate a discount into the rooms if you have a large wedding order at a hotel banquet hall.

- Put guests up at a nearby bed and breakfast, which is generally less expensive than a hotel. Just pick a good one that is rated well.

Don't try to save everyone money by letting them stay at your house or your parents' house. That's inviting chaos.

Buying Time

P*ut someone in charge of booking and confirming the block of rooms a few days before the wedding. You won't have time, and it's a simple job for an honor attendant or a parent.*

14

INVITATIONS

A PERFECT PRESENTATION TO A PERFECT DAY

Y our wedding invitations catch a lot of attention when they show up in your guests' mailboxes. The recipients get not only a grand pronouncement of your upcoming event, but also their first "taste" of what kind of wedding you've planned. A lot shows in the invitations. The design and style of wording shows the formality, giving your guests an idea of what they ought to wear. The inclusions show them what kind of reception yours will be—formal, outdoor, at-home. Most importantly, they learn where and when to show up.

You might expect choosing your invitations to be a horrendous, time-consuming job. After all, those fat sample books at the store contain *thousands* of styles, and there are so many rules about the wording. But done correctly, your invitation selection process could take no more than a day. Follow this advice, and you'll get through this task unscathed—with a beautiful, applicable invitation that's perfect.

The First Steps

BEFORE you get to this job, have several decisions already made:

- The wedding date, location, and time of day

- The formality of the wedding

- The style of the wedding

- The street addresses of the ceremony and reception locations

- The full, correct spellings of the names of all people who will be mentioned on the invitation (more on this later)

- Whether you'll need separate cards for reception invitations. (This decisive paper is needed for cases in which some guests may be invited only to the church. Know if you've had to do that with your guest list.)

- Your full guest headcount for ceremony and reception (two counts if they're different)

What do we do with the leftover invitations?

They're great for mementos, but many brides like to use them as part of gift photo albums, framed displays for special family members, even anniversary gifts.

I ended with the guest headcount issue because you know that many of your guests will be named as couples on their invitation. So two people get one invitation. Families with several children under sixteen may all be named on one invitation. Take a few minutes to go through your guest list and add up the number of invitations you'll actually need. But do not order just that many. You will need more. Have you included the bridal party in the guest-list count? Many brides forget that the bridal party does have to be officially invited. As a general rule of thumb, order 20% more invitations than you expect to need. For example, if your careful count says you need 100 invitations, order 120.

You and your fiancé can save the most time by knowing what style invitation you have in mind. Going into this job blind will mean looking at hundreds of different types of invitations. Even without a pushy salesperson, the task can be overwhelming. You might be torn, for instance, between a simple, classic, elegant style and a catchy, stylish, modern style in just your wedding colors. With each flip of the catalog page, another attractive option appears. The more you look, the more confused you become, and the further you get from your decision.

The best bet is to have some idea of what you want. Decide ahead of time if you want simple and elegant to match your formal dinner, a more romantic look, an informal look with a graphic and color, or a modern look that says *you*. Look at samples in magazines or on the Internet ahead of time, without ordering at this point, and see what the salesperson can show you.

> ## Wedding Day Reflections
>
>
>
> We just walked in there, said we wanted to see the Crane invitations, said we wanted a simple invitation on cream-colored paper. No frills, no extras, no little glittery swans or cherubs. The salesperson was great and flipped the catalog right open to a selection of three suitable designs. It took us only three minutes to decide.
>
> —Justina and Regg

Know, too, the many other elements of the invitation that require decisions from you—different types of paper, different types of printing styles, different fonts, all with different prices. So while you may see a style you like, you're not ready to check another job off your list and head out the door for a latte. The fun is only just beginning.

Again, without the information provided in this chapter, your head might be spinning. Armed with these explanations, though, you can make your choice and move on to the more fun stuff. Granted, planning invitations isn't the most enjoyable part of the wedding, but it is the one most ruled by etiquette, and you'll still have to play within the boundaries to a point. So let's talk about invitations as a whole.

What Type of Paper?

INVITATIONS don't just come on one kind of stiff paper. You can choose from dozens of paper styles, and you'll be looking at even more options as the world of print experiences even more artistic changes. By looking at invitations, holding them, feeling them in your hand, you'll see which kinds of papers will complement a more formal wedding invitation style. No doubt, you've seen plenty of invitations before, and have noticed that some papers are thicker than others. There is a reason for that, and it applies to formality, print, and price. So choose from these kinds of papers:

- *100% cotton:* This is the most common type of invitation paper, and also one of the least expensive. A good company will make a pure paper for the crisp capturing of print.

- *Corrugated:* More suitable for informal or at-home weddings with an artsy flair, this type of paper is thick and may have that "homemade paper" look. Very often, it is presented with a center fold or two middle folds, with print inside.

- *Jacquard:* Uses the layered-paper look through a printing that gives the impression of an overlay of fabric or lace on parts of the invitation. This is very popular, as brides and grooms look to make their invitations stand out from the usual forms.

- *Laid:* A lighter feel, a smoother blend like cotton, but with noticeable bumpy grain. It comes across as a natural paper, which is a great choice if your wedding is outside.

- *Linen:* A popular choice for all wedding styles. You have seen linen papers before in boxed stationery, and its less-smooth finish may be the perfect complement to the style of your invitation.

- *Moiré:* A smooth finish with watermarks pressed into the grain. Very often, the watermark gives a classic look to a plain-lettered invitation, giving that something extra without the need for adornment. It's there, but subtle. It catches your eye, but does not take away from the wording.

- *Parchment:* This type of paper is not just used as an insert in the invitation anymore. It's becoming the main attraction, as parchments are becoming slightly thicker, shaded, colored, and able to hold print. An invitation that comes on a piece of parchment creates an illusory, dreamy effect. It's a romantic image, one that even the most famous brides have sent their guests.

What Kind of Type?

THE print may all look the same to you, but invitations are printed using different technology. The kind of type you get could be very expensive or more moderate, depending on which of the following you choose:

ENGRAVED

This is the most expensive type, the kind you see with raised lettering and letter indentations on the back of the invitation. This print type is used for very formal weddings, by brides and grooms who have a large budget and some extra time to wait. Since the printing process is more involved, delivery time may require a few weeks, but the flawless product that comes out is the essence of style.

THERMOGRAPHED

This style of print is the most popular. The letters come out raised and formal-looking, just like engraved invitations, only you'll see no indentations on the back of the invitation. It's also a less expensive

> **Penny-Wise**
>
> **$**
>
> Keep in mind that heavier paper means a heavier invitation packet. The invitation may seem light, but your full envelope will have that invitation, a response card, two envelopes, and other items. Thus thicker paper will mean a heavier packet, and that will mean more postage for each of your invitations—perhaps enough to double or triple your postage bill, which does make a dent in the budget. So choose a lighter paper stock if you have a lot of heavy invitations to send.

option, with less turnaround time. In sense of appearance, this is a wise choice. Most printing companies use this printing method a majority of the time, so the process is much more finely tuned.

CALLIGRAPHY

Handcrafting adds a special touch, but you do not have to spend months learning to perfect each line of calligraphy. Nor do you have to spend a lot of money on professional calligraphers, unless you choose to do so. Computer programs now come with calligraphy fonts and services, so you may be able to choose a calligraphy style that's as simple as typing in your wording. If, however, you only have a few invitations to do, hiring someone to do a fine calligraphy job is a great way to go. Be sure to get referrals, see samples, and choose the style of calligraphy you want, from gothic to Celtic to more modern styles, and a good calligrapher who can write in your chosen model.

COLOR

Several of the above-mentioned print types can be done in color. Although the most widely accepted wedding invitation is black ink on white or cream-colored paper, color is creeping into the picture. Now, some brides and grooms are choosing a subtle blush pink paper with a deeper rose-colored print. Thermography, offset printing (where available), laser printing, and calligraphy can handle this task. So if you want color in your invitations, consider your options and the fact that color is often more expensive.

MELANIE AND TOM'S STORY

It was Melanie's second wedding and Tom's first wedding. They agreed upon everything, except for the fact that Melanie really had her heart set on a pretty invitation with hearts around the border and a pale green print (to match the colors of her wedding). Tom gave her that decision, and the invitations went out in the mail.

A few weeks later, the guests started calling with questions. What should they wear? Was it a formal wedding? They simply couldn't tell from the invitation they had received, and Melanie found herself constantly on the phone telling everyone that yes, it was a formal wedding, and formal was the dress code.

Looking back, the couple realized that the invitation was more than Melanie's own personal design statement; it was a tool of information for their guests. Melanie's simple choice to add color actually made more work for the couple and confused the guests. Some guests actually came in less-formal attire, not knowing that the wedding was one of those black-tie events.

Choosing a Style

I'VE already discussed the issues of choosing a style of invitation that adequately reflects the formality of the wedding. Now we'll tackle the issue of choosing a specific style of invitation.

While the decision is completely up to you, depending upon how the pieces of your wedding fit together, here is further advice about choosing invitation styles.

- *Simpler is better.* Just choose a plain invitation with a simple border and easily readable wording.

- *Skip the glittery stuff.* It may look nice, but guests have complained to me over the years about that darn glitter getting all over the place.

- *If you're having a less formal, theme wedding, let your invitation reflect that.* One bride who was planning a beach-themed wedding chose an invitation with a delicate starfish and some shells in the top corner. Her guests could figure out the theme, and some gave her gifts with starfish and beach themes that she could proudly use in her home.

♦ *Make sure it says you.* If you're a laid-back couple, go for a simple style that suits your personalities. If you're worldly and sophisticated, flashy and unique, choose a style that speaks of your essence.

Wedding Day Reflections

We *found a great way to go with our golf-themed wedding. My fiancé and I had met at a golf course, so we did the whole golf-theme thing. Our invitations had golf phrases like "tee time" and had little golf tees all around the edges. Of course, our wedding was an outdoor tea party held at the country club, so this was perfect.*

—Arielle and Jacob

The Little Inserts

OF course, your invitation packet will include not just the invitation itself, but several little notable extras. The invitation catalog will almost certainly offer matching styles of the following:

RESPONSE CARDS

Sunday, the fourteenth of March
_____ *will attend*
_____ *will not attend*

RECEPTION CARDS

Reception
following cocktail party
at
The Highlawn Pavilion
Eagle Rock Reservation
8 o'clock in the evening

HOTEL INFORMATION CARDS

On these, list the name of the hotel where the block of rooms is reserved, the last name to provide for identification as a member of that block of rooms, prices, the reservations phone line, and the availability of non-smoking rooms.

PRINTED DIRECTIONS

You might help your guests find the ceremony, reception, and possibly hotel locations—and avoid the otherwise inevitable "How do

I get there?" calls—by enclosing printed directions in your invitations. For example:

From Route 287: Take Exit 22 to Bedminster, turn left . . .

AN AT-HOME CARD

Print your after-wedding residence and contact number and enclose with your invitations to save additional correspondence.

Annabelle and Scott Johnston
1121 Pleasant Valley Way
Hanover, New Hampshire 00000
(300) 555-0000

INVITATION CARDS

You might enclose invitations to whatever other events will be going on that weekend, such as brunches, barbecues, and other outings. For cxample:

You are invited
To a pre-wedding brunch
In the main dining room
of the Ramada Hotel
Saturday morning
7:00 A.M. to 10:00 A.M.
Dress is casual.
Mr. and Mrs. Anderson are hosting this event

Buying Time

Have the ceremony site and reception site managers provide you with maps or clear step-by-step directions from all major approaches to your area. Often these directions are already available and ready for use, and your simple request can save you hours in researching all the rights and lefts, merges and stop signs along each route to your wedding.

Remember to order the same number of each extra as you do of the invitations, so that extras are available to include in all packages.

Envelopes

AGAIN, the invitation package you choose will most often come with its own matching envelope pairings. Speak with the invitation salesperson about the number of enclosures you'll have, and she should be able to help you select the size of envelopes you'll need.

Remember that most formal and even informal invitations packages include an inner and outer envelope for your use, and a smaller envelope for the return of the response card. So order 20% more envelopes of both sizes than you think you'll need, as mistakes are almost always made when hand-addressing all your envelopes. We'll talk more about assembling your invitations below.

Stay away from designed envelopes, ones with décor on the outside, colored envelopes, and ones with glitter on them. Not only do most people find these tacky, but my friends at the U.S. Post Office say that large envelopes with lots of details sometimes get stuck in the processing machines. Postal workers also find it difficult to process some shades of colored envelopes. So keep your choices clean and clear.

Stress Relief

Do not attempt to save time by using your computer to print out a merged list of all your wedding guests onto labels that you can just slap onto the envelopes. It doesn't matter how pretty a font you have, even if it looks just like calligraphy. Printed envelopes are tacky, they'll always be tacky, and your guests will notice.

Finding the Right Words

EVEN I hate this part. Of all wedding elements, finding the correct wording to put on an invitation is perhaps the worst task of the entire preparation. Weddings used to be pretty much cookie-cutter events—first marriage for both the bride and groom, the bride's family paying for most of it, the bride's parents "giving her away." In other words, the formal wedding was pretty much standard.

With all the changes in the wedding industry and in the types of couples who marry—with their own resources, their own histories, their own likes and dislikes, and a general panning away from etiquette rules—the invitation remains the last bastion of strict rules, at least to parents.

You probably have an eyebrow raised right now, and may be thinking, "But I thought anything goes these days, that we're moving away from etiquette." Although that's true in general, in this area you're not only dealing with information on a piece of paper; you're dealing with family dynamics. Let me explain:

Countless brides have come to me to ask what they should do about the wording of their invitations. The couple is paying for the wedding, but their parents want to be listed on the invitation. The couple said no, and now a war is raging. The parents want to *not be left out*. What would their friends think of this snub? They are, after all, honored guests and should be mentioned on the invitation. The bride, in this case, stood firm and said that since she and her fiancé have planned it, paid for it, and arranged it, it's their wedding, and only their names will be on the invitation. The parents, of course, scoffed and gave the couple's plan an icy reception.

Other brides with less stubborn and selfish parents have not had the same problem result from their assertiveness. You have to know your own parents to gauge whether or not they'll be okay with this, it seems; but it's even more important to have your invitation honor the right people.

BRIANNA AND ETHAN'S STORY

Brianna has about four mothers and three fathers, when you add up all of her biological parents, adopted parents, step-parents, and others. They've all played an important role in her life, yet she didn't want her wedding invitation to read like a Who's Who list. Her now-divorced adoptive parents, who ranked first in her mind, should be listed as her parents, but that would undermine the relationships she's been building with her step-parents and her recently found biological parents.

Rules for Invitation Wording

- For formal weddings, you'll go with the old English spellings of some words, like honour and favour.

- Spell everything out, such as "Street" and "Avenue."

- Times, for example 3:00 P.M., should be spelled out as "three o'clock in the afternoon."

- Provide a street location and town for sites.

- Spell out all names in full, formal spelling.

- Use appropriate titles where necessary. For example, if your fiancé is a captain in the navy, his name would be "Captain James Anderson."

- Don't use bold lettering. All print should be the same.

- Make sure your wording is accurate, check and double-check, have the salesperson read it back to you, and be sure your order is perfect.

For more complete descriptions of the various invitation-wording etiquette standards, consult *Emily Post's Complete Book of Modern Wedding Etiquette* by Elizabeth L. Post.

Always the problem-solver, Ethan jumped in with a wonderful solution: They would begin the invitation with, "The many loving parents of Brianna Marie request the honour of your attendance. . . ." It was a simple solution, one that actually satisfied all her parents. No one was ranked. No one was left out. Brianna had suggested that idea to her many friends with only two sets of divorced parents, and the trend continues to roll on.

The best way to deal with this problem is to have a frank discussion with both sets of parents about your decision as to the wording of the invitation. They may balk about your phrasing or the ranking (or absence) of their names, but it is your decision. Of course, if you have gone the traditional route and had your parents pay for everything or help out a lot, don't snub them now. Just go by the rules and exercise good family diplomacy for the sake of future happiness.

Now, we get into the standard wording for the various types of wedding situations out there. Follow these models and create your own correct style of wording for your invitations.

Following are examples for various invitation situations.

BRIDE'S PARENTS HOSTING WEDDING

Mr. and Mrs. Stephen Kelly
request the honour of your presence
at the marriage of their daughter
Eleanor Lorraine
And
Lawrence Kennedy Kasdan
son of
Mr. and Mrs. Michael Kasdan
Saturday, the twenty-fifth of May
at three o'clock in the afternoon
St. Mary's Church
12 Bishop Street
San Francisco, California

. . . .

BOTH SETS OF PARENTS HOSTING

Mr. and Mrs. Stephen Kelly
And
Mr. and Mrs. Michael Kasdan
request the honour of your company
at the marriage of their children
Eleanor Lorraine
And
Lawrence Kennedy Kasdan

. . . .

DIVORCED PARENTS HOSTING

Mr. Allan Riesdale
And
Mrs. Jessica Riesdale
request the honour of your company
at the wedding of their daughter
Annabelle Claire
To
Mr. Scott Henry Johnston

. . . .

MULTIPLE SETS OF PARENTS HOSTING

The loving parents of
Annabelle Claire Riesdale
request the honour of your company
as their daughter unites in marriage with
Mr. Scott Henry Johnston

. . . .

BRIDE AND GROOM HOSTING

Ms. Annabelle Claire Riesdale
And
Mr. Scott Henry Johnston
Request the honour of your presence
as they unite in marriage

. . . .

LESS FORMAL INVITATIONS

You may have noticed some subtle differences in the wording within the invitation. Not all styles and formalities are suited to the ultra-deluxe English spellings of invitation words. Less formal wedding invitations may be worded as such:

We're finally tying the knot!
You're invited to join us on our wedding day,
To share in our celebration,
Drink a toast,
Watch the sunset,
And dance all night with us
As we light up
Pier A
In Hoboken, New Jersey
At Frank Sinatra Park
On Friday the sixteenth of June
At 7:00 P.M.

Other, more personalized invitations fit for informal or home weddings can use any number of fun wording styles. If you aren't going the traditional route, you have more freedom with your invitations. All you have to do is remember that your invitation includes some very important cues for your guests, and it will become a forever keepsake for yourself.

KENDRA AND MICHAEL'S STORY

We were planning a beach wedding—before the whole *Survivor* television series came along and threatened to make us look cheesy. But we kept it within our tastes, and we did an amazing thing with our invitations. We printed our invitations out on paper that we had "aged" with wet teabags and a short, safe bake in the oven. We scribbled out our invitation information on each, rolled them into scrolls, and stuffed each in a worn, sea-glass bottle with a cork that we found for fifty cents each at a gift shop near the shore. Each of our guests got a "message in a bottle" as their invitation, and they loved it. It was easy, inexpensive, and we didn't have to wait for ordering.

Ah, ordering. All the style-choosing, correct wording, and enve-lope-stuffing in the world will not make up for the time it takes to order and have invitations delivered. Most standard invitation com-panies whose books you looked at in the stationery store have a turn-around of eight to ten weeks. Add that to the six to eight weeks' notice you should give your guests, and a good week for addressing, stamp-ing, and sending all those invitations, and you're looking at a large lead time—around four months! Those invitations might have to be ordered *now* if you're to get them in time before your wedding.

Standard Orders Through Stationery Stores

THE best companies, such as Cranes, can deliver in that standard time of eight to ten weeks, but will charge extra for rush orders. Check on what delivery time is as you go, and whether you have the time for standard ordering in the first place. Be sure to fill in the order form carefully. In most cases, the salesperson at the shop will help you fill it out, will let you proofread and give it your final okay, and then start talking about payment.

Mail-Order Invitations

WHILE mail-order selection may not be as large as what you'd see in a lineup of books in a stationery store, this is still a good option. Many brides report good results with mail-order invitation companies, and even Leah Ingram, author of *Your Wedding Your Way* suggests this as a viable alternative to the standard invitation mills. If you've sent for the right catalogs, you'll find that the collections of these individual com-panies have more off-beat invitations, very graphics-oriented choices with a large degree of individuality. Such orders are likely to take less than the standard eight to ten weeks, and will almost certainly be less expensive. If you do choose this option, fill out your order form very carefully to prevent errors, and allow enough time for the company to reprint in case any errors do occur. Also, be sure you have a refund and reprint guarantee in your contract.

Note that invitation catalogs are trying hard to compete with online competitors. Many are offering amazing lines of invitations packages at cut rates, in addition to a 10% to 15% discount. For both online and mail-order invitations, you will have to pay a shipping fee and insurance, so be sure to factor those costs into your budget.

Online Invitation Orders

By "online invitation orders," I do *not* mean sending invitations online. While some sites are trying that trend on for size, it is just not working in the wedding industry. Some people do not have e-mail, some don't get all their e-mail messages, some save it and forget to print it out, some lose all their e-mail to a computer virus, and so on. Not only are the logistics dangerous; it's just plain tacky to send out your invitations via an e-mail "CC" option. By online ordering, I mean searching online invitation ordering catalogs and companies. As with any other wedding industry, I'd suggest you check these companies thoroughly. An image on a computer screen will not give you an accurate preview of what your invitation will look like, or feel like, so you're in essence ordering blindly. Plus, you'll need to create a rock-solid contract, give your personal information out over the computer, and trust a company in the new world of e-commerce to meet your understandably great need for reliability and quality. I can't sway you either way, but I do urge you to research this one carefully.

Say the Word

If you're in a dire rush and are placing your order over the phone, take these extra steps. Direct the salesperson not only to read your order back to you, but to spell every word, specify every capitalized letter, note when a new line is started, and name again the type of print and catalog style order.

The Do-It-Yourself Route

IF you're really short on time—and money—or if you want total control over your invitations, you can design them yourselves. A great many brides and grooms have done this, following the steps listed below:

♦ *Have all the pertinent information at the ready.* This includes the day of the week, date, time, location of the ceremony, street address of the ceremony site, reception location name and address, and the correct spellings of all of your entries.

♦ *Get a supply of good invitation paper stock or suitably designed paper.* You can find it at a stationery store, or even at a business supply store such as Staples and OfficeMax. These chains know that a proliferation of couples are using their own computers to print out wedding invitations and other paper items so they stock attractive, high-quality papers at a steep discount.

♦ *Use a good computer design program.* Even a standard one such as Microsoft Word can give you a beautiful layout, hundreds of fonts and sizes to choose from, borders, even clip art and graphic design elements. If you're a true computer genius, you can use other design programs, scanners, and your own clip art.

♦ *Fine-tune your design on inexpensive paper.* Spend some time arranging the wording on the page, then practice printing it out onto regular paper so you can see how it would lay out on the official paper.

♦ *Test your design on your chosen card stock.* Create your invitation and print it out on your chosen card stock to see how the final product will look.

♦ *Consider getting your creation professionally duplicated.* While I would suggest using your own printer for all your invitations, you might not want to put your machines through that kind of drain. Instead, take a solid, crisp printout of your invitation on regular white paper, along with your card stock, to a reputable printer in town and have him duplicate your invitations and smaller cards. In the end, you may not save as much as if you printed everything yourself, but it does ensure a quality invitation on every copy, no computer foul-ups, and a great outcome with less time wasted.

LEILA AND DAVID'S STORY

Leila and David had the most beautiful wedding invitations I've ever seen. Leila painted lilacs (her favorite flower) onto a card stock, and David designed an officially worded invitation in a unique font that captured their ethnic backgrounds. They not only provided all the "stats" of their wedding, but they put in some Hawaiian quotes at the bottom to complement the theme of their wedding.

With her artwork, and his choice of quotes—something that could never have been created by any other professional invitation designer—the couple created a wonderful, unique invitation that took their guests' breath away.

Leila confided that it only took her a half-hour to do the painting, and that David only spent an hour in front of the computer doing the wording. They took the final product to the printers, and had their invitations the next day. Now that may be the way to do it!

Getting Ready to Assemble the Invitation Packets

THE invitations have arrived with no mistakes, and you have all the inserts in piles on the kitchen table, waiting to be assembled into packets and sent out. Hold it right there! First take the following time-saving steps:

Assemble one packet completely, with all response cards, reception cards, maps, paper inserts, and so on. Then take that complete packet to the post office and ask the postal worker to just weigh it, not stamp it. You'll find out whether it will require a single stamp or a double stamp. If you've chosen smaller invitations, thinner paper, and have not included lots of inserts, a single stamp should do. Remember, too, that you'll need a stamp for the inside response card, and then you can calculate your stamp order. Always get twenty or so extra. They won't go to waste.

Before you begin addressing your envelopes and assembling your invitation packages, make sure you have the full, correct addresses for everyone on your list. Your fiancé's side of the family should have provided theirs already, and you should have all the addresses for your side's guest list. But if any street numbers, apartment numbers, or zip codes are missing, you can tackle the job quickly with a phone call to that recipient.

> ### *Buying Time*
>
>
>
> *Go to the post office as soon as they open so you're less likely to face long lines, busy times, and stressed postal workers.*

With your postage needs set, your list complete, and everything in front of you ready to go, there's just one step left: assembling the packages.

In most cases, figuring out how to do it is fairly easy. You put the invitation down first, the tissue paper over the print. Lay on top of these any enclosure materials such as the stamped response card, reception card, at-home card, and folded map or directions sheet. That's your first part of the package.

Then, slip these into the slightly smaller inner envelope, print side up. Address this envelope with just the names of the people invited, again going by formality. If you're having a formal wedding, you will write *Mr. and Mrs. John Smith*. If you're having a more informal wedding, write *Donald and Janice*. If this envelope is for a family, the inner envelope will read *Mr. and Mrs. Smith* with the children's names *Sarah, Aimee, and Dennis* centered below their parent's names.

It is very important that you list the names of the actual guests you are inviting on this inner envelope. Without this information, your guests may assume their kids are invited or not invited. It leaves room for questions, and assumptions may be made.

After you write the names on each inner envelope, immediately do the outer envelope. A sample reads as follows:

Mr. and Mrs. Andrew Bennett
343 Jefferson Road
Houston, Texas 87369

Again, spell out all words, and always include the fundamentally important zip code.

One item that trips up brides and grooms is guests who will be bringing a "date." You may not know who this person is, yet writing "Paul Meyers and Guest" on an inner envelope does seem odd. For this situation, ask Paul who he's bringing, record her name, and write the name on the envelope. Even though you don't yet know her, she still is one of your guests, and should be called by her name.

Buying Time

Before you call friends and family all over the country to verify addresses, check—for free—the Internet White Pages at www. whitepages.com. They can give you addresses for anyone in the United States. If it's just a zip code you need, use the U.S. Post Office's Web site at www.usps.gov/ welcome.htm.

When to Send?

TRADITIONALLY, wedding invitations go out six to eight weeks before the wedding. If your wedding is just a few short months away, think about sending your invitations earlier. Take into consideration the fact that your guests may have travel or business plans. Their kids may be out of school on break at that time. Or, it may be a big travel weekend for a busy holiday.

If you're asking guests to travel across several states to attend your wedding, respect their planning time by giving them even more notice than those eight weeks.

With short-time notice, you ought to give all of your guests the most advance information as possible. Too many brides and grooms report disappointment that loved ones who already had previous unbreakable commitments were unable to attend. Scheduling problems are an inevitable fact of timing, but you can cut down the odds of hassles and disappointments by sending your invitations sooner rather than later.

Wedding Day Reflections

We tried to be formal and kind with our single guests' friends, so we sent our friends' invited guests their own invitations. While it did take extra time and cost us some extra money, the guests very much appreciated it. Who knows? We may be going to their weddings someday!

—Sonia and Charles

RSVPs

Your invitation should spell out an RSVP date early enough to enable you to provide a solid headcount to the caterer, florist, cake baker, and all other professionals. Most guests do respond in time, but there are always stragglers who do not send the response card back on time. That will take a simple call to ask the guest whether he or she is or isn't coming to the wedding. Many brides have had to take a stand here, due to an irresponsible guest. Some waffle with the "I don't know yet . . ." or "I have to check my schedule still. . . ." Again, this is not the time to be a people-pleaser. Simply explain that you're on a rushed deadline and need to know right away. Tell him he has until tomorrow, or he's off the list. Say it nicely; don't attack. He'll get the message. It just may be that no one's ever made him be responsible before.

You might also find that your guest is embarrassed that she lost her response card. Just be understanding, assure her that you're misplacing things left and right, and that you're happy she's coming. Everyone's off the hook.

The Additional Mailer

THE time has come for the additional mailer trend. As weddings become more expansive events, with activities planned throughout the weekend, brides and grooms often provide bigger informational packets to their guests. I've seen couples send veritable packets of material for their guests' use, and the guests were thrilled when these packages arrived. Here are some of the more ingenious inclusions I've seen:

- A personal message from the bride and groom, sharing how the planning is coming along (This is almost always humor-laced, as their guests may not want to know about the push and pull between the bride and her future mother-in-law, the testy cake baker, or the bratty flower girl's fitting.)

- A brochure of the hotel at which the guest will be staying (Just ask the manager for as many as you need. It's free publicity!)

- A list of nearby hotels if the guests will be making their own plans

- A travel guide or tour book of the surrounding area, landmarks, spots to see

- A list of activities for kids to do in the area, such as playgrounds, zoos, even what movies are playing that weekend at the local theater

> ## *Stress Relief*
>
>
>
> **H**ere's another "Anti-Timesaver." Some brides set the RSVP up so they can get them via e-mail or through their Web site. It sounds like an easy step, and indeed some wedding programs out there can "take care" of RSVPs for you. But e-mail sometimes does not get through, and there is no replacement for having a response card in hand. So, it is best to skip the e-mail responses, for reliability's sake.

♦ Invitations to family events during the long weekend (Barbecues, brunches, mini-golf tournaments, and spa days have all been listed with complete directions, prices, and "coupons.")

♦ Maps to all wedding-specific sites

One bride even made little care packages for the kids who would be coming by long train, plane, and car rides. She collected little games, crossword puzzle books, joke books, crayons and pads, and other thoughtful items that would get the kids into town without major tantrums . . . from either the kids or their frazzled parents.

Penny-Wise

*Y*ou don't have to buy stationery and letterhead that matches the style and print of your other wedding papers. In fact, you're likely to find a better deal through another company. American Stationery, for one, offers a wide range of cards, papers, and letterheads in a variety of prints, colors, and formalities. Their prices are competitive, and they deliver in just three to four weeks. Address labels take six to eight weeks for this company. You can get their catalog by calling (800) 822-2577. I've sampled many stationery companies, and American Stationery is the best I've worked with.

Thank-You Notes and Other Stationery

Most brides and grooms order these now, in addition to their invitation packages. You'll save time by ordering while you're already entrenched in the world of calligraphy, papers, fonts, and borders.

Choose a simple style, an elegant letterhead, and personal stationery. One advantage of placing this order now is that you will have professional and official stationery that declares your name. Whether or not you take your groom's name is your personal choice, and your pronouncement through the printing of these papers means that no one will need to ask your name, call you by the wrong name, or get the spelling of your new name wrong. They'll also have your new address and phone number, which saves your having to send post-

Wording for Thank-You Notes

Here are a few examples to give you ideas for the wording of your thank-you notes.

Thank you so much for sharing our day with us, and for your generous gift. Mark and I will use it toward a down payment on our first home. And you'll be one of our first guests! We were so happy to have you as part of our day.

Our thanks and love, Mark and Eliza

Thank you so much for the beautiful wedding gift. We love the vase so much — it reminds us of our trip to Venice — and we will display it in our living room. It was so wonderful to have you there on our wedding day, and that dance we shared was forever a memory for me.

Love, Crystal and Tom

Thank you so much for being a part of our wedding day. We couldn't have pulled it off so well without your help. You truly added to the beauty of our day, and we will be forever grateful for your help and for your friendship and love.

Always, Megan and Sam

According to etiquette experts throughout the years, you do have up to a year to send your thank-you notes, so don't start stressing about that yet. Just choose a simple style right now, and place your order.

cards to your friends. It's a simple win-win situation—one that does not have to cost a fortune if you choose your styles well.

For your thank-you notes, a simple style with perhaps a cutout for a wedding photo will suffice. Choose a style that is blank inside, rather than one with a pre-printed message. Since you do have to write a handwritten message anyway—that's a must! This will save you time, room, and money.

15

PLANNING THE HONEYMOON

MAKING A DREAM GETAWAY COME TRUE

THIS ISN'T LIKE planning any ordinary vacation. This is the big one: your honeymoon—the vacation you'll remember for the rest of your life. It's your getaway, your reward for these months of planning, and the symbolic start of your new life together.

Many brides with lengthy planning time have the luxury of looking at every honeymoon package out there—spending days at the travel agency flipping through full-color, splashy brochures and considering every option open to them. At this late date, however, you're facing some monumental efforts, depending upon when and where you want to go. Remember, most places have been booked for a while. Availability is limited, especially if you're marrying during one of the crowded times of the year.

BEVERLY AND MICHAEL'S STORY

Being quite young themselves, Beverly and Michael knew enough about spring break time to avoid the college scene hotspots. Their honeymoon would be during spring break season, and they didn't want their romantic walks on the beach to be disturbed by wet T-shirt contests, keg parties, and hot buns competitions. They also knew that spring breakers were not just flocking to the beaches. In some parts of the country, they were going skiing, so the big ski resorts were also full of rowdy, hard-drinking young people.

So, knowing their travel time, they chose a non–spring break destination, a four-star bed and breakfast in South Carolina, and thus found the quiet and peace they wanted in an idyllic, romantic setting.

While you may think that nothing will be available and you'll be stuck at the Motel 6 down the road, you should know that tens of thousands of honeymoon opportunities are out there. You'll just have to begin your search by asking yourself a few important questions to help you narrow down the overwhelming number of choices. Spend some time discussing with your fiancé what you want as far as style of honeymoon, what your budget is, and how much time you have. We'll take these one at a time.

When Will You Be Honeymooning?

You've booked your wedding, say, three months in advance. That works for most aspects of your wedding. Now, it's time to book something that really fits what you want for your honeymoon. At this late time, you may find that the major resorts in your chosen destination have no honeymoon packages or suites. So, what are your options? You might ask whether regular rooms are available. You may not get the king-sized bed, the Jacuzzi, and the marvelous view of the azure sea, but you may only use your room at night (ahem), so the accommodations may not mean that much to you. If you're planning your honeymoon late, you may have to be flexible about the kind of room you'll book and the package you buy.

Or perhaps you didn't think about the fact that your honeymoon coincides with high travel time, and you find all the flights booked. You may have to book an airline other than the one you usually take. Again, flexibility is important, as is taking time to work with an established travel agent to create your own honeymoon package where none exists. With the help of the right professional, you can quickly find a great resort at a perfect honeymoon destination that is *not* experiencing peak time.

Do yourself a favor and stay away from hot travel times if you can. Prices will be up, availability will be low, and your options will be frustratingly limited.

What Do You Want in Honeymoon Style?

YOUR preference of honeymoon style is one of the first details you'll need to know. Do you want that relaxing week at a beach resort, with miles and miles of pristine sand stretching on either side, clear blue ocean waters ahead, steel drum music playing in the background as you lazily sip piña coladas from a hammock swinging between two palm trees? Or do you want an adventure honeymoon filled with tours and sports, horseback riding on the beach, hiking through the Mayan ruins, wreck diving, and white-water rafting? "Honeymoon" does not mean the same thing to all people. Some couples' lifestyles and personalities lend themselves to the laidback vacation; others would climb the walls if they didn't have something to do every minute. So decide what the two of you want—quiet, adventurous, or a mix of both—before you start the hunt for the greatest vacation of your life.

Avoid a Crowded Honeymoon

These are times you'll find availability is limited:

♦ High honeymoon season (July through September)

♦ School-time vacation breaks (March through April)

♦ High tourism seasons in your chosen destination (varies)

♦ Holiday weekends (Christmas/ New Year's, Memorial Day, 4th of July)

What Is Your Honeymoon Budget?

IT all comes down to what you can afford. While some lucky couples get their honeymoon package as a wedding gift from one or both sets of parents (don't you hate them?), you're more likely to swing your honeymoon on your own dime. That said, you'll have to look carefully at what you can spend. A long-distance honeymoon, such as a trip from Florida to Hawaii, will cost plenty for airfare alone. A European honeymoon will cost a fortune. On the other hand, a week at a nearby four-star beach resort will cost less. Compare the package and airfare costs for each of your desired destinations, and you'll soon see what kind of honeymoon is within your budget. This step will often eliminate some unrealistic options, and will help you zero in on your best choices.

Say the Word

It may seem as though you can save a lot of time by booking your honeymoon package and flights through the Internet. While that may prove true for some, I'm hearing a lot about travelers who did not seek the professional knowledge that travel agents have and failed to do enough homework on their own. As a result, they experienced honeymoon nightmares. Those "inexpensive flights" were actually on sub-par airlines, and those "great hotel rates" included no extras. So go with a pro, especially with your short planning time.

How Much Time Do You Have?

IF you're planning a late-stage wedding, with just a few months or even weeks to spare, you may have very few vacation days accumulated at work. Last-minute planners especially have to assess the number of vacation days they have available for their honeymoon—perhaps only a week, or maybe just enough for a long weekend. If, for instance, you have only a week, you might forgo a faraway honeymoon that requires two or three of your seven days be taken up by travel time. If you have just five days, your cruise options will be limited. By looking at how much off-time each of you has, you may further narrow your honeymoon choices.

By knowing what you have in mind, you've eliminated lots of unnecessary search work. You can walk into the travel agent's office and tell her what kind of honeymoon you want, and be guided by a professional toward booking a great getaway.

Start Looking *Now!*

THIS is not a job you can leave until the last minute. You'll have so many details to think about, ask about, and arrange—perhaps as many as you faced when planning the rest of the wedding—that you'll need plenty of time to sort through your options so you can create the best honeymoon package for you and your fiancé.

Yes, you know that it's possible to get a great airfare through on-line price clubs at the last minute, or that it's not high tourism season on Hilton Head Island. But that doesn't mean you'll get the ideal vacation out of it. Online price clubs may indeed get you to Hilton Head, but you may have to take an out-of-the-way flight or several connecting flights. The Westin in Hilton Head may be booked—even during the off-season—with conferences. Leave nothing to the last minute, as booking a honeymoon entails a host of responsibilities and the threat of major extra expenses if it's not handled well.

So set out on this planning stage by sitting down with your fiancé and talking about what you want. If he's an action guy, and you'd prefer reading the latest Tom Clancy novel on the beach, choose a location that provides activities for both of you. If you don't like to fly, consider a short boat trip to a nearby island or resort town, or take the train.

With this detailed discussion, you're then able to go to your travel agent, together, with your list of wants and don't-wants. A good travel agent loves working with decisive couples who come in for short-term planning sessions. Their time is important, too, and they hate having

Honeymoon Decisions

No doubt you've traveled together before and know one another's likes and dislikes, and you generally know what kind of honeymoon you want. But it's important that you discuss ahead of time details such as these:

- *What are our dream destinations?* Start with this one, even though other questions may bring you back to reality.

- *How much time do we have and want to spend on vacation?* You may want to leave a few days for relaxing after your return before you have to head back to work.

- *How much money do we have and want to spend?* Check the list of extra expenses later in this chapter.

- *Do we want a relaxed vacation or an active one?*

to show a waffling couple ten thousand brochures. So when you walk in the door, have this information ready for the best and fastest first steps toward planning your honeymoon:

- The dates you'll be traveling or honeymooning
- Your budget
- The locations you're interested in
- Whether or not you currently have valid passports
- The activities you want available at your location
- The style of vacation you want (such as relaxed or active)
- The resort chains you're interested in

- *What kind of activities are we looking for?*

- *Do we want to travel far away, or stay close by?*

- *Should we fly, take the train, or drive?*

- *Are cruises a possibility?*

- *Do we have time for the paperwork, red tape, and planning we might need?* This might include getting a passport, shots, and so on.

- *Should we travel the day after the wedding, a few days after, or when?* This does make a difference in price, as leaving-on-Saturday fares may be significantly lower.

Another important factor to consider is what kind of room you want. Stay away from the honeymoon suite, as mentioned earlier. It's more expensive and highly booked, and most resorts are of such high quality right now that there really is no difference between the honeymoon suite and the higher-end regular rooms. You can do without a Jacuzzi in your room if there's one down by the pool. Think about what you really need in your room, and be ready to state which of the following choices you want to book:

- King-sized bed or two doubles (two can fit snugly in a double!)

- Smoking or non-smoking

- Terrace or non-terrace

- ◆ Ocean view, pool view, or not-too-great view

- ◆ Refrigerator in room

- ◆ Mini-bar

- ◆ Shower and bath

- ◆ Air-conditioning (very important if you're going to a hot climate)

Wedding Day Reflections

The whole place was like honey-moon central. During dinner, the whole night, the DJ kept calling out couples' names to get the crowd to applaud, and if the couple wasn't there, the DJ would say something tacky like "Well, we know what they're doing right now." It was very annoying, and we all felt like we were under a microscope.

—Tania and Richard

If you know exactly what you want, you won't waste time trying to weigh so many options—plus travel agents and reservations clerks will love you!

Another consideration is whether you want to go to a place that is honeymoon-exclusive or couples-only. Some couples-only resorts are geared toward couples in love or out on flings as well as honeymooners. You'll find dance parties and beach parties, nude beaches, skinny-dipping, and so on.

On the flip side, find out whether your chosen destination is a family-oriented resort spot. Just as annoying as couples having open sex on the beach could be packs of screaming kids brandishing water pistols or following their camp leader on scavenger hunts. While you can't control who will be at your resort during your honeymoon, you can get a feel for the clientele likely at that time of the year. Ask your travel agent whether your destination is a couples' resort, a family resort, or some other type of specialty place. One befuddled couple, not knowing the lingo, booked over the Internet for a weekend at a "naturalist resort." Being nature-lovers and bird-watchers, they expected a place that catered to eco-friendly people. Instead, they spent the entire weekend as the only couple who kept their clothes on at a nudist resort.

Don't Spend Your Honeymoon in Hiding

One last detail to consider is the weather. Will you be facing hurricane season out where you want to go? In late August, for instance, the Caribbean and Atlantic islands are known for getting smacked with hurricanes of all levels, and the eastern coast of the United States is also at risk. So ask the travel agent about weather advisories during that part of the year, and check with weather Web sites such as www.weather.com. Choose your destination based on the projected weather, so you can avoid high heat, humidity, rainstorms, hurricanes, tornadoes, or other uninvited guests Mother Nature may send.

Honeymoon Packages Versus Regular Packages

ONE thing you'll face that might confuse and tempt you at first is the honeymoon travel package presentation. The lineup of offerings—travel, transportation, lodging, dinners, and activities all for one price—may have you thinking: "Great, that's easy!" A package, however, may not be all that it appears. Never take a honeymoon package that you haven't checked out fully. Yes, some are amazing, such as one that Aruba's tourism department recently offered, but it's important that you investigate carefully each element of a package. Anything can be explained in glowing terms, but the realities may be less "interesting."

Although pricing the individual items in a package may take time, you might learn that you can book your honeymoon at that same resort as a regular guest, and pay less than you would as a honeymooning couple. Use these criteria to decide whether a package is worth its cost:

Know Where You're Going

Do a bit of research on your desired sites before you visit your travel agent. For example, if you've heard that the locals are quite unfriendly if not dangerous in some parts of Jamaica, or that there are uprisings in Peru, call the U.S. State Department's Travel Advisory Board at (202) 647-5225 to see whether any major situations are going on that may hamper your vacation. Brewing coups could necessitate spending your honeymoon in a bomb shelter. A dangerous location could mean that you can't leave the resort grounds—which are fenced in by unattractive barbed wire—without an armed hotel escort. Ask questions and do your own research as well.

Wedding Day Reflections

We so wanted to go scuba diving during our honeymoon that we had underwater cameras and everything. But our resort, which offered the lessons for free, required you to sign up for this three-day course that took all day. So we couldn't do it, and we were really disappointed.

—Cindy and Ken

♦ *Travel is included.* What kind of travel rates are they offering? What airline? Can you get a better fare yourself on another airline? Can you get discount fares or use your frequent-flier miles? Check it out!

♦ *Accommodations for seven days and six nights. Itemize this bill.* This is where the savings are likely to be legitimate, as some rooms go for $500 a night. Again, check out what a lower-ranked but still beautiful room goes for, and see whether you might save by booking your own room.

♦ *All meals included.* This feature could be great if you were to eat every meal in the same dining room at the hotel or at the same snack bar by the pool. But most honeymooners want to travel the area, eat at different places, and sample the local cuisine. So you'd be wasting money if you're paying for uneaten dinners at the hotel's bistro while shelling out additional cash for lobster bisque at a nice place across the island.

- *Breakfast included.* Do they serve full breakfasts, or continental? Will a tray of exotic fruits and freshly baked breads, coffees, and juices be brought to your room, or will you be eating mini-bagels along with other guests in the hotel lobby?

- *Activities available.* Watch this one! *Available* does not mean *free.* The golf course may be nearby, but exorbitant greens fees might prevent your playing it. The tennis courts may be affordable, but a three-day wait for courts might rule out your playing a match. Find out exactly what activities are available, what the fees are, and what's involved as far as reservations.

> ### Say the Word
>
>
>
> Speaking of unwelcome guests, think about the fact that many islands are densely populated with insects, especially during the hot, humid months. You may find it worth calling your resort to ask when they're spraying for bugs. One honeymooner who didn't take that step had an allergic reaction to the pesticide used in a regularly scheduled spraying and wound up sick for the rest of her stay. A simple phone call and a simple question may prevent you from facing palm-sized mosquitoes and crawly things in your bed.

- *Transportation included.* Free shuttle buses to and from the airport could be a savings. Some resorts run shuttles to the various touristy spots in their area, and those are a big savings. Always find out about transportation availability and costs at your location. Too many couples find themselves paying high prices for taxis and mopeds to get around their island or area, a high drain on spending money that most couples don't expect.

◆ *Tips and taxes included.* Sounds great, doesn't it? Especially when those tips could be as high as 22%. If there's no way around this built-in charge, be sure you keep a straight spine during your stay at the resort. It's tempting to be nice to extra-friendly wait staff or towel boys and hand over an additional tip, but you'd really be paying double. Know what's in your contract.

◆ *Free extras.* Most honeymoon packages come with extras such as a complimentary bottle of champagne, fruit platter, and more. Find out what these extras are and whether they really add up to a great deal.

JENNA AND MARCUS' STORY

Jenna and Marcus wanted that Hawaiian honeymoon. They'd saved up for years, and really had no question as to where they would honeymoon. But when the time to book their package came, they spent a lot of time going over the elements of the packages and figuring out what they could arrange on their own.

With a few simple phone calls, they figured out the room rate for a regular room, then investigated the terms of an all-inclusive package that meant all meals and drinks were included (they planned to get their money's worth at every buffet and with every Blue Hawaiian!). They knew they weren't the activities type, but still checked out the individual prices of rafts and kayaks and helicopter tours. In the end, after crunching the numbers and figuring what they'd really spend during their week's stay, they chose to avoid the honeymoon package and pay individual prices. They spent $2,000 less on their honeymoon than if they'd taken the same resort's honeymooners' package, and they had a lot more freedom and control over their vacation. "The little time that we spent crunching numbers was worth it," says Marcus, "because we didn't have to worry about spending too much. We knew we had it all in line."

This by no means suggests that you should avoid all-inclusive honeymoon packages. Many of the best resorts know what they're doing, and offer phenomenal honeymoon packages. Just check all the details so you know what you're getting for your money.

Assessing Short-Term Fares

AT no other time have brides and grooms had more opportunity to find great travel rates, even on short notice. Major airlines are warring against one another to lower their rates and attract fliers. Discount services such as Priceline.com and the many other services are offering dirt-cheap prices; and many of the credit cards, phone companies, and hotel chains are offering frequent-flier miles for every purchase, stay, and minute you buy. You can save up all of these and cash them in for discounts on your travels, and you can even find great hotel rates with the points you've earned.

Since each plan is different, explaining all the individual companies' rules and cash-in requirements would take an entire book, which would be outdated before it could be printed. So I'll just warn you of a few things:

- *You may need some time to cash in frequent flier miles for the destination you want.* Some programs do have restrictions, and the cash-in progress can be long and tedious. Start asking your company for its rules and regulations now.

- *Look for the small print.* A Web site may offer a great price on flights, but may have conditions attached, such as your having to fly stand-by. No one wants to go through that at the airport, so be sure you have a solid ticket to use.

- *Book your travel as soon as possible.* Last-minute flights are going to cost you. If your wedding is just weeks away, you might be better off finding another mode of travel.

- *Always book through a reputable company such as an airline, AAA, or a well-known online travel company.* These companies have standards to uphold, and you'll want to be sure you're dealing with true professionals.

♦ *Do not take the free vacation offers you get in the mail.* Sure, you may think that sitting through a condo lecture is a small price to pay for a trip to Florida, but you might pay a large price in the end for a great vacation through one of those deals.

♦ *If you're facing nothing but late fees, all you can do is shop around for the least oppressive one.*

Say the Word

*B*e *sure you and your fiancé agree on whatever alternative honeymoon plan you choose. If he loves hiking, fishing, camping, and all things outdoors, but you would die without your curling iron, perhaps you can compromise—such as visiting a great mountain resort with all the amenities, including outdoor activities you can share a few days out of the week. You'll run into trouble if you go way out of your comfort zone just to please your partner or pursue a completely original honeymoon that no one else has ever attempted.*

Alternative Honeymoon Ideas

ESPECIALLY at this late time, and if your budget is limited, you might plan an alternative honeymoon. For some couples, this means avoiding the usual honeymoon spots such as Hawaii, the Caribbean, Europe, or Florida. For others, it means doing something completely different for their honeymoon, such as an adventure trek including a climb up a mountain. For still others, a simple getaway at a bed and breakfast for the weekend after the wedding will do for now, with a more elaborate honeymoon postponed until later in the year.

The idea of the honeymoon is changing as are many ideas within the wedding industry. It's no longer a given that couples go to beach resorts for ten days. No longer are those with less ample budgets limited to the mountain resort. Now, couples are creating truly individual getaways set to their liking.

I'll start with the bed and breakfast idea. Many couples are beginning their post-wedding time with a short stay at a romantic inn, completely surrounded by the elements of love. They may choose a quaint, antique town that offers wine tasting, balloon rides, bicycle rides through historic districts, mansion tours, and outdoor concerts. This getaway is not too lofty in price, and you can almost always find openings in this realm. It's a simple vacation to plan, leaves lots of room for individual choice, and is relaxing and conducive to cuddling. Plus, those early-morning breakfasts are amazing.

JENNIFER AND TROY'S STORY

Jennifer and Troy spent their honeymoon within driving distance in charming Cape May, New Jersey. A friend had given them a gift certificate to one of the most lavish and upscale bed and breakfasts in the area, suitable for a high-end dinner in style. Their accommodations were a few blocks from the ocean, and they toured lighthouses, mansions, did some antiquing, and spent some quiet time together after the hassle of the wedding planning. Jen and Troy loved the place, and they return every few years to reminisce about their honeymoon.

The delayed honeymoon may be a solution for you if you don't have enough vacation time accumulated for a two-week trek through Europe. Or, you may be expecting, and would rather wait until the baby is born before you take a major vacation. One couple who put off their big getaway said they celebrated the wedding for a weekend at a nearby resort hotel (The Marriott offers inexpensive "Two for Breakfast" plans that add up to just $79 to $199, depending upon where you are in the country), but put off their big getaway for a year or two so they could save for the vacation they wanted. Spending the money to throw a big wedding with all the trimmings was important to them. The big honeymoon would have to wait.

If someone you know has a time-share or a condo at a nice resort area, perhaps they'll allow you to stay there for your honeymoon as their wedding gift to you. Many couples have found beautiful places to stay at lovely destinations for a fraction of usual honeymoon costs due to the generosity of loved ones. The kind-hearted wedding guests receive a bonus: They won't have to spend extra money for your wedding gift!

Be diplomatic if you request this. Realize that you may be asking them to give up their own vacation time. Limit your stay there, and be a good houseguest.

Another great idea is renting a private villa at an overseas location. Private villas and chateaux come in all price ranges, give you access to marvelous sights and cultures, and some come with maid and cook service. Check the Web site at the back of this book to start your research on this one.

ANNAMARIE AND CHET'S STORY

While Annamarie could not afford to fly her Italian relatives in for her wedding, she decided to take her wedding celebration— in part—to them. The week after her big family wedding, she and her husband took a discount flight to Italy, where they rented a lovely little villa with a view of the Italian countryside.

During their stay, they invited Annamarie's Italian relatives over for dinner, and everyone was able to celebrate the wedding with a big, traditional meal and plenty of red wine toasts. After that event, the couple enjoyed their freedom to roam the towns, take side tours, shop, and spend time alone where her family had its roots.

Gilligan jokes aside, private cruises are becoming more popular for honeymooners. While the major cruise lines may be booked by now, and no one wants a room deep in the ship's "dungeon," you might find a high-end yacht with an experienced crew who can take you to any port of call or even just to float out in the Pacific for a while.

Many of these yachts are breathtaking, and some millionaire owners do rent out these playthings to good clients who refer other people.

LAINIE AND MITCH'S STORY

Lainie and Mitch had seen enough romantic movies to know that a romantic night on the ocean, counting the brilliant stars and enjoying the ocean breeze and gentle waves rocking them, was just what they wanted. They did some research and found a yacht company that rented sixty-footers for weekend sails.

The yacht, which they carefully inspected before booking, had mahogany walls and gold trim, spotless details, a full entertainment center, and a spacious bedroom with a king-sized bed and plush bedding. The captain explained about the champagne brunches served on deck, the gourmet meal, the luscious desserts, and the privacy afforded by the crew on their own sub-deck.

During their cruise, Lainie and Mitch spoke of how the captain knew right where to anchor the yacht so that they could dive off and swim in the safety of a cove. The captain also knew all about astronomy and pointed out the Milky Way and various constellations. They saw shooting stars in the sky and frolicking porpoises in the sea.

All in all, the couple report, it was the perfect honeymoon. Just the privacy and relaxation they wanted, special events they would remember forever, first-class service, and—luckily—beautiful weather. They plan to spend their fifth anniversary on the same boat.

As these few suggestions demonstrate, honeymoons come in all variations. You might choose to go skiing, climb a mountain, work on an eco-friendly volunteer trek. You might spend weeks crossing the country to visit family and friends. You might pack up and head off to

Disney World for that youthful and magical experience you miss from when you were a kid. The choice is up to you. Do your homework, assess your needs, and make all the right decisions through reputable companies.

Honeymoon Red Tape

IT'S a problem that many couples who want to go on a distant honeymoon face: the passport and paperwork hassle. For some, it's a matter of finding that dusty, old passport that happens to still be valid, ugly photo and all. For others, it's the task of getting a new one—or their first one ever. Is there time? What's the process?

If you're short on time, I'd suggest you skip the destination sites where passports, paperwork, and immunizations are necessary. Instead, opt for a foreign-type honeymoon that doesn't require a passport (and new passport photo) for entry by choosing one of these destinations:

+ Hawaii

+ Puerto Rico

+ U.S. Virgin Islands

Beyond the States and their above-mentioned territories, the following locations will let you in with just your photo-ID driver's license and your birth certificate (an official one with a raised, notarized seal): Anguilla, Antigua, Aruba, Barbados, Bonaire, British Virgin Islands, Cayman Islands, Curacao, Dominica, Dominican Republic, Grenada, Guadeloupe, Haiti, Jamaica, Martinique, Nevis, St. Kitts, St. Lucia, St. Maarten, St. Vincent, Turks, and Caicos. Notice that all are tourism islands, but each has adapted its rules so you can gain entry without carrying an official passport. That doesn't mean, however, that your job is easier. Notice that you do still need an official notice of your birth certificate with a raised, notarized seal. Tracking one of those down could take some doing. Whether you can or can't accomplish this task depends upon how much time you have.

As far as distant or exotic travel, if you're going that route, always call the tourism department of the destination you've chosen to ask about their rules on inoculations and customs. Do not trust what you find written on Internet sites, as rules change every day. Be sure you're up to date, and that you know the rules about safe travel in your area. Again, ask the consulate for any bulletins on safe or unsafe areas, health hazards, and anything else you need to know before setting foot into the country of your destination.

Buying Time

To get a new passport, pick up an application at your post office and fill it out. Have your passport photo taken at any photo shop or AAA. Return the application with photos and payment as directed, then wait a month or so for your valid passport to arrive.

The Honeymoon Packing List

THIS will save you time and money. After all, you'll be able to pack everything you need and not have to buy necessities at your honeymoon location. You'll be organized, stress-free, and ready to take off for your big getaway right after the wedding with your bags packed and your mind ready for relaxation.

Label all your luggage clearly, use a garment bag for your dresses and suits, and make sure your carry-on will fit in the overhead compartment. Make sure you keep all toiletries in a tightly sealed plastic bag to prevent leakage, and put a paper with your name and destination's phone number inside your luggage in case your tags get torn off during transit.

Items for Your Carry-On Bag

_____ Plane tickets

_____ Hotel confirmation

_____ Traveler's checks

_____ Foreign currency

_____ Maps

_____ Travel guides

_____ Driver's license

_____ Passport (if necessary)

_____ Birth certificate (if necessary)

_____ Credit cards

_____ Checkbook and cash (don't forget small bills for tipping)

_____ Your marriage certificate

_____ Address book

_____ Cameras and film

_____ Batteries for the cameras

_____ Portable CD player

_____ Contact lens supplies

_____ Jewelry (don't put it in your suitcase)

_____ A change of clothing (in case of travel delays)

_____ A change of underwear (for travel delays)

_____ Prescription medication

Items for Your Suitcase

_____ One casual outfit per day

_____ One formal outfit per day

_____ Two pairs of underwear per day

_____ Two pairs of socks per day

_____ Ties

_____ Belts

_____ Sports wardrobe

_____ Sports underwear

_____ Bathing suits

_____ Bathing suit cover-ups

_____ Beach sandals

_____ Pajamas

_____ Lingerie

_____ Robe

_____ Slippers

_____ Slip

_____ Stockings

_____ Sneakers

_____ Walking shoes

_____ Dress shoes

_____ Casual jacket

_____ Dressy jacket

Toiletries

_____ Deodorant

_____ Toothpaste

_____ Toothbrush

_____ Dental floss

_____ Mouthwash

_____ Breath spray

_____ Face cleanser

_____ Face creams

_____ Hand cream

_____ Aloe cream (for sunburn)

_____ Sunblock

_____ Shampoo

_____ Conditioner

_____ Hair mousse or gel

_____ Hair dryer

_____ Curling iron

_____ Hair brushes

_____ Hair clips or bands

_____ Electrical adapters for overseas use

_____ Women's razor and disposable blades

_____ Men's razor and disposable blades

_____ Shaving cream

_____ Perfume/aftershave/cologne

_____ Nail polish remover

_____ Nail polish

_____ Cotton balls

_____ Cotton swabs

_____ Emery board
_____ Nail clipper
_____ Tweezers

Makeup

_____ Foundation
_____ Loose powder and brush
_____ Pressed powder
_____ Lipstick
_____ Lipliner
_____ Lip gloss
_____ Eye shadow
_____ Eyeliner
_____ Mascara (waterproof)
_____ Blush
_____ Lip balm
_____ Makeup remover

Other Items

_____ Birth control
_____ Pain medication
_____ Upset stomach medicines
_____ Copies of vital prescriptions
_____ Eyeglasses
_____ Sunglasses
_____ Spot remover
_____ Small sewing kit
_____ Sun hat
_____ Throwaway cameras (underwater, panoramic, etc.)

Honeymoon Specialties

_____ Candles
_____ Massage oil

_____ Aromatherapy products (essential oils on light rings, potpourri, sprays)

_____ Bubble bath

_____ Body paint

_____ Romantic music CD and player

_____ Journal for recording great honeymoon memories

_____ Article or book on giving great massages

_____ Extra tape for videocamera

Don't Forget!

HERE are a few more suggestions for enhancing your honeymoon stay.

♦ *Leave a complete copy of your travel itinerary with someone you trust back at home.* Leave instructions where you can be reached in case of emergency only.

♦ *Get all your honeymoon package plans in writing, down to the smallest detail.*

♦ *Be sure you have room on your credit card to pay for your honeymoon.*

♦ *Factor a few hundred dollars of "play money" into your budget.* Include tips, travel, late-night snacks, and souvenir shopping.

♦ *Call and confirm your travel and hotel reservations 48 hours in advance.*

♦ *Remember to leave your room once in a while.* Get great pictures of the two of you at sunset, by landmarks, looking your best and just having fun. Ask other vacationers to snap pictures of you, so there's proof that you were there together.

♦ *If you're unhappy with anything, tell the hotel manager.* Even if he can't do anything about the construction noise at the next resort over, he may send a fruit and cheese platter to your room. If you're truly unhappy with your room, barred windows and all, he may upgrade you to a new room. Just remember to be friendly and diplomatic while making your requests.

- *Make friends with other honeymooners.* Some couples strike up lasting friendships for the future, and you may find other people to go out with occasionally. It may mean you can share taxi fare, or you might hear about a great spot for a few hours out on the town.

- *Go for the grand gesture.* Write your names in the sand. Sprinkle rose petals on your bed. Drink champagne at sunrise. Slow dance until the band packs up and leaves. Share breakfast in bed. Do the limbo. Take a bubble bath together. Wish on shooting stars. Make the most of every minute. This is the start of your new life.

16

THE LITTLE THINGS

MAKING SURE NOTHING GOES UNNOTICED

Y OU THOUGHT THE big issues were a handful! As you may well know, you'll also face a mountain of little tasks and to-do's that are going to take up your time, energy, and some of your budget. Here are suggestions for the most efficient ways to get these little things done. The good news is that you can ask for and accept help from your friends, family, and bridal party.

Wedding Programs

AT many weddings, couples provide their guests with a printed program of the elements of the ceremony, the names of bridal party members, and any number of additional pieces of information. The size and design of program is up to you. You can choose from the styles (and prices) offered in stationery catalogs, as some brides do, or you might take the more popular route of making the programs yourselves:

The first step is determining the style of your program. Will you have a tri-fold of a large, business-sized piece of card stock? The result will be a long, narrow program that is the size and shape of a wine list.

Or will you have a folded piece of 8 ½ × 11-inch card stock? Several pages stapled or bound together? Your first decision is to choose the shape: third or half pages? Halves makes it easier for most brides and grooms, as their home computer allows them to print in this style much more readily than in three-column.

The next step is to get the wording of your program. The cover may say something as simple as "The Wedding of _____ and _____," or it may be more poetic and romantic, such as "Join us as we begin a life of love." The cover usually has a beautiful, soft graphic, but I have seen lovely program covers with just an underlay of water-marked design.

For inside the program, your wording will usually go by the standard outline of the ceremony you've chosen. For the sake of brevity, and since you may have a plan to create a unique ceremony, I've just included a standard sample of a Roman Catholic program:

Front Cover

Our Wedding Service
Anne and Michael

Left Inside Page

The Wedding of
Anne Marie Smith
And
Michael James Olsen
Saturday, August 14, 2000
3:45 P.M.
St. James Church
Riverton, Oklahoma

Prelude:
"Songbird"
by Christine McVie

Processional:
"Bridal Chorus"
by Wagner

Greeting
Reading:
"How Do I Love Thee"
by Elizabeth Barrett Browning,
read by Denise Strohman

Musical Interlude:
"More" (The Theme from Mondo Cane)
sung by Anthony Vienetta

Exchange of Rings
Blessing of the Marriage

Recessional:
"Wedding March"
by Mendelssohn

Pastor Presiding:
Father Henry Baker

Organist:
Helen Doran

Right Inside Page

Matron of Honor:
Shelby Lynne Blake

Bride's Attendants:
Theresa Aviano
Stephanie Aviano
Carianne Blake

Flower Girl:
Maria Taylor

Sprucing Up the Program

You may choose to include the following on your program in addition to the information given:

♦ Your parents' names

♦ Your phone number at home

♦ A dedication of the floral arrangements to departed loved ones

♦ Quotes or poetry

♦ Individual notes of love to each other

How many programs should we make?

The general rule of thumb is one program per guest, plus twenty extras for keepsakes, albums, and gifts to guests who could not attend the wedding.

Ring Bearer:
Benjamin Wood

Best Man:
Kenneth Olsen

Groomsmen:
Daniel Wood
Frank Wood
Patrick Blake

Guest Hostesses:
Daria Taylor
Marina Wood
Eleanor Olsen

Photographs are not permitted during the ceremony, nor are rice, birdseed, or confetti after the ceremony.

Back Cover

We would like to thank all of you for being here to share in our day. Over the past few months, as we planned this wedding, we've had the opportunity to count our blessings for having each of you in our lives. As we begin this new life together, we know we are richer for having you in it. We would also like to thank our parents, sisters, and brothers, for all of the unconditional love and support they have given us over the years. You have taught us, through your example, how to be wise, loving, gentle, and kind, and we take these gifts with us as we venture forth into the future.

Michael and Anne Olsen
321 Harvard Street
Manning, Oklahoma 74000

Of course, you may choose to word and design your programs any way you wish.

Now, for putting it all together. . . .

As mentioned in earlier chapters, stationery stores and office supply stores now carry a wide range of wedding-appropriate papers and card stocks. You'll find lovely paper designs with soft, pastel-hued images of flowers, wedding cakes, wedding bands, doves, and even just romantic scrolls that suit your wedding style. Know the amount of paper you'll need. That means making a mock copy of regular paper on your printer, counting the pages, and multiplying that by the number of programs you'll be making.

Some brides and grooms do choose a do-half-of-it-yourself route, printing the wording out on their home computer, controlling

---

Buying Time

Be sure you've checked everything thoroughly, from the spelling of every name to the order of every step of the ceremony. Don't rely on spell-check. Have someone else look over your program print as well, in order to spot those flaws that will mar your perfect handout. Mistakes at this stage may mean double the effort and double the expense when you have to print them all over again.

the font and style, and then taking their masterpiece to the local printer for a professional job done on high-quality paper. This option may cost slightly more than a total at-home job, but you may find the final outcome worth the expense. Just check around for printers' fees, ask whether they have the capability and the time to do your job (never pay extra just for the sake of getting it done), and always be sure to request collating and stapling, if necessary.

Assign a trusted friend of the family, perhaps a guest hostess in her teenage years, to hand out the programs as the guests arrive. The ushers will be too busy seating the rush of guests to be sure each has a program in hand, and your maids will be too busy gushing over how gorgeous you are. So make a simple phone call, ask someone to serve as a "program honor attendant," and give simple but clear instructions for that job.

Professionally Speaking

Our wedding favors come in two-piece boxes, four-piece boxes, and larger boxes for less than you'd pay for other favors. We can arrange any kind of box décor and imprinted ribbon you desire, to match your colors.

—Julie Croft, Godiva

Favors

THIS one is a budget headache for most brides and grooms. They want to get something special for their guests as a memento of their wedding, but the nicer gifts such as the crystal vases and the silver frames are just way too much per piece when you're looking at a large guest count. In times past, favors were very similar: inscribed wine glasses, cognac snifters, and tulle-wrapped sugar-coated almonds. Now, the wedding industry offers a wide, wide variety of new favors from which you can choose.

For high-end weddings, favors are expensive and notable. Some brides give Lalique crystal figurines, mini-Lladros, bottles of expensive port, and designer-name goods. For the average bride with a moderate budget, though, there is a world of inexpensive favors that *look* pricier than they are. I've interviewed hundreds of brides who shared their ideas with me and I've seen many favors such as these handed out to the great pleasure of the guests:

- *Godiva chocolates:* Still the gold standard by which all favors are measured, Godivas state elegance with their gold-foil wrappers, their classy ribbons, and their reputation as the finest chocolates available for weddings.

- *Candy store chocolates:* You have to compare carefully to find a truly gifted chocolate artist, but when you do, you'll find a wide selection of fine chocolates in many wedding-oriented shapes. A good confectioner will be able to supply you with different styles, colors, sizes, and shapes of boxes with ribbons and labels to match.

> ### Wedding Day Reflections
>
>
>
> We thought we were saving time and money by having the printer do our programs, but when they came back to us in six different piles, we had a long, long night of assembling and stapling ahead of us. It wasn't the great idea we thought it was, and we would have paid extra for the assembly.
>
> —Tara and Richard

- *Candy store candies:* Some brides and grooms are bypassing the chocolate route and going with fun candy snacks in tulle wraps or boxes. One couple chose rock candy as favors for guests attending their beachside wedding, as that was something they ate on their first boardwalk date together.

- *Candleholders:* Have you seen the selection out there lately? From the $2 variety at craft stores to the $10 variety at stores such as Pier 1, you can't miss with a pretty, decorative votive holder and candle in a color that matches your wedding tones. For extra décor, wrap the holder in tulle and tie it up with a ribbon.

- *Potpourri bowls.* I'm not talking about the bags of mixed potpourri that you find at any bath shop. These are the pretty glass potpourri bowls stocked en masse in craft stores. You then fill these up with a small amount of fragrant potpourri, label, and set out on your aromatic favors table.

• *Plants.* It may sound strange, but brides and grooms are giving their guests live plants and potted flowers as favors to take home. The idea is to give their home a piece of "new life," a breath of "fresh air," and a living thing to "plant and watch grow." These favors are incredibly popular now, with couples even leaning toward packages of seeds and bulbs for guests' gardens. One of the prettiest weddings I've attended was an outdoor garden wedding with a sunflower theme. Sunflowers abounded, and the favors were packets of seeds and planting directions to grow sunflowers. The seed packets were adorned with a little sunflower magnet to add charm (and a little more expense to that $1.99 cost of the seeds per guest).

Say the Word

Be sure to arrange with your banquet hall manager or coordinator ahead of time as to the arrangement of your favors. Specify whether they'll be piled in groups on each table, arranged on a gift table, or if you'll be handing them out personally throughout the night.

• *CD mixes.* While this is among the pricier of the ideas, it's popular for couples to choose to create music mixes of special songs for their guests to enjoy in years to come. Some couples do choose to take on this task themselves, creating specialized tapes for categories of their guests—relatives, friends, clients—and some are hiring the professional companies that make CDs in bulk order. Guests love this idea, as it is truly a favor that they can use in the future.

• *Silver frames.* Even the little silver frames found in Pier 1 and in craft shops can be dressed up with poetry typed on parchment paper, or with a framed photo of the two of you.

- *Tickets to events.* Depending upon which kind of event you choose, your guests will be thrilled to get as their favor a ticket to their favorite team's playoff game or even to a minor-league game with a big tailgate party for all of you to attend. The idea is the thing, and guests love getting something new and different as a favor.

The ideas are endless. Some brides do get favors in categories, choosing less expensive gifts for their acquaintances and the more impressive, whopping gifts for their very generous relatives. In this case, the favors should be presented wrapped with labels to prevent confusion.

> ### *Wedding Day Reflections*
>
> I plan on getting my maid of honor two gifts—a piece of jewelry for all that she is doing for me and a massage, something to help her relax once the wedding is over.
>
> —Stephanie

Gifts for Your Bridal Party

WHAT would you do without your bridesmaids to make sure you look perfect on your wedding day? What would your groom do without someone to make sure he gets to the church on time? Your bridal party brings love, friendship, support, and fun to your wedding celebration—and giving each a special gift is a great way to show your appreciation for all they have done from your engagement to the big day.

Whether you want to give your bridal party a traditional gift or something unique and completely different, gifts for the bridal party are a great way to say "thank you" for making your wedding day magical.

GIFTS FOR YOUR PARENTS

At this special time, you'll almost certainly want to give your parents a little something special as a commemoration of this transition in your life. Whether or not they've footed the bill for your wedding, they've still given to you, loved you, and supported you all your life

Gifts for the Bridesmaids

Gift	Price	Description
Jewelry	$25 to $50	Earrings, a string of pearls, or personally engraved bracelets will be a perfect accent to the bridesmaids' dresses.
Tickets to a play	$50 to $80	Take them to a show, and give each woman a small purse filled with mints, hand cream, and chocolates on the night of the play.
Picture frame	$10 to $25	Frame a picture of you and your bridesmaids or a poem you wrote especially for them.
Day at the spa	$45 to $85	Giving them a facial or massage gives your bridesmaids a chance to chat, relax, and unwind.
Initialized silk makeup bag	$10 to $15	What woman couldn't use another makeup bag? Your bridesmaids can bring the bag with them on your wedding day for any last-minute touch-ups.
Topiary or plant	$15 to $35	Give the gift that keeps growing—a potted plant or topiary is a lasting reminder of your appreciation.
Perfume	$30 to $45	Get each woman a bottle of her favorite perfume.
Keepsake box or jewelry box	$7 to $20	Fill each box with personalized notes for each woman, telling her how grateful you are for her support.
Pottery	$10 to $20	Buy or make each bridesmaid a vase, bowl, or set of coffee mugs.
Basket of goodies	$30 to $35	Fill a basket with candles, body lotion, incense, and scented soaps—the perfect pampering gifts for any woman.

Gifts for the Groomsmen

Gift	Price	Description
Silver cigar case	$10 to $20	Fill a monogrammed cigar case with your groomsmen's favorite cigars.
Cologne	$35 to $50	Give each man a bottle of his favorite cologne.
Engraved money clips	$10 to $15	Put an old picture of the groom and his men from when they were younger in each money clip.
Cufflinks	$15 to $25	Give each man initialized cufflinks to wear on the wedding day.
Tickets to a sporting event	$30 to $40	The men can go to a ball game or spend a day at the horse races and get some of that male bonding out of their systems.
Day of golf	Price depends upon location and greens fees	After the men enjoy a day on the green, give each groomsman a box of Titleist golf balls to remember the day.
Daily planner	$25 to $60	The groomsmen can keep track of important dates (your wedding day) in a leather, monogrammed daily planner.
Bar glasses	$15 to $25	Give each man a set of initialized bar glasses for entertaining friends.
Engraved watch	$45 to $80	If each groomsman is wearing a watch on the big day, chances are the groom will get to the church on time.

Gifts for Your Parents

Gift	Price	Description
His and her watches	$40 to $60	Give your parents a timepiece that reminds them of the time they've spent raising you.
Engraved silver frame	$30 to $50	Find a great picture of the two of them (or the four of you) and encase it in a beautiful frame for their home.
Weekend getaway	$75 to $100	After all of that planning, they deserve their own vacation, so make their reservations at a bed and breakfast, get them a travel tour guide, and a little wicker basket for a picnic out in the apple grove.
Spa day	$40 to $150	Not just for Mom, but also for Dad. The experts at a wonderful day spa can groom and pamper both your parents, working out those kinks and smoothing out those worry lines.

(even though they may have made you crazy at times), and you may want to give them a special gift now:

GIFTS FOR EACH OTHER

Brides and grooms often get each other very special gifts on the day of the wedding. For most, it's the groom giving the bride her wedding-day jewelry, such as a strand of pearls. The bride may give the groom a flask of whiskey to calm his nerves. Here, from other couples who've come before you, is a list of great from-me-to-you wedding gift ideas that break with the traditional mold and speak of the modern partnership you have:

Videotape of your growing-up years	$40 to $100	Hire a good videographer to transfer your old home movie reels, videotape, and still pictures onto a tape that your parents will love watching after you've gone away on your honeymoon. Include your baby footage, snuggling photos, fun family vacations, special family events, and a recent "speech" that you and the groom deliver on tape.
Parents' jewelry	$25 to $50	Get a mother's ring and a father's ring or tie clip bejeweled with your birthstones for an incorporation of your family and bond.
Tickets to a special event	$40 to $100	If your parents have always wanted to see Andrea Boccelli in concert, or even Don Henley, get them front-row seats and allow them to enjoy a special night out.

+ Name a star (You can actually "buy and name" a star in the sky!)

+ Mountain bikes

+ Perfume or cologne with a meaningful name

+ Membership to a gym

+ Luggage for the honeymoon

+ Engraved watches

+ Favorite book in a leather-bound edition, signed by the author

+ Skis

Guest Room Baskets

If your bridal party and out-of-town guests will be staying in a hotel or at some other place of lodging, a nice gesture is supplying them with gift baskets or gift bags filled with treats, sodas, bottled water, candies, guidebooks to nearby sites of interest, and even luxuriant items such as bath gels, candles, and aromatherapy kits. Make your guests feel welcome and pampered for your special day.

If kids are in the mix, get them their own baskets filled with small toys, activity sets, word game books, joke books, and kid-friendly snacks and juice boxes.

- Professional nameplate with the bride's new name
- Personalized license plates for the car
- A pedigree dog or cat
- Professional framing of the other's best accomplishments, pieces of art, contracts, articles, acceptance to a prestigious school or organization
- A much-wanted collector's item, licensed and appraised
- An heirloom valued item
- A mailbox or doormat with your last names hyphenated, if applicable

Throw-Outs

BIRDSEED and rice may be out of the options list, and confetti may be banned from the reception site due to cleanup rules, but your first hailed dash to the limo need not exclude all throw-outs. Choose, instead, to have your guests blow bubbles to signal your first passing as husband and wife. You can find little bubble containers at party store, gift stores, craft shops, and on Internet wedding sites.

Another option is not a throw-out at all, but the ringing of little bells to symbolize the celebration of your union. Again, check at craft stores and fabric stores for a bulk buy of little bells, and tie them onto imprinted cards that tell the guests to ring loudly when you pass. It's a great option—one that gets a lot of attention, and avoids the discomfort of getting birdseed down your dress.

The Unity Candle and Ring Bearer's Pillow

You're likely to find these in the same place. I'd avoid the pricey bridal salons, although they'll have the widest selection. You can find these items in card shops, dollar stores, fabric stores, online, and even at craft stores. More enterprising brides are choosing non-wedding silky pillow of a hued color for their ring bearers, or they're allowing a crafter guest to make the pillow for them (it's really a simple task). As for the unity candle, new kits are stocked in craft stores and party stores, and some of these kits allow you to personalize your unity candle with pierce gems, glitter, press-in words, and custom bases. Check out all your options, and price carefully.

> ### *Wedding Day Reflections*
>
>
>
> *We had our guests "play" on kazoos as we went by. They broke into "The Wedding March," and it was hysterical. Our wedding photos from that moment caught us with enormous smiles and our happy guests in the background. Best of all, they were only 75 cents each at a gift shop at the mall.*
>
> —Kristin and Warren

Wedding Cameras

If you'll provide throwaway cameras for your guests to capture candid shots at your reception, remember that you'll only need one per table.

Penny-Wise

——— $ ———

Do not get your throwaway cameras in camera shops, where they tend to be higher-priced. Check in less obvious places. In my hometown, our local discount beauty supply store stocks these cameras for just a few dollars, and prospective brides stocked up on these rather than pay higher prices at another establishment.

Buy them in bulk through one of the suppliers listed in the back of this book, or compare prices in party stores.

Go for brand name throwaways, get some panoramic styles for more interesting shots, and remember to assign someone to collect the cameras at the end of the night. Many brides have reported confused guests taking the cameras home with them.

The Bride's Emergency Bag

You've undoubtedly read plenty of articles about having an "emergency bag" at the ready in case of stocking runs, nail chips, or onsets of headaches. The best organized brides do arrange ahead of time their emergency bag—assembling their most-needed items in a decorated large wedding gift bag—and they assign a family member to take it to the ceremony and the reception for easy access.

Here, then, are the most popular items stocked in emergency bags:

- Several extra pairs of pantyhose (for you and for your maids)
- Your makeup (lipstick, pressed powder, eyeliner)
- Extra bobby pins for those runaway curls
- Hairspray or hair gel
- Pain medication
- Allergy medication
- Emery boards
- Clear nail polish for runs
- Colored nail polish for pre-picture touchups

- Cell phone

- List of all necessary phone numbers and vendors' cell phone numbers

- Camera

- Extra film

- Contact lens solution, case, holder

- Breath spray or mints

- Extra earrings (in case you lose one in a hug or during the night)

- Facial tissues

- Small baby powder for chafing legs beneath the dress

- Gift for groom (unless it's that mountain bike)

- Band-Aids

- Safety pins

- Needle and thread

- Tweezers (for removing stingers and splinters)

- Small water bottle

- Prescription medications you'll need during the day

- Superglue for broken heels

- And (this gets my vote for the most unusual!) a small container of meat tenderizer to take the pain out of bee stings at outdoor weddings

- All other necessary items

Delegation List

As a short-time planning bride, you are going to get plenty of offers to help out with the wedding. Some will be well-meaning, the very

Who's Doing What?

To help you begin, here is a list of common jobs brides and grooms report delegating to their relatives and friends. Feel free to fill in your own checklist (see "Task Delegation List" in the "Helpful Lists and Forms" section in the back of the book).

- Calling for ceremony site brochures
- Calling for reception site brochures
- Calling for reception menus
- Calling for baking menus
- Pricing limos
- Pricing photographers
- Pricing videographers
- Pricing honeymoon packages
- Going with bride to look at gowns
- Going with bride to look at bridesmaids' gowns
- Going with groom to look at tuxes
- Going with bride to reserve gown
- Going with bride to reserve bridesmaids' gowns
- Going with bride to reserve flower order

- Choosing favors
- Making favors
- Choosing gifts
- Wrapping gifts
- Labeling gifts
- Making seating arrangements
- Writing out place cards
- Making programs
- Making maps
- Writing out invitations and envelopes
- Picking up "Love" stamps
- Making some reception food
- Making reception desserts
- Performing music at ceremony
- Performing music at reception

least you'd expect from your friends and the same you'd do for them. Some will be cloaked offers to grandstand or to have more control over your wedding than you are willing to give. In your position, you have the power to decide who will do what, you'll be able to set boundaries and deadlines, and you'll be able to assess who is right for what task.

- Extra hand at shooting video
- Extra hand at taking pictures
- Driving the bridal party around
- Driving guests around
- Picking up guests at the airport and bringing them to the hotel
- Booking hotel block
- Dropping off favors at the reception site
- Setting up favors at the reception site
- Setting out place cards
- Setting out framed photos
- Setting out guest book
- Decorating ceremony site
- Decorating reception site
- Assembling rented tables and chairs
- Assembling tent
- Assembling lights
- Getting permits
- Picking up non-delivered items and having them delivered to the right place
- Bringing wedding gifts from the reception back to your home
- Bringing guest book from reception back to your home
- Collecting throwaway cameras and having film developed
- Collecting framed family albums and bringing them home
- Dropping off your getaway car at the reception location
- Confirming your honeymoon
- Bringing all your honeymoon luggage to your hotel room so that you have access to it for your trip.
- Other to-do's

Today's bridal parties and grooms are doing far more than just showing up on the wedding day. They all work together to create a wonderful event, one that's shared equally by all on the big day, as they all had a hand in planning it.

Indeed, trust is going to be a main issue here, as is reliability. Assign no task to your resident "slacker," and do not let your control-freak friend try to take on too much. Just sit down, plan it out, discuss the needed jobs with your helpful friends, see what they can realistically take on, give a firm deadline, and tell them to get back to you ASAP. Your friends may see something on the list that they'd prefer doing. They may suggest other tasks that you don't even have on your list. Just hear their suggestions and use your own judgment as to which ones to incorporate.

Some important duties that are not on the list have to do with while you are away. You must ask someone to watch your home, your cars, your pets, water your plants, take in your mail and newspapers, water your garden, even watch out for important packages to be delivered. Give your caretakers all home security codes, lessons in where the fuse box and gas switches are, and the name and number of a neighbor who can help in case of emergency.

Again, choose someone responsible who can ideally stay at your place while you are gone. Stock the refrigerator with great gourmet foods and snacks, specify rules on long-distance calls and houseguests, and make sure all Fido's care requirements are written down and all his supplies are easy to find. A little pre-planning in this department means you won't come home to disaster.

Wedding Day Reflections

W*ith just four weeks to go, we had no choice but to divide up our to-do list and ask our friends and relatives to help out. We just gave them our wish lists, the money, and specific orders, and they were off to do their thing. They really enjoyed having the free spending spree—even if it was for our wedding—and we trusted that they'd follow through in time.*

—Deanna and Chris

TIFFANY AND DOUG'S STORY

Tiffany and Doug had heard all the stories about newlyweds' homes being robbed while they were honeymooning, so they asked a family member to stay at their place for a week. Doug's younger brother, who had just graduated from college, volunteered—with pleading eyes and heartfelt promises—for this chance to have his "own place" for a while. With no other option, they let Doug's brother stay and returned home to find their entire stash of liquor gone (including the cooking wine), their Jacuzzi broken, their glass-topped table smashed, beer cans all over the place, unidentifiable stains on the carpets, and a strange couple sleeping on their couch. Doug's brother confessed to having a party that "just kind of happened, man," and he spent months re-paying the unhappy couple for the repairs to their home.

My first advice would be to ask a couple to stay at your place. A young engaged couple might see the "living together" aspect as fun, and a married couple will see it as a free getaway with good food and cable. I'd avoid asking parents to sit for you (unless you want to spend days before the wedding cleaning the house furiously and hiding your naughty lingerie!). Always go with someone you know, and leave solid instructions for them.

Say the Word

You can call your local police department, tell them that you will be away for a week and that someone will be watching your home. Ask the police to include your home on their regular drive-by schedule so they can keep an eye on your place for you. Then let the house sitter know that the cops will be circling . . . for their own protection and yours. There should be no loud frat parties and no bodies on your couch when you get home.

17

THE REHEARSAL AND REHEARSAL DINNER

A FLAWLESS PREPARATION

THE TIME IS upon you. You've gotten everything done, completed all your arrangements, started writing checks, and made your confirmations. Your dress is hanging up safely in your bedroom for tomorrow morning, and all the main players are assembled and buzzing with excitement for the coming celebration.

The Rehearsal

YOU'VE booked your rehearsal (usually for the night before) with the officiant, and all members of your bridal party, musicians, and readers should be in attendance. Start the evening off by gathering outside the church or site, taking some pictures, and sharing some hugs and kisses. This is no time to be a stress case—to rush in there, get the job done, and move on to the next task. Although the rehearsal is an important event, it is also your first chance to shine as the bride. It's your first official, non-shower, on-site radiant presence, and this is the point

Bridal Party Reflections

Our bridal party was so rambunctious, with participants laughing, joking, not paying attention, that the priest actually walked out on the rehearsal. He said he wouldn't waste his time. We were all shocked, and had to do the wedding the next day without a rehearsal. My bridal party was mortified, on their best behavior then, but we were all really confused.

—Tania and Rich

My two ushers, the groom's loser brothers, thought they were being funny by marching their mother down the aisle in a Nazi-like military step. My grandmother, a survivor of a Nazi camp, completely freaked out, and it was a very, very bad scene.

—Auriana and Stephan

My bridal party just didn't take the whole thing seriously. They were too busy checking out who they were attracted to on the other end of the altar, planning who they'd hit on the next day. On the wedding day, they didn't know what they were doing.

—Sonia and Louis

One of my bridesmaids didn't know what to do with the communion wafer, so she stuck it in her bouquet. That's a major sacrilege, and all my guests noticed. No one would talk to her for the rest of the night.

—Arlene and Warren

where you should start taking everything in and enjoying all that goes into creating your day.

The rehearsal is usually a relaxed affair—casual and filled with laughter, joking, and some nerves (especially at the first run-through). This is the time when the officiant or the coordinator will walk you step-by-step through each element of the ceremony, explaining what is happening when, who is doing what, and what everything means.

Usually, the bridal party is lined up according to the tradition of your chosen site, or of your faith. Couples are paired off according to your specifications or perhaps by height, and you get your first look at how the child attendants are likely to behave. That said, practice by having someone stand at the end of the aisle to lure them down, and to tell them how pretty they'll look and how special their job is.

If it's your attendants who are being juvenile, not paying attention, or are still drunk from the bachelor or bachelorette parties the night before, take some advice from couples who have been there:

Any number of wedding nightmares can happen if you don't take time to treat the rehearsal as a serious event. A lot of work has gone into this wedding, even if your bridal party is not aware of it or is just looking at it as a free party, so you're best served by taking matters into your own hands.

- *Plan your own entrance.* If you're not doing the traditional down-the-aisle thing, decide whether you'll be coming down a staircase, up from the beach, through a hallway, or from some other direction. Arrange with the groom where he will meet you as well.

- *Practice with whomever is "giving you away."* These days it's not necessary to follow the tradition that Dad walks you down the aisle and hands you off to the groom. Now brides are choosing to have their dad and step-dad share the honor, have their mom do it, have their child do it, or simply come down the aisle alone. Couples are also making their entrance together in a grand show of unity. Decide ahead of time what the processional will look like in its entirety, and make it happen during your rehearsal.

Say the Word

This is one area where brides report major rehearsal headaches. Even though your parents half-heartedly agreed to having your stepfather escort you down the aisle, you may sense some major "attitude" (if not outright interference) about the decision. Remember that this is your wedding. Do not cave into manipulative guilt trips, and keep your vision in focus. Do not make changes at this point to appease everyone; and even if you have to be blunt, you've earned the right to say, "This is my wedding."

♦ *Ask for run-throughs.* Some officiants, knowing what they're doing, think it's fine if you do just one run-through. Ask for two or three to be sure everyone gets it right.

♦ *Ask that the music be played for your rehearsal.* Music cues are important for your entrances, so be sure your maids are coming in at the right time.

♦ *Ask for clarification of the traditions so everyone knows what is going on.* The salt and the coin traditions may be old news to you, but some of your bridal party members may have no idea that the presentation of these gifts symbolize the riches and flavor of a future life. So ask the officiant to give a brief explanation.

♦ *Have musicians perform.* If your friend will be playing a guitar piece at your ceremony, have him perform the song at your rehearsal. He may need to get used to the acoustics of the room, assess his sound system, and get a feel for the space. This also gives you a chance to sit back, hear that special song, and know that the next time you hear it, you'll be one step away from wearing that wedding ring.

♦ *Have your readers read.* They will be nervous, so this is an important run-through. They'll have to know when it's time for them to come to the podium, have their reading in hand or noted, and practice speaking into the microphone. You may have to give some good-natured coaching, such as "louder" or "more slowly." Remember, they will be nervous, and they're doing the best they can in honor of your marriage.

♦ *Ask "stupid" questions.* Even if they're not your questions, ask when your father should sit down after giving you away. Ask when the maid of honor should take your bouquet.

♦ *Ask for cues during the ceremony.* Explain to your officiant that your bridal party is not all made up of Catholics/Jews/Protestants, or whatever, so they'll need prompting. Ask him to say "Please stand" or "Please kneel" where appropriate, and arrange to have him give hand signals when it's time for the bridal party to do the recessional.

♦ *Practice the befores and afters.* Let the ushers practice seating guests. Tell them to walk slowly, to offer their arm to ladies (some guys may not know about this practice), and that the gentleman walks behind. Give specific instructions about who is seated where. This is an important one. Let them know for whom the first few rows are reserved, so that an irate aunt is not seated in the back of the room on the wrong side of the church. Tell them your wishes, point out the designated spaces, and ask them to make small talk with guests as they are escorting them to their seats. One bride reports that it's a good idea for an in-the-know usher to keep an eye out for any undesirable guests, such as the father's new girlfriend who has been bitterly allowed to come. She should not be placed in the first row with him, if that's against the bride's wishes, and it's up to the usher to handle that situation. As for after the ceremony, practice escorting guests back down the aisle and the lineup of the receiving line, if you will have one.

♦ *Talk about the mechanics of the site.* Ask the manager what time the air-conditioner will be turned on, whether the doors will be opened, when the florist can get in to decorate, when candles will be lit.

♦ *Leave instructions for delivery.* Make sure the manager of the site is aware that the flowers for the men will be delivered at 2:00 P.M., and he should be on the lookout for them.

♦ *Ask whether anyone else has any questions.* Make it clear that you don't want any problems the next day. If someone has a question, he or she should speak up now.

♦ *Find out what the process is for signing the marriage certificate.* After all, this is the paper that makes it all legal. So ask when the certificate will be signed, and designate now who your witnesses will be. Instruct those honor attendants to be at the ready right after the ceremony so you can sign and go.

The Rehearsal Dinner

ONCE all the details are set and all participants seem clear on their roles for the ceremony, it's time to go out, pop some corks, and have a little fun. Rehearsal dinners are time for relaxation and celebration, good food, the mingling and introduction of members of both families and the bridal party, toasts and tributes, and the anticipation of what is to come.

Traditionally, the groom's family pays for the rehearsal dinner, and the industry is seeing a rise in more lofty expenses. Grooms' families frequently create elegant buffet dinners with a wide variety of foods, champagnes, wines, and desserts, and the effect may rival that planned for the wedding day itself. On the flip side, the rehearsal dinner can be a casual dinner at a favorite Italian family restaurant, where the family is known by the owners and staff, kisses abound, and your favorite meals are made-to-order. A festive atmosphere is created as you seat your party of sixteen at long tables, and you take your position as guests of honor.

The groom's family will likely start the evening off with a toast, with well wishes, and with assurances that all will go well on the wedding day. After that, there is usually a time of drinking wine and cocktails, with groups of bridesmaids and ushers, family members from both sides talking excitedly and making introductions. You're watching your future support system blend together here, seeing them all in the same place for the first time, perhaps, and knowing that your wedding has brought them all together.

Throughout the night, there will of course be wedding talk. Eager family members may ask about your dress, the band, the food. "Just checking" questions will be asked, such as "Did you remember to book your ride to the airport?" and you should answer with a smile. Soon, the food will come, everyone will stuff themselves with baked chicken parmigiana, salmon provençal, and chocolate mousse cake. Toasts will be given, and rolls and rolls of informal pictures will be taken. You may even keep a videocamera running for those candid interviews with all the bridal party members.

As the evening winds down, it's time for the giving of gifts. You'll hand out your chosen gifts to your maids and ushers, to the flower girls and ring bearers, to your parents, and to each other. Everyone will delight in your good taste, cherish the gift, and perhaps make another toast to you for your kindness.

Just before midnight, if you're old-fashioned and go by the old rules, you and your fiancé will part for the night, knowing that tomorrow you'll see each other again, dressed in all your finery, ready to take vows from your hearts and join yourselves together forever. It will be sweet dreams tonight, because you have a busy day ahead!

IRENA AND GEORGE'S STORY

Irena and George's rehearsal dinner was a blast. It was a small, intimate gathering, and everyone gathered together over cognac and Grand Marnier after the meal to talk about how the couple met five years ago, how they were both so afraid to fall in love, their ups and downs, and what it took for George to finally get up the courage to ask her to marry him. It was such a touching conversation—captured, thankfully, on videotape—that Irena and George felt it added so much to the fullness of their wedding. They included that footage on their wedding videotape, sharing it with the rest of their loved ones.

Rehearsal dinners are not always so formal, though. Perhaps needing a break from all talk of china and crystal, filet mignon,

292   THE REHEARSAL AND REHEARSAL DINNER

bacon-wrapped scallops, and roses, some couples are going with a far more informal rehearsal dinner. Some budgets demand it.

Consider, if you will, the idea of an at-home rehearsal dinner, with all of your guests enjoying your famous sausage lasagna or lobster bisque. A backyard barbecue with all the trimmings may make its mark on the relaxed atmosphere you want, as will a picnic in the park. Your guests can play boccie ball, badminton, even a pickup game of whiffle ball. (Keep sports activities low contact so no one gets injured today!) Some rehearsal dinners take place at wineries, at sporting events, at sushi bars, even at formal brunches at a nearby hotel.

The options are up to you. Just make sure all your rehearsal dinner guests are there, and that they get a chance to unwind and be themselves, in clothes they're comfortable in, before the big day of beauty, formality, and responsibility is upon them.

Before Bed

THIS will be the last night you spend as a single person. So before you lay your head on that pillow, vow to make this a restful, last single sleep. Be sure you have all the little details arranged, such as your honeymoon luggage packed, tagged, and your carry-on waiting for your last-minute items.

Have a big button-down shirt ready to wear to the salon tomorrow, and be sure your gown and all your accessories—stockings, shoes, and veil—are laid out and ready for your easy dressing in the morning. Set your alarm clock, give your sweetie a goodnight call, or a goodnight kiss, and get your eight hours of sleep. You're going to need it!

18

THE BIG DAY

TURNING A LIFELONG DREAM INTO REALITY

IT'S FINALLY HERE! This is the day you've been waiting for, planning for, and dreaming of for a long, long time. And even if your planning process took only a few months, the outcome of that work is coming to fruition through every step of this twenty-four-hour period. All the details are in place, all the plans made, and all you have to do is show up and enjoy.

When the alarm clock rings, it may take a few seconds before you realize just what day it isthat is, if you were able to sleep at all. The best advice I've heard from brides is to start the day off with some kind of relaxing, solitary activity. Go for a short walk. Do some yoga. Spend some time on the back porch alone with your journal. Use this time to charge your batteries, clear your head, and get ready for the day's events.

Getting Everyone in Place

IN most cases, the maids will come to your house to dress, but you may find it easier and more roomy to all assemble at a suite you've rented at a hotel. It may be your honeymoon suite for the night, and there

293

will surely be full-length mirrors for you all to use. Have the women arrive early for their bridal brunch—be it homemade, catered, or delivered as room service. This is an important part of the morning, as you all will need to be well fueled and hydrated. You might not be eating again for another seven hours, so fill up on bagels and waffles, fresh fruit, and freshly squeezed juice. Go easy on the mimosas, as getting tipsy now will only make you tired later. Be sure you do eat something, though. No matter how nervous you are or how tight that gown is, not eating is the easiest way to pass out during the wedding.

Across town, the men should be gathering at the groom's house to spend a few hours together before they have to dress. Most male attendants report that they went out early to play a round of golf, or they went out to breakfast for a last "single guy meal."

Wedding Day Reflections

We actually went outside and threw a football around and then went in to watch some WWF wrestling. Charlie's fiancé doesn't let him watch it, so it was the ultimate last-stand activity for us.

—Anonymous
(for obvious reasons!)
groomsman

At this time, car arrangements need to be established. Will the attendants leave their cars in front of your house? Will they drop them off at the hotel or at the reception site? Have a plan with this foresight, and the car delivery system can be worked into the earliest part of the day.

The Salon Trip

HERE'S where the fun begins for the women. You all pile into the car or the limo, and head to the beauty salon where your hair, makeup, and nails will be done. Hopefully, you've made these reservations several weeks in advance, and you'll have the majority of the salon to yourselves. Many salons that cater to wedding parties will bring out coffee, tea, juice, water, or champagne to you and your attendants, and you'll receive the royal treatment as you all have your hair braided, pinned, wrapped, or tucked just the way you all want it.

As for you, your veil will be placed perfectly, pinned, and—if necessary—shellacked into place. It will withstand even the wildest of beach breezes and the snags of dance-time flailing arms. Tiaras can also be placed well and pinned for a secure look. No bride wants a wobbly crown when she's walking down the aisle.

Makeup application may be done by a professional, if you choose, with your maids assured ahead of time that they should speak up if the blush is too pink or the lipliner too severe. With your okay, even the meekest of bridesmaids will feel confident speaking up for herself at this point, and you'll all feel better knowing that you look your best. For further suggestions, see "Bridal Beauty" in the appendix.

With nails done, the bills paid, and those generous tips handed out to your beauty team, you're ready to go home and get dressed.

Wedding Day Reflections

I *was trying to get into my gown on my own, and I stepped on the dress, tried to wiggle it on, slipped sideways on the silky fabric, and wiped out in the bathroom. Luckily, I wasn't hurt, but my elbow was sore for the rest of the day. Good thing the videographer wasn't there to catch that moment!*

—Cynthia

Getting Dressed

ALLOW yourself and your entire bridal party plenty of time to get dressed. Have someone help you into your gown, zip the zipper, button that lineup of Victorian cloth-covered buttons. You will need help easing yourself into the dress, as you're going to try to avoid the most common dressing blunders:

- Snagging your veil on your engagement ring
- Getting lipstick marks on the wedding dress
- Pulling your carefully arranged hair out of place

- ◆ Tearing a dress seam

- ◆ Stepping through a dress seam

- ◆ Taking a bad fall

Once you're all dressed, primped, and ready to go, avoid that bridal brunch buffet. It may be tempting to go for another round of quiche,

but now it's time to avoid getting spills and stains on the dresses. Have someone put the food and drink away—except, perhaps, one more mimosa.

Check your details in the mirror: Hair in place? Makeup shine-free? Lipstick non-smudged? Eyeliner in order? Earrings hanging the right way? Necklace clasp not showing? Veil centered on your head? Once you're in good shape, you can help your bridesmaids check for their own little flaws, fix earrings and chains, finish up a zip. It used to be that the bride was off on her own, with only her maid of honor helping her, but now she spends time with all of her attendants, including the children.

> ### Wedding Day Reflections
>
>
>
> *O*ne of the best things was when my nieces saw me in my gown for the first time, and I saw them in their pretty dresses. They looked like little princesses, and they looked at me with wide eyes like I was the most beautiful person they'd ever seen. It was priceless.
>
> —Heather

Taking the Pictures

You're probably going to be nervous at this point, so that smile may be a little shaky. A good photographer knows how to handle nervous brides, and may be very good at putting you at ease. Try to lighten up and enjoy the photo session.

One thing about these pre-wedding picture times is that they can be long and tedious. Especially if your maids and attendants can't seem to stay in one place for very long, getting through the list of required shots can take an hour or more. Just talk with your photographer, explain that you don't want this session to last forever, and ask whether he can speed the process along.

Remember to ask for fun shots as well as posed, and get a great one with the flower girls.

Leaving for the Wedding

ALL the neighbors are gathered out on their lawns, holding their hands over their hearts, watching the little girl you used to be getting swept away in a limousine on her way to her wedding. After a few pictures, you'll be on your way with your maids in close tow. Enjoy this ride. Sure, play with the buttons, learn how everything works. Do some deep breathing. The big moment is quickly upon you, and soon you'll be going down that aisle, knowing that every element of your wedding will go as smoothly as possible.

You and your new husband will slip the rings on one another. You'll be pronounced husband and wife and share that public kiss. Then you'll be rushing down the aisle to dive into the limo and enjoy your first private kiss and a few moments of solitude before the rest of the evening progresses. Take this time to share some thoughts, look into each other's eyes, and remember this moment forever.

Throughout the Reception

EVEN during the reception, as each step rolls out and you're dancing to your favorite songs, make sure you don't forget a few more tasks. Be sure to greet all your guests, accept all compliments with a genuine smile, and introduce your husband to people he may not know.

Don't get drunk, and don't go hide out with your groom for some alone time during the reception. You'll have plenty of time for that later.

In many cases, the father of the bride takes on the role of host, and the mother of the bride becomes the hostess. All minor details are up

Wedding Day Reflections

W*hen my sister was married, she forgot her garter, so I had to run home to get it. We missed the conga line, but it was a job that someone had to do for her.*

—Karen, bridesmaid

to them, and they make the last-minute decisions—sometimes without the bride even knowing. At one wedding, an overzealous dancer knocked off the top layer of the cake, and the mother of the bride distracted the bride long enough for the cake to be wheeled away and fitted with a new top layer. In some instances, fathers of the groom have stepped in to drive drunk guests home at the end of the night. While it may seem as though someone will always be there to fill in the blanks when tasks need to be done, it's smart to designate someone beforehand who will take charge of all the little crop-ups that can happen at any wedding.

At the End of the Reception

WHEN the clock strikes 10:00—or 11:00, or 12:00—and it's time to leave your reception for your "chariot" ride to your honeymoon suite, be sure to say goodnight to everyone. Make your grand exit to a wonderful song of your choice, be it "What a Wonderful World" or even "I Know Who I Want to Take Me Home." The party will likely run on after your departure, but you have many more important things to think about.

ALONE AT LAST!

With a little forethought, again, your first night together as husband and wife can be the most romantic of your lives. Brides and grooms of all ages have told me about how they sprinkled rose petals on the bed, filled the room with long-stemmed roses, took a relaxing bubble bath together, gave mutual massages, drank champagne with strawberries in it, and spent intimate hours just cuddling and talking about the day.

While they all say they were exhausted by the wedding day, they still cherished this first night of intimacy. Some chose to skip the love-making. They knew they were too tired to make the earth shake, and wanted their consummation to be a memorable experience. Besides, as one confided, it wasn't like it was a new thing for them. So they used that first night to just be close, to talk or be silent together, to relax and look back on the wonderful wedding they'd just pulled off. They laughed about their nervous vows, about how they almost tripped getting out of the limo, and what was Aunt Mina *thinking* when she bought that dress?

This is what you've been waiting for. To *be* married. After all, there is a big difference between *being* married and *getting* married. Being married is more important, and is far more rewarding hard work than your months of planning for a wedding and reception that lasted just a few hours. But as elated as you feel now at creating a wonderful wedding despite your time disadvantage, you'll feel exponentially elated when your marriage withstands the trials of time and fate, when it soars with the good times and remains faithful during the bad.

Your vows will be tested. You will change and grow as individuals and as a couple, and you will learn new skills you can't even imagine now as you gloriously replay this wonderful day. You have a bright future ahead of you; you can do anything, and you have each other.

I wish you a lifetime of love, luck, and joy; the ability to share, to laugh, to be loyal and faithful, and to be each other's first priority. Congratulations on your marriage.

HELPFUL LISTS AND FORMS

Phone List

Role	Name	Phone Number
Bride:		
Groom:		
Bride's Parents:		
Groom's Parents:		
Maid of Honor:		
Bridesmaid:		
Bridesmaid:		
Bridesmaid:		
Bridesmaid:		
Bridesmaid:		
Flower Girl:		
Flower Girl:		
Guest Hostess:		
Guest Book Attendant:		
Best Man:		
Usher:		
Usher:		
Usher:		
Usher:		
Ring Bearer:		
Ceremony Site Manager:		
Ceremony Officiant:		
Organist:		
Ceremony Musician:		
Ceremony Musician:		

Role	Name	Phone Number
Ceremony Reader:		
Other Ceremony Participants:		
Wedding Coordinator:		
Reception Hall Manager:		
Caterer:		
Baker:		
Bar Manager:		
Bridal Shop Manager:		
Seamstress:		
Bridesmaids' Bridal Shop Manager:		
Bridesmaids' Seamstress:		
Shoe Shop Manager:		
Accessories Shop Manager:		
Tuxedo Manager:		
Florist:		
Photographer:		
Videographer:		
Reception Entertainers:		
Limousine Company:		
Hotel Manager:		
Travel Agent:		
Babysitters:		
Drivers:		
Housesitters:		
Beauty Shop:		
Spa:		
Other Numbers:		

Bridesmaids' Dress Order Form

THIS checklist is to be used by the maid of honor, bridemaids, and flower girls.

Name:_____

Title:_____

Address: _____

Phone: _____

E-mail: _____

Cell phone:_____

_____ Measurements taken professionally by deadline date: _____

_____ Card sent in to gown company by deadline date: _____

_____ Measurements called in: _____

_____ Order placed: _____

_____ Size ordered: _____

_____ Deposit left: _____

_____ Fittings scheduled: _____

_____ Shoes bought: _____

_____ Accessories bought: _____

_____ Final payment: _____

Notes:

Tuxedo Rental Order Form

This checklist is to be used by the groom, groomsmen, and the fathers of the bride and groom.

Name:_____

Title:_____

Address: _____

Phone: _____

E-mail: _____

Cell phone:_____

_____ Measurements taken professionally by deadline date: _____

_____ Card sent in to tuxedo company by deadline date: _____

_____ Measurements called in: _____

_____ Order placed: _____

_____ Size ordered: _____

_____ Deposit left: _____

_____ Fitting scheduled: _____

_____ Shoes bought: _____

_____ Accessories bought: _____

_____ Final payment: _____

Notes:

Task Delegation List

Name	Task	Deadline	Instructions	Completed

RESOURCES

Bridal Gowns

Alfred Angelo: 800-531-1125
America's Bridal Discounters: 800-326-0833,
    www.bridalgallery.com/bridaldiscounters
Amsale: 212-971-0170, www.amsale.com
Brides-R-Us.com: 800-598-0685, www.e-brides.net
Christos, Inc.: 212-921-0025, www.christos.com
E-Brides.net: 800-598-0685, www.e-brides.net
Emme Bridal: 281-634-9225
Forever Yours: 800-USA-BRIDE
Galina: 212-564-1020
Impressions: 800-BRIDAL-1
Jasmine Collection: 630-295-5880
Jessica McClintock: 800-333-5301
Jim Hjelm: 800-686-7880
L'Amour: 800-664-5683
Lili: 626-336-5048

Melissa Sweet Bridal Collections:
    404-633-4395, www.melissasweet.com
Michelle Roth: 212-245-3390,
    www.michelleroth.com
Mon Cheri: 212-869-0800
Mori Lee: 818-385-0930
Pallas Athena: 818-285-5796
Priscilla of Boston: 617-242-2677,
    www.priscillaofboston.com
Private Label by G: 800-858-3338
Signature Designs: 800-654-7375
Silvia Designs: 760-323-8808
Sweetheart: 212-947-7171
Tomasina: 412-563-7788
USA Bridal: www.usabridal.com
Venus: 818-285-5796

Bridesmaids' and Mother of the Bride's Gowns

Alfred Angelo: 800-531-1125
Bianchi: 800-669-2346
Bill Levkoff: 800-LEVKOFF
Chadwick's of Boston Special Occasions:
    800-525-6650
Champagne Formals: 212-302-9162
Entourage: 212-719-0889
Fashion: www.fashion.net
Galina: 212-564-1020

Macy's: 877-622-9274,
    www.macys.weddingchannel.com
Melissa Sweet Bridal Collection: 404-633-
    4395, www.melissasweet.com

MOTHER OF THE BRIDE'S GOWNS

Spiegel: 800-527-1577, www.spiegel.com
Watters and Watters: 972-960-9884

Shoes and Accessories

Kenneth Cole: 800-KENCOLE
Dyeables: 800-431-2000
Fenaroli for Regalia: 617-723-3682

Nina Footwear: 800-23-NINA
Shoe Buy: www.shoebuy.com
Watters and Watters: 972-960-9884,
www.watters.com

Veils and Headpieces

Dream Veils and Accessories: 312-943-9554, www.dreamveilsacc.com
Fenaroli for Regalia: 617-723-3682
Homa: 973-467-5500, homabridal@aol.com
Renee Romano: 312-943-0912, www.Renee-Romano.com

Invitations

FOR additional savings of up to 30%, contact Informals at 800-6-INVITE with the catalog book and model number of the invitation you like. This company offers discounts on retail invitation sales

Anna Griffin Invitation Design: 404-817-8170, www.annagriffin.com
Botanical PaperWorks: 888-727-3755
Camelot Wedding Stationery: 800-280-2860
Cranes: 800-572-0024, www.cranes.com
Embossed Graphics: 800-325-1016, www.embossedgraphics.com
Invitations by Dawn: 800-332-3296
Julie Holcomb Printers: 510-654-6416, www.julieholcombprinters.com
PaperStyle.com (ordering invitations online): 770-667-6100, www.paper style.com
Papyrus: 800-886-6700, www.papyrusonline.com
Renaissance Writings: 800-246-8483, www.RenaissanceWriting.com
Rexcraft: 800-635-3898
The Precious Collection: 800-537-5222

Rings

American Gem Society: 800-346-8485, www.ags.org
Benchmark: 800-633-5950, www.benchmarkrings.com
Bianca: 213-622-7234, www.BiancaPlatinum.com
DeBeers: www.adiamondisforever.com
EGL Gemological Society: 877-EGL-USA-1, EGLUSA@worldnet .att.net
Honora: 888-2HONORA
Keepsake Diamond Jewelry: 888-4-KEEPSAKE
Novell: 888-916-6835, www.novelldesignstudio.com
OGI Wedding Bands Unlimited: 800-578-3846, www.ogi-ltd.com
Paul Klecka: 888-P-KLECKA, www.klecka.com
Rudolf Erdel Platinum: 212-633-9333, www.rudolferdel.com
Scott Kay Platinum: 800-487-4898, www.scottkay.com
Wedding Ring Hotline: 800-985-RING, www.weddingringhotline.com

For information on how to design your own rings, check out www .adiamondisforever.com

Honeymoon

AIRLINES
Air Canada: 800-776-3000, www.aircanada.ca
Air France: www.airfrance.fr

Alaska Airlines: 800-426-0333, www.alaskaair.com
Alitalia: www.zenonet.com
Aloha Airlines: 800-367-5250, www.alohaair.com
America West: 800-247-5692, www.americawest.com
American Airlines: 800-433-7300, www.amrcorp.com
British Airways: 800-247-9297, www.british-airways.com
Continental Airlines: 800-525-0280, www.flycontinental.com
Delta Airlines: 800-221-1212, www.delta-air.com
Hawaiian Airlines: 800-367-5320, www.hawaiianair.com
KLM Royal Dutch Airlines: 800-374-7747, www.klm.nl
Northwest Airlines: 800-225-2525, www.nwa.com
Southwest Airlines: 800-435-9792, www.southwest.com
TWA: 800-221-2000, www.twa.com
USAir: 800-428-4322, www.usair.com
United Airlines: 800-241-6522, www.ualservices.com
Virgin Atlantic Airways: 800-862-8621, www.fly.virgin.com

DISCOUNT AIRFARES

Air Fare: www.airfare.com
Cheap Fares: www.cheapfares.com
Cheap Tickets: 800-377-1000
Discount Airfare: www.discount-airfare.com
Mr. Cheap: 800-MR-CHEAP
Priceline: www.priceline.com
You Price It: www.youpriceit.com

CRUISES

Cruise Lines International Association: www.cruising.org
A Wedding for You (weddings aboard a cruise ship): 800-929-4198
American Cruise Line (east coast from Florida to Maine): www
    .americancruiselines.com
American Hawaii Cruises (weddings aboard a cruise ship): 800-474-9934
Carnival Cruise Lines: www.carnival.com
Celebrity Cruises: www.celebrity-cruises.com
Cunard: www.cunardline.com
Delta Queen: www.deltaqueen.com
Discount Cruises: www.cruise.com
Disney Cruises: www.disneycruise.com
Holland America: www.hollandamerica.com
Norwegian Cruise Lines: 800-262-4NCL, www.ncl.com
Princess Cruises: www.princess.com
Radisson 7 Sevens Cruises: www.rssc.com
Royal Caribbean: 800-727-2717, www.royalcaribbean.com

    For further comparison-shopping, check out Personalogic at www.personalogic.com for detailed information on a variety of destinations. The site provides critical looks at each cruise line's offerings that mention price lists for grade of room, ratings, dress code, cuisine style, surcharges, tipping, amenities such as pools and saunas, and whether or not you can expect to be surrounded by couples, families, singles, or seniors. Yes, the reviews are subjective, but the information is there for your own comparison shopping.

RESORTS

Beaches: 800-BEACHES
Club Med: www.clubmed.com

Hilton Hotels: www.hilton.com
Hyatt Hotels: www.hyatt.com
Marriott Hotels: www.marriott.com
Radisson: www.radisson.com
Sandals: 800-SANDALS, www.sandals.com
Super Clubs: 800-GO-SUPER, www.superclubs.com
Swept Away: 800-545-7937, www.sweptaway.com/weddings.htm
Westin Hotels: www.westin.com

HOTELS

To find a suitable hotel in your destination, look up the All Hotels on the Web site at www.all-hotels.com

Bed and Breakfasts, Country Inns, and Small Hotels:
    www.virtualcities.com/ons/Oonsadex.htm
Bed and Breakfast—International Guide: www.ibbp.com
Fodors: www.fodors.com
Hilton: www.hilton.com
Hyatt: www.hyatt.com
Leading Hotels of the World: www.lhw.com
Marriott: www.marriott.com
Radisson: www.radison.com

STATE AND LOCATION TOURISM DEPARTMENTS

Tourism Office Worldwide Directory:
    www.towd.com
Alabama: 800-252-2262
Alaska: 907-465-2010
Arizona: 602-542-8687
Aruba Tourism Department:
    201-330-0800
Australian Tourist Commission:
    800-445-4400
Bahamas: 800-228-5173
Barbados: 212-986-6516
Bermuda: 800-223-6106
British Virgin Islands: 800-888-5563,
    ext. 559
California: 916-322-1396
Canadian Consulate: 213-687-7432
Caribbean: 212-682-0435
Colorado: 800-433-2656
Connecticut: 800-282-6863
Delaware: 800-441-8846
Disney's Fairy Tale Weddings:
    407-828-3400
Florida: 904-487-1462
France: 212-757-1125
Fiji: 310-568-1616
Georgia: 800-847-4842
Germany: 212-661-7200
Hawaii: 808-923-1811
Idaho: 800-635-7820
Illinois: 217-782-7139

Indiana: 800-289-ONIN
Iowa: 800-345-IOWA
Ireland: 212-418-0800
Italy: 212-245-4961
Jamaica: 800-233-4582
Jersey/Cape May County:
    800-227-2297
Kansas: 800-2-KANSAS
Kentucky: 800-225-8747
Key West: 800-648-6269
Las Vegas: 800-426-8695
Louisiana: 800-227-4386
Maine: 207-289-6070
Maryland: 800-543-1036
Massachusetts: 617-727-3201
Mexico: 800-44-MEXICO
Michigan: 800-543-2937
Minnesota: 800-345-2537
Mississippi: 800-647-2290
Missouri: 314-751-4133
Monaco: 212-759-5227
Montana: 800-541-1447
Nebraska: 800-228-4307
Nevada: 800-638-2328
New Hampshire: 800-542-2331
New Jersey: 800-JERSEY-7
New Mexico: 800-545-2040
New York: 800-255-5697
Niagara Falls: 800-338-7890
North Carolina: 800-847-4862

North Dakota: 800-437-2077
Oahu, Hawaii: 877-525-OAHU,
    www.visitoahu.com
Ohio: 800-BUCKEYE
Oklahoma: 800-654-8240
Oregon: 800-424-3002
Pennsylvania: 800-VISIT-PA
Puerto Rico: 800-223-6530
Quebec: 800-363-7777
Rhode Island: 800-556-2484
South Carolina: 800-872-3505
Wyoming: 800-225-5996

South Dakota: 800-843-1930
Spain: 212-759-8822
Tahiti: 800-828-6877, www.islandsinthesun.com
Tennessee: 615-741-2158
Texas: 512-483-3705
Utah: 800-222-8824
Vermont: 802-828-3236
Virginia: 800-248-4833
Washington: 206-753-5630
West Virginia: 800-CALL-WVA
Wisconsin: 800-432-TRIP

TRAIN TRAVEL

Amtrak: 800-872-7245, www.amtrak.com
Eurailpass: www.eurail.com
Orient Express Hotels, Trains and Cruises: www.orient-express.com

TOURING COMPANIES

Backroads Active Adventures: 800-GO-ACTIVE, www.backroads.com
Brendan Tours: 800-421-8446, www.brendantours.com
Collette Tours: 888-261-8483, www.collettetours.com
iExplore: 800-IEXPLORE
Geographic Expeditions: 800-777-8183, www.geoex.com
Grand European Tours: 800-552-5545, www.gctours.com
Orient Lines-Cruise Tours: 800-333-7300, www.orientlines.com
Saga Holidays: 800-291-0786, www.sagaholidays.com
The United States Tour Operators Association: 800-GO USTOA, www.ustoa.com
Trafalgar Tours: 800-854-0103, www.trafalgartours.com

TOURING PROGRAMS

Concierge (for the wealthy, upscale traveler): www.concierge.com
Expedia (for a selection of flights and discount fares): www.expedia.com
Travelocity: www.travelocity
Travelsmith: www.travelsmith.com
Wimco (for luxurious, overseas vacations): www.wimco.com

COTTAGES AND VILLAS

Country Cottages (cottages and villas in the U.S. and Europe):
    800-674-8883

Bridal Assocations

BRIDAL SHOW AND CONFERENCE

Great Bridal Expo: 800-422-3976, www.bridalexpo.com

ORGANIZATIONS FOR WEDDING-RELATED SERVICES

Association of Bridal Consultants: 860-355-0464
American Federation of Musicians: 212-869-1330
American Rental Association: 800-334-2177, www.ararental.org

American Society of Travel Agents: 703-739-2782
Better Business Bureau (to find the Better Business Bureau of your state or locale):
    www.bbb.org/bureaus
National Limousine Association: 800-NLA-7007
Professional Photographers of America: 800-786-6277,
    www.ppa-world.org

Wedding Web Sites

Bride's Magazine: www.brides.com
Elegant Bride: www.elegantbridemagazine.com
Martha Stewart Living: www.marthastewart.com
Modern Bride: www.ModernBride.com
Premiere Bride: www.premierebride.com
The Best Man: www.thebestman.com
The Knot: www.theknot.com
The Wedding Channel: www.theweddingchannel.com
The Wedding Helpers: www.weddinghelpers.com
Today's Bride: www.todaysbride.com
Town & Country Weddings (upscale): www.tncweddings.com
Ultimate Internet Wedding Guide: www.ultimatewedding.com
Wedding Bells: www.weddingbells.com
Wedding Central: www.weddingcentral.com
Wedding Details: www.weddingdetails.com
Wedding Spot: www.weddingspot.com
Wedding World: www.weddingworld.com

Wedding Registries

Bed Bath and Beyond: 800-GO-BEYOND, www.bedbathandbeyond.com
Bloomingdales: 800-888-2WED, www.bloomingdales.com
Crate and Barrel: 800-967-6696
Dillards: 800-626-6001, www.dillards.com
Fortunoffs: 800-777-2807, www.fortunoffs.com
Gift Emporia.com: www.giftemporia.com
Home Depot: www.homedepot.com
JC Penney: 800-JCP-GIFT, www.jcpenney.com
Macy's Wedding Channel: 888-92-BRIDES,
    www.macys.weddingchannel.com
National Bridal Service: www.weddingexperts.com/nbs
Neiman Marcus: www.neimanmarcus.com
Pier 1 Imports: 800-245-4595, www.pier1.com
Sears: www.sears.com
Service Merchandise: 800-582-1960, www.servicemerchandise.com
Target's Club WeddGift Registry: 800-888-9333, www.target.com
The Gift: www.thegift.com
The Wedding List: 800-345-7795, www.theweddinglist.com
Wedding Network (Internet wedding registry): 800-628-5113, www.weddingnetwork.com
Williams Sonoma: 800-541-2376, www.williams-sonoma.com

Wedding Supplies and Services

BOOKS AND PLANNERS
Amazon.com: www.amazon.com
Barnes and Noble: 800-242-6657, www.bn.com
Borders: www.borders.com

CALLIGRAPHY
Petals and Ink: 818-509-6783, www.petalsnink.com

CAMERAS
Best Camera: 888-237-8226
Boecks Camera: 800-700-5090
EPP Wedding Products: 412-823-6748

FAVORS AND GIFTS
Beverly Clark Collection: 877-862-3933, www.beverlyclark.com
Chandler's Candle Company: 800-463-7143, www.chandlerscandle.com
Double T Limited: 800-756-6184, www.uniquefavors.com
Eve.com: www.eve.com
Exclusively Weddings: 800-759-7666, www.exclusivelyweddings.com
Forever and Always Company: 800-404-4025,
    www.foreverandalways.com
Gift Emporia.com: www.giftemporia.com
Godiva: 800-9-GODIVA, www.godiva.com
Gratitude: 800-914-4342, www.giftsofgratitude.com
Personal Creations. 800-326-6626
Pier 1 Imports: www.pier1.com
Seasons: 800-776-9677
Service Merchandise: 800-251-1212
Tree and Floral Beginnings (seedlings, bulbs, and candles):
    800-499-9580, www.plantamemory.com; in Canada,
    www.plantamemory.on.ca
Wireless: 800-669-9999

PAPER PRODUCTS
OfficeMax: check your local listings
Paper Access: 800-727-3701, www.paperaccess.com
Paper Direct: 800-A-PAPERS
Staples: 800-333-3330, www.staples.com
The Wedding Store: www.wedguide.com/store
Ultimate Wedding Store: www.ultimatewedding.com/store
Wedmart.com: 888-802-2229, www.wedmart.com

WEATHER SERVICE
For checking the weather at your ceremony, reception, or honeymoon sites, including five-day forecast and weather bulletins:

AccuWeather: www.accuweather.com
Rain or Shine (five-day forecasts for anywhere in the world, plus ski and boating conditions):
    www.rainorshine.com
Sunset Time (precise sunset time for any day of the year): www.usno.navy.mil
Weather Channel: www.weather.com

WEDDING ITEMS
For toasting flutes, ring pillows, and such:

Affectionately Yours: www.affectionately-yours.com
Beverly Clark Collection: 877-862-3933, www.beverlyclark.com
Bridalink Store: www.bridalink.com/store2
Chandler's Candle Company: 800-463-7143, www.chandlerscandle.com
Magical Beginnings Butterfly Farms (live butterflies for release):
    888-639-9995, www.butterflyevents.com
The Sarina Collection: 888-6SARINA, www.sarinacollection.com
The Wedding Shopper: www.theweddingshopper.com/catalog.htm
Treasured Moments: 800-754-5151, www.treasured-moments.com

If you will be making your own wedding cake, baked favors, or desserts, check out the Wilton site for the best in supplies: 800-794-5866, www.wilton.com

Beauty and Health

BEAUTY PRODUCTS AND SERVICES
Check these sites for makeup and skincare products, assessments, and services:
Avon: www.avon.com
Beauty.com: www.beauty.com
Beauty Jungle: www.beautyjungle.com
Clinique: www.clinique.com
Elizabeth Arden: www.elizabetharden.com (Choose the shades and treatment products that are
    right for you, and find the perfect perfume for your big day.)
Eve (carries Lorac, Elizabeth Arden, Calvin Klein, and others): www.eve.com
iBeauty: www.ibeauty.com
Lancome: www.lancome.com
Mac: www.maccosmetics.com
Makeover Studio: www.makeoverstudio.com (Choose your face shape and experiment with
    makeup shades and looks.)
Revlon: www.revlon.com
Sephora: www.sephora.com

GENERAL FREE STUFF
Some Internet sites give away promotional items to lure online shoppers. So check out the top 50 freebie hits at:

    www.top50.com
    www.always4free.com
    www.freestuffcentral.com
    www.freebies.com

Hilton Honors (allows you to earn points and frequent flier miles): 800-548-8690
Marriott Rewards: 800-MARRIOTT (You earn ten points for every dollar you spend at one of
    their hotels. Points can be used for travel and shopping.)

INDEX